Rumble and Crash

THE SUNY SERIES

HORIZONS OF CINEMA

MURRAY POMERANCE | EDITOR

Rumble and Crash

Crises of Capitalism in Contemporary Film

∾

Milo Sweedler

Cover art: Clive Owen in *Inside Man* (2006), directed by Spike Lee / Photofest.

Published by State University of New York Press, Albany

© 2019 State University of New York

All rights reserved

No part of this book may be used or reproduced in any manner whatsoever without written permission. No part of this book may be stored in a retrieval system or transmitted in any form or by any means including electronic, electrostatic, magnetic tape, mechanical, photocopying, recording, or otherwise without the prior permission in writing of the publisher.

For information, contact State University of New York Press, Albany, NY www.sunypress.edu

Library of Congress Cataloging-in-Publication Data

Names: Sweedler, Milo, [date] author.
Title: Rumble and crash : crises of capitalism in contemporary film / Milo Sweedler.
Description: Albany : State University of New York Press, 2018. | Series: SUNY series, horizons of cinema | Includes bibliographical references and index.
Identifiers: LCCN 2018009218 | ISBN 9781438472799 (hardcover) | ISBN 9781438472805 (pbk.) | ISBN 9781438472812 (ebook)
Subjects: LCSH: Motion pictures—History—21st century. | Capitalism in motion pictures. | Politics in motion pictures.
Classification: LCC PN1995.9.C33255 S94 2018 | DDC 791.436/553—dc23
LC record available at https://lccn.loc.gov/2018009218

10 9 8 7 6 5 4 3 2 1

*This book is dedicated to the memory of
William V. Spanos (1924–2017)*

Contents

List of Illustrations		ix
Acknowledgments		xiii
Introduction		xv
1	Exceptions and Rules: States of Emergency in *Children of Men*	1
2	Mapping *Syriana*	29
3	Corporate Murder in *The Constant Gardener*	53
4	Secrets of Primitive Accumulation: *Inside Man*	79
5	Fictitious Capital and Narrative Spin in *The Wolf of Wall Street*	107
6	The Meltdown and the Bailout without the Recovery: *Blue Jasmine*	133
Conclusion: Allegories for the Present		153
Notes		159
Bibliography		175
Index		181

Illustrations

Figure 1.1 Theo strolls past refugees quarantined like animals in cages (*Children of Men*, Universal, 2006).   7

Figure 1.2 The inclusion in the frame of a commuter rushing to catch the train at the end of the Alresford station scene shows how normal the state of exception has become (*Children of Men*, Universal, 2006).   7

Figure 1.3 The fate of labor. A plastic sheet covering an inverted chair on a desk at the Ministry of Energy evokes layoffs and redundancies more than the prospect of human extinction (*Children of Men*, Universal, 2006).   9

Figure 1.4 If we were to imagine Mr. Griffiths trying to stand up from his desk, we would realize that there is no room for him to pull out his chair (*Children of Men*, Universal, 2006).   11

Figure 1.5 Dead cows, an oil drum on its side, and scattered debris lie in a pool of stagnant water while factories belch flames and smoke (*Children of Men*, Universal, 2006).   13

Figure 1.6 The wall of heroes in the Palmers' house commemorates half a century of social protest. Photographs of Rosa Parks, Angela Davis, John Lennon, Rigoberta Menchú, Aung San Suu Kyi, and Naomi Klein lead to a photomontage that sets the iconic hooded Abu Ghraib prisoner on the Statue of Liberty's pedestal (*Children of Men*, Universal, 2006).   15

Figure 1.7	The scene of the arrival at the Bexhill refugee camp derives its imagery from the infamous photographs of tortures conducted at the US-run Abu Ghraib prison (*Children of Men*, Universal, 2006).	19
Figure 1.8	The Bexhill uprising visualizes what the "real state of emergency" evoked by Walter Benjamin might look like (*Children of Men*, Universal, 2006).	23
Figure 2.1	The walls of the Connex boardroom are covered with maps dividing the world into color-coded regions belonging to various energy corporations (*Syriana*, Warner Bros., 2005).	30
Figure 2.2	CIA operative Bob Barnes's nonchalance and his subtle glance up to the corner of the frame are the only indications that he just orchestrated the assassination of two arms dealers (*Syriana*, Warner Bros., 2005).	37
Figure 2.3	Bryan Woodman illogically places Prince Nasir's kingdom outside of the Eurasian triangle in the map that he draws in the sand (*Syriana*, Warner Bros., 2005).	43
Figure 3.1	An eight-second static shot of Arnold Bluhm watching Tessa Quayle nurse a newborn infant leads the spectator to believe that Tessa has given birth to Arnold's child (*The Constant Gardener*, Focus Features, 2005).	59
Figure 3.2	By successively depicting ThreeBees as a drug company, an agrochemical corporation, and a multinational food company, Meirelles disperses the image of the corporation across numerous sectors (*The Constant Gardener*, Focus Features, 2005).	63
Figure 3.3	ThreeBees employees wear white coats reminiscent of those worn by Nestlé's "milk nurses" during the 1970s (*The Constant Gardener*, Focus Features, 2005).	65
Figure 4.1	As Dalton Russell recounts the story of Arthur Case's collaboration with the Nazis during World War II, the camera does a reverse dolly shot, pulling Case and his desk forward and thereby creating the effect that the wall behind him is receding into the	

	background. Photos of Case posing with the first President George Bush, with Prime Minister Margaret Thatcher, and with New York's Mayor Rudy Giuliani are visible on the credenza (*Inside Man*, Universal, 2006).	92
Figure 4.2	Objects on display in Arthur Case's office include a commemorative plate recognizing the banker's achievements at Manhattan Trust, a framed letter on White House stationery, a plaque bearing a Star of David, and a plaque adorned with a menorah (*Inside Man*, Universal, 2006).	92
Figure 4.3	A wide high-angle shot of Detective Frazier crossing the dining room of the Four Seasons restaurant enlarges the field of prospective criminals (*Inside Man*, Universal, 2006).	105
Figure 5.1	The Stratton Oakmont logo at the beginning *The Wolf of Wall Street* creates the impression that the company coproduced the film we are about to watch (Paramount, 2013).	110
Figure 5.2	The mock ad for Stratton Oakmont shows rows of confidence-inspiring stockbrokers speaking calmly on the phone (*The Wolf of Wall Street*, Paramount, 2013).	111
Figure 5.3	The first shot inside the Stratton Oakmont investment firm presents the company as an outlandish fraternity house (*The Wolf of Wall Street*, Paramount, 2013).	113
Figure 5.4	Scorsese uses an aesthetic borrowed from infomercials to film Jordan Belfort's opening monologue (*The Wolf of Wall Street*, Paramount, 2013).	116
Figure 5.5	The infomercial for *Jordan Belfort's Straight Line* seminar is an audio-visual mise-en-abyme of the movie as a whole (*The Wolf of Wall Street*, Paramount, 2013).	117
Figure 5.6	Continuities in editing, costume, dialogue, sound, and mise-en-scène lead the viewer initially to perceive the sales-call scene as a continuation of the sales-training scene (*The Wolf of Wall Street*, Paramount, 2013).	121

Figure 5.7	Alden Kupferberg reads from a typewritten script while Jordan lip-syncs every word that should be coming out of his trainee's mouth (*The Wolf of Wall Street*, Paramount, 2013).	122
Figure 6.1	The opening sequence of *Blue Jasmine* gradually reveals Jasmine's sociability and self-confidence to be antisocial self-absorption (Sony, 2013).	136
Figure 6.2	The similarities between the flashback of Jasmine and her friend Nora strolling down Madison Avenue and the film's opening sequence reinforce the similitude between the fashionable New York socialite and the babbling woman on the plane (*Blue Jasmine*, Sony, 2013).	137
Figure 6.3	A flashback of Jasmine hosting a dinner party at her posh Fifth Avenue residence shows the glamorous socialite in her element (*Blue Jasmine*, Sony, 2013).	138
Figure 6.4	Jasmine's eerie reenactment of the dinner party scene as she sits alone, homeless and penniless, in her sister's apartment conveys the severity of the heroine's condition (*Blue Jasmine*, Sony, 2013).	139
Figure 6.5	*Blue Jasmine*'s gut-wrenching last shot shows Jasmine in freefall, with nothing to prevent her inevitable crash (Sony, 2013).	145

Acknowledgments

The idea for this book grew out of a conversation with Marc Olivier Reid. Abderrahman Beggar, Hugo De Marinis, Colman Hogan, Penelope Ironstone, Marta Marín-Dòmine, Herbert Pimlott, Natasha Pravaz, Alicia Sliwinski, Margaret Toye, and Alexandra Zimmermann were important interlocutors as the project developed. Discussions with students in the Cultural Analysis and Social Theory program at Wilfrid Laurier University helped me formulate my ideas. I wish to thank, in particular, Rachel Bangura, Corey Clarisse, Dalia Elawad, Madeline McCaffrey, Jalal Midani, Allison Leonard, and Virginia Pecjak for sharing their thoughts on the material.

The "Representing the Great Recession" panel that John McCullough organized for the Society for Cinema and Media Studies annual conference in 2018 offered an opportunity to get feedback from my peers. Jennifer Sweedler and Christopher Treadwell provided insightful comments on the work in progress. Marilyn Zeitlin went through the entire manuscript with a fine-tooth comb, correcting innumerable mistakes and making countless suggestions for improvements. The anonymous peer reviewers at SUNY Press also offered helpful comments, which significantly enriched portions of the book.

I thank Murray Pomerance, editor of the Horizons of Cinema series at SUNY Press, for his belief in the project's importance, his encouragement, his suggestions for revisions, and his good humor. James Peltz, Rafael Chaiken, Ryan Morris, and Anne Valentine at SUNY Press were a pleasure to work with. My copyeditor, Eric Schramm, did stellar work. Finally, I am grateful to Todd Ifft at Photofest for helping me locate the image on the book's cover.

Introduction

AT THE BEGINNING OF THE twenty-first century, as the contradictions of capitalism became more apparent than they had been in the living memory of anyone born after the 1920s, numerous films gave allegorical form to the crises of contemporary capitalism. Some of the films were overtly political in nature, while others refracted the vicissitudes of capital in stories that did not, on the surface, have anything explicitly political about them. This book examines six particularly rich and thought-provoking films in this vein. Analyzing four movies from before the global financial crisis of 2008 and two that allegorize the financial meltdown itself, *Rumble and Crash* explores the ways that films as different as a bank-heist thriller like *Inside Man* and an intimate psychological drama like *Blue Jasmine* allegorize one of the defining crises of our time.

The films examined in this book are works by well-known auteurs such as Woody Allen, Spike Lee, and Martin Scorsese, international political thrillers by Stephen Gaghan and Fernando Meirelles, and a dystopian science fiction film by Alfonso Cuarón. What unites the films is not a particular genre, the shared cultural heritage of the filmmakers, or a common aesthetic, but their refraction of a common problem. Combining social history and political theory with detailed film analysis, this study situates the movies in their historical context and examines how they reflect recent sociopolitical and economic developments. It offers original interpretations of six culturally significant films released between 2005 and 2013 while showing how very different movies give narrative and audio-visual form to one of the most pressing issues of the twenty-first century.

The book is organized chronologically in the order of the historical moments that the movies allegorically evoke rather than by film date, spanning from the "war on terror" of the early 2000s and the US-led invasion of Iraq in 2003 to the global financial crisis and the bank bailout of 2008. Its themes include globalization and its discontents, interventionist mapmaking in the Middle East, the rise of finance capitalism, and the ways that multinational corporations literally get away with murder in the developing world. Analyzing representations of both sides of the yawning class divide, it examines the class war between the super-rich and the rest of the world's population, and diverse ways that an international capitalist class is inadvertently digging its own grave. Although numerous books have appeared in recent years confronting these and related issues, no book-length study has analyzed the role of film as the platform and allegory as the narrative device used to express the increasingly pervasive sense that the economic system that we have known and accepted as inevitable and ubiquitous is riddled with self-destructive flaws.

Allegory

The term "allegory" implies a distinction between a work's manifest narrative content and its latent or implicit meaning. Thus Alfonso Cuarón's *Children of Men* (2006), for example, a science fiction film set in the year 2027, is ostensibly a movie about the future, but, like many sci-fi narratives, its vision of the future invites comparisons with the present. Similarly, Martin Scorsese's *The Wolf of Wall Street* (2013) is explicitly the story of a dodgy stockbroker in the late 1980s and early 1990s, but it is implicitly a critique of the esteemed financiers of the 2000s who brought the global economy to the brink of collapse. Spike Lee's *Inside Man* (2006), set in the historical present, uses the bank-heist genre to allegorize class struggle, while Stephen Gaghan's *Syriana* (2005) and Fernando Meirelles's *The Constant Gardener* (2005) use the conspiracy-thriller genre as a vehicle to expose and critique the machinations of global capital. Finally, Woody Allen's *Blue Jasmine* (2013), which presents itself as a retelling of Tennessee Williams's *A Streetcar Named Desire*, transposes the global financial crisis of 2008 onto the story of the meltdown and the subsequent bailout of a New York socialite.

The decision to examine allegorical refractions of recent sociopolitical and economic developments, as opposed to films that depict frontally the vicissitudes of contemporary capitalism, stems largely from the richness and diversity of films that have adopted the allegorical mode and the relative paucity of smart, engaging, and thought-provoking movies that have opted for a more straightforward approach. There are noteworthy exceptions, J. C. Chandor's *Margin Call* (2011) and Adam McKay's *The Big Short* (2015) among them, but by and large the recent movies that have thematized directly the fluctuations of contemporary capital have been less compelling than the generally subtler, more engrossing, and further-reaching cinematic allegories that have come out in the past decade or so. I agree on the whole with Alberto Toscano and Jeff Kinkle's overall assessment, in their analysis of films on the financial crisis of 2008, that "it will be necessary to take a far greater distance from capital's ubiquitous *clichés* than works 'about' the crisis and finance have done hitherto."[1] Too many of the recent films that address frontally the crises of capitalism offer versions of what Christopher Sharrett calls "Hollywood's false criticism." This form of criticism, which "prefers to place blame on a dubious concept of human nature rather than on political-economic frameworks," relies on the specious notion that "any answer to social disorder under patriarchal capitalism must be absolutely personal."[2] Although the films examined in this book occasionally fall prey to clichés of different sorts, they do not for the most part present managerial altruism, family values, or individual acts of charity as the key to overcoming the challenges posed by an increasingly virulent form of capitalism.

There may be historical reasons for the recent profusion, both inside Hollywood and out, of interesting allegories of capitalism. "In the simplest terms," literary theorist Angus Fletcher writes in his magisterial study, *Allegory: The Theory of a Symbolic Mode*, "allegory says one thing and means another."[3] Rather than "saying what it means," allegory means something that it does not say. It offers an image of something—a person, an idea, a quality or characteristic, a process, or an event—that does not or cannot appear as such. Defined by the Roman rhetorician Quintilian as a "continuous metaphor," allegory lends itself particularly well to the figuration of phenomena that elude direct representation.[4] As Rita Copeland and Peter Struck bring to light in their introduction to *The Cambridge Companion to Allegory*, one of the earliest allegorical studies, dating to the fourth century BCE, explicitly presents itself as a search for the concealed cosmological meaning of a poetic "enigma" (*aenigma*).[5] In this context, the recent revival of allegory—a revival that is by no means limited to the cinema—beckons us to consider whether there is something peculiarly enigmatic about the present age. The title of David Harvey's *The Enigma of Capital* gives us an initial hint of what that "something" might be.[6] Allegory had fallen out of fashion in the early nineteenth century. Its resurgence in recent decades gives pause for thought.

In his afterword to the 2012 edition of his book, Fletcher offers a fascinating interpretation of the popularity that allegory is currently enjoying. He begins his 2012 afterword by remarking that much has changed since 1964, when *Allegory* was first published. He then specifies for his reader the fundamental changes, as he sees them, that took place over this forty-eight-year period: "The rich countries want yet more natural resources to support their standards of living, while the divided and hence troubled poorer nations have experienced sectarian religious wars characterized by chaotic internal power struggles."[7] The author goes on to enumerate further developments that typify the shift that took place over the preceding half-century. His examples include the Wall Street banks that were deemed "too big to fail" in 2008, the astronomical spending in recent years of political action committees (PACs) and so-called super PACs on political candidates (in particular, following the Supreme Court's ruling in *Citizens United v. Federal Election Committee* [2010]), the resulting disenfranchisement of the working people that cannot afford to bribe politicians with substantial monetary gifts, and the concomitant demise of US democracy as a bona fide form of participatory government. In sum, capitalism has reached a new stage in its development, Fletcher proposes, with decidedly deleterious consequences for the majority of the people who find themselves on the socioeconomic and political margins of the system.

Fletcher calls this new situation a "crisis of scale."[8] He likens it to the phenomenon that philosopher Immanuel Kant dubbed "the mathematical sublime" in the *Critique of Judgment* (1790). "Recall that the sublime is whatever is too massive, often too monumentally impressive for our mind's eye to hold," Fletcher writes, glossing Kant.[9] Similarly, Fletcher proposes, the "runaway expansion of the Numbers in society"—by which he means the billions of bits and bytes of information in our electronic devices as well as outsized multinational corporations, banks that are "too big to fail," and the enormous sums of money that those institutions (legally defined in the United States as "people" with a right to unlimited "free speech") give to lawmakers—inhibits the individual subject's ability to form a mental image of the vast social structure in which she exists.[10] We find ourselves immersed in a system too big and boundless for us to conceive of it as a totality.

Given the extent of the changes that Fletcher outlines, and the emphasis that he places on them in his 2012 afterword, the reader might anticipate an attendant change in the author's appreciation of the narrative mode he analyzed nearly fifty years earlier. On the contrary: "When many years ago I began this study, the seeds of the present were in the ground or at least ready to plant, and for decades it seemed to me a foregone conclusion that not only in the West, but everywhere in the world, the allegorical mode would recapture the prominence it possessed during the Middle Ages, which in fact has transpired, as predicted."[11] In sum, Fletcher concludes, making a broad claim for the relevance of his study: "My book . . . may illuminate the present and the oncoming global future."[12] As long as global capitalism is allowed to continue on its current trajectory of limitless expansion, Fletcher suggests, allegory—the mode of representation that corresponds to this monstrous system—will be in fashion.

I am struck by the resemblance between Fletcher's remarks here on the pertinence of allegory in the age of late capitalism and eminent Marxist critic Fredric Jameson's theory of "cognitive mapping." First developed in the mid-1980s, in the early years of the neoliberal onslaught (about which I have much to say in chapter 4), Jameson's proposed strategy of "cognitive mapping" would enable individual subjects to form a mental image of the vast nexus of global social relations.[13] Derived from urbanist Kevin Lynch's studies of the mental maps that people make of cities by observing their surroundings, Jameson's concept of "cognitive mapping" extrapolates Lynch's analyses of the ways people unconsciously map urban space to "the realm of social structure, that is to say, in our historical moment, to the totality of class relations on a global (or should I say multinational) scale."[14] Observing "a most interesting convergence between the empirical problems studied by Lynch in terms of city space" and French Marxist Louis Althusser's definition of ideology as "the representation of the subject's *Imaginary* relationship to his or her *Real* conditions of existence," Jameson proposes that "this is exactly what the cognitive map is called upon to do . . . : to enable a situational representation on the part of the individual subject to that vaster and properly unrepresentable totality which is the ensemble of society's structures as a whole."[15] Unlike Fletcher, who proposes that allegory is the representational mode endemic to late capitalism, Jameson argues for the invention of a new aesthetic that would give form to this amorphous beast. Like Fletcher, he perceives that the "vast and properly unrepresentable totality" of capitalist globalization calls for an art form adequate to this sublime object.

As Toscano and Kinkle emphasize in *Cartographies of the Absolute*, the aesthetic that Jameson was calling for in the eighties did not exist, in the theorist's opinion: "He didn't announce its existence . . . but stressed instead the political need for its elaboration in both theory and practice."[16] The latter specification—its elaboration *in both theory and practice*—is crucial. Whereas, according to Jameson, there were no cognitive maps of global capital in the realms of arts and culture, his own critical work in those areas constitutes a "cognitive map" in its own right. Jameson's numerous studies on an impressively wide array of media and genres—from postmodern historical fiction to cyberpunk novels, experimental video to the Hollywood retro film, avant-garde architectural designs to towering glass skyscrapers, hyperrealist sculpture to pop art—theoretically derive from the works the "cognitive map" of multinational capitalism that the artifacts cryptically encode.

Jameson explicitly calls his general approach to literary and cultural interpretation allegorical. "Interpretation is here construed as an essentially allegorical act," he writes, for example, in his preface to *The Political Unconscious*.[17] Jameson's use of the term "allegory" here is different from Fletcher's acceptation of the term. Whereas, for Fletcher, allegories are things that artists produce, for Jameson "allegory" refers first and foremost to a way of interpreting cultural artifacts. For both theorists, the term designates artworks that say one thing but mean another, but they locate the moment of meaning creation at different stages in a work's production and reception. What Jameson designates by the term "allegory" is primarily a reading strategy, not a particular type of art.

These two meanings of "allegory" have a long history. As Copeland and Struck explain: "In its most common usage ['allegory'] refers to two related procedures, a manner of composing and a method of interpreting."[18] The latter operation, called "allegoresis," is in fact the older of the two procedures, dating to the time of the ancient Greeks. "Allegoresis" designates what people *read into* a text, rather than what a given cultural producer meant to communicate in creating the work. It is more or less synonymous with "interpretation" in the broad sense of the term. If, as Copeland and Struck suggest, glossing an argument by deconstructionist Paul de Man, "all reading, all critical practice, is allegoresis, that is, allegorical interpretation,"[19] it follows that any critical analysis that strives to do more than faithfully reproduce the source material (if such a procedure is even possible outside of the fictional world of Jorge Luis Borges)[20] is to some extent allegorical.

What I do in this book is cinematic allegoresis. Rather than making claims about what filmmakers intended to communicate in making their movies, I analyze the films themselves, placing them in their historical context and exploring the diverse ways that they synthesize and visualize that context, regardless of their creators' intentions. This disregard for the filmmakers' intentions enables us to view their movies as expressions of what Jameson famously called "the political unconscious" in his 1981 book of that title. Although I find Jameson's pronouncement that the political interpretation of texts is "the absolute horizon of all reading and all interpretation" hyperbolic, I agree with him that "the convenient working distinction between cultural texts that are social and political and those that are not" fails to account for the deep penetration of politics into private life.[21] Such a distinction, which tacitly sanctions the idea that the individual artist or lone genius can somehow transcend her conjuncture, reinforces, intentionally or not, the fundamentally ideological idea that some of us are outside of ideology. In sum, I agree with Jameson that cultural artifacts, whether they are explicitly "political" or not, can profitably be read as socially symbolic acts bearing witness to a "political unconscious."

Jameson's allegorical approach to cultural interpretation also resolves the apparent paradox of using a particularly capital-intensive and commodified art form to shed light on the prospective self-destruction of capitalism. Before getting into the ways that Jameson's allegorical reading strategy enables us to "read into" (if not necessarily "against") the cultural commodities produced by film studios, let us take a moment to consider how the motion picture industry works. This brief consideration, based in large part on philosopher-sociologists Max Horkheimer and Theodor Adorno's influential essay "The Culture Industry" and media analyst-*cum*-social activist Mark Crispin Miller's piercing analysis of the entertainment industry (but see also Robert Sklar's monumental *Movie-Made America*),[22] provides a glimpse into the intricacies of capitalism and the movie industry. The image that emerges from these authors' studies leaves little doubt as to the interests and motivations of movie studios' boards of directors, making the idea that these industry leaders might produce cinematic works that undermine the basic tenets of capitalism seem far-fetched. I then turn to the work of film theorist Siegfried Kracauer, which offers an implicit response to Horkheimer and Adorno, and finally to Jameson's allegorical approach to film criticism.

Capitalism and Film

Films studios are, of course, major corporations. They are quintessential capitalist institutions. As Horkheimer and Adorno, prominent members of the "Frankfurt School" of social research, argue in their 1944 treatise on the culture industry—a treatise that remains as pertinent today as the day it was written—the Hollywood moguls obey the same rules as executive board members of the most powerful sectors of industry. "The captains of the film industry . . . accept only more or less ephemeral box-office success as evidence," Horkheimer and Adorno assert. "Their ideology is business."[23]

Two important corollaries follow from this initial observation. First, the cultural commodities that film studios produce are as standardized and interchangeable as the articles coming off a factory assembly line. If a movie performs well at the box office, film producers are liable to replicate the formula in countless iterations in an effort to repeat the success of the earlier film. As a result, the differences between Warner Bros.' movies and those produced by MGM are no more appreciable, in Horkheimer and Adorno's eyes, than the "fundamentally illusory" difference between the models of Ford and General Motors.[24] A visit to the local mall cinema or megaplex confirms the ongoing relevance of this observation in the twenty-first century.

Second, the chances that the products coming out of film studios might constitute an attack on the institution of capitalism are virtually nil. The tycoons of the culture industry are unlikely to yearn for the demise of the economic system that generates their wealth. Consequently, the films that they produce, which (in Horkheimer and Adorno's view) implicitly or explicitly reflect their class position, function to buttress rather than to erode the credos and institutions of capitalism. The authors could not be clearer on this point: "To impress the omnipotence of capital" on the viewer's heart "is the purpose of all films, regardless of the plot selected by the production directors."[25]

Granted, the motion picture industry has undergone changes since the 1940s, when Horkheimer and Adorno penned their treatise. However, as Mark Crispin Miller shows in his incisive introduction to *Seeing through Movies* (1990), those changes have by and large been in the direction of increased monopolization and a more narrowly defined mission to maximize profits. Miller enumerates key transformations, both inside and outside the film industry, that account in various ways for this shift. In the 1980s, for example, a wave of mergers and acquisitions combined an array of diverse enterprises (TV production companies, cable distribution networks, record companies, theme parks, merchandising operations, and so on) into vast entertainment conglomerates. Many of those conglomerates' parent companies are not film studios at all but companies traditionally associated with selling soft drinks or managing investment portfolios. These corporate realignments enable synergies across sectors. The purchase of Columbia Pictures by the Coca-Cola Corporation, for instance, enabled wonderful new synergistic opportunities in the form of product-placement advertisements for Coke in Columbia-produced movies (the subject of Miller's own contribution to his edited volume). In sum, Miller concludes, sounding like a latter-day Horkheimer or Adorno taking stock of the changes in the culture industry that have taken place since the days of his predecessors, "the movies now are made deliberately to show us nothing, but to sell us everything."[26]

Some of the elements discussed in Miller's penetrating critique of the entertainment industry have gone through further changes since his volume appeared in 1990. However, those changes have not altered the basic parameters of how the movies themselves movies are made. "Hollywood is, somewhat surprisingly, a remarkably stable industry," columnist Adam Davidson wrote in the *New York Times Magazine* in 2012. "Over the past 80 years or so, its basic model . . . has been largely unaltered."[27] Even Miller, who documents and brilliantly interprets the changes that the entertainment industry has undergone since the heyday of studio filmmaking, sees these changes as simultaneously telling two different stories: one of transformation and another "of smooth continuation, of predictable fulfillment."[28] In sum, the important changes documented by Miller notwithstanding, the contemporary film industry follows more or less the same dictates, if not the exact same procedures, as it did during Hollywood's golden age. Horkheimer and Adorno, for their part, are quite clear about what those dictates are: "the general laws of capital."[29]

Published in 1947, Siegfried Kracauer's *From Caligari to Hitler* offers an oblique but unmistakable response to the thesis that Horkheimer and Adorno put forward in the pages of "The Culture Industry." Written at the suggestion of Horkheimer (a fellow Frankfurt exile), Kracauer's *Caligari* book examines the ways that the cinema of the Weimar Republic (1918–1933) reflects social tensions in Germany over the course of a decade and a half. In his introduction to the book, in which he lays out his agenda and his premises, Kracauer justifies his investigation in the following terms:

> The films of a nation reflect its mentality in a more direct way than other artistic media for two reasons:
>
> First, films are never the product of an individual. The Russian film director Pudovkin emphasizes the collective character of film production by identifying it with industrial production: "The technical manager can achieve nothing without foremen and workmen and their collective effort will lead to no good result if every collaborator limits himself only to a mechanical performance of his narrow function." . . .
>
> Second, films address themselves, and appeal, to an anonymous multitude. . . . It has occasionally been remarked that Hollywood manages to sell films which do not give the masses what they really want. . . . However, . . . Hollywood cannot afford to ignore spontaneity on the part of the public. General discontent becomes apparent in waning box-office receipts, and the film industry, vitally interested in profit, is bound to adjust itself, as far as possible, to the changes of mental climate.[30]

This justification responds virtually term for term to the central argument of "The Culture Industry." Like Horkheimer and Adorno, Kracauer likens cinematic production to industrial production, but unlike his colleagues, who use the comparison to illustrate the intrinsic seriality of

Hollywood films (as well as other mass-produced cultural commodities), Kracauer makes the comparison in order to emphasize the inherently collective nature of filmmaking. Kracauer's second point, which moves from the context of production to that of consumption, similarly democratizes (or "massifies") the process. Rather than foisting their ideology onto the passively receptive masses, studio executives must engage in a process of negotiation with the public in order to respond to the multitude's desires. Kracauer is clear here that the movie magnates do not engage in this give-and-take with the audience out of respect for the latter's opinions but out of self-interest. Film studio executives seek, above all, to generate a return on investment. If a movie that "speaks to" the masses' concerns stands to turn a bigger profit than one that champions the corporate bosses' worldview, then the best way for those bosses to further their self-interests may be to make pictures that do not openly promote those interests. Indeed, in certain contexts, it may lie in condemning them. In the current context—a context in which wealth inequality is at its highest level in recorded economic history, in which the US government calls upon taxpayers to bail out the very banks that swindled countless investors of their savings, in which labor-saving technologies render redundant an ever-increasing number of workers, and in which multinational corporations restlessly shift operations from region to region in pursuit of lower taxes, weaker labor laws, and rock-bottom wages—the relevance of this argument is immediately apparent.

Kracauer subtitles his book *A Psychological History of the German Film*. However, he clarifies that this idea of "a psychological history" does not presuppose an essentialist determination of a people's national character but, on the contrary, implies a historical conception of collective fears and desires at a given moment in time: "To speak of the peculiar mentality of a nation by no means implies the concept of a fixed national character. The interest here lies exclusively in such collective dispositions or tendencies as prevail within a nation at a certain stage in its development."[31] He speaks elsewhere of the "*symptomatic* value" of cinema, implying at once both film's capacity to express a society's unconscious desires and a distinction between a movie's "manifest" and its "latent" content.[32] It is in this "psychological" sense that Kracauer's frequent references to films' ability to "reflect" or "mirror" historical and social events must be understood. The horizon of cinema is "a culture's *unconscious*."[33] Recurrent cinematic themes, motifs, and figures condense a society's anxieties and wishes at a moment in time into visual and narrative form. To conceive of movies as necessarily an expression of the ideological class position of film studio executives or the conscious intentions of the filmmakers whose work they bankroll is to fail to take into account the larger sociopolitical context in which the cultural producers work. Intentionally or not, explicitly or not, in different ways and to varying degrees, filmmakers respond to what is happening in the world around them. The films that they make cannot fail to reflect in some way that larger context.

Fredric Jameson makes a similar point in the preamble to his exemplary allegorical reading of Sidney Lumet's *Dog Day Afternoon* (1975). Arguing that commercial film is the "medium where, if at all, some change in the class character of social reality ought to be detectable, since social reality and the stereotypes of everyday social reality are the raw material with which commercial film and television are inevitably forced to work," he writes:

> This is my answer, in advance, to critics who object a priori that the immense costs of commercial films, which inevitably place their production under the control of multinational corporations, make any genuinely political content in them unlikely, and on the contrary insure commercial film's vocation as a vehicle for ideological manipulation. No doubt this is so, if we remain on the level of the intention of the filmmaker who is bound to be limited consciously or unconsciously by the objective situation. But it is to fail to reckon with the political content of daily life, with the political logic which is already inherent in the raw material with which the filmmaker must work.[34]

In sum, Jameson suggests, whether or not they mean to and whether or not they want to, filmmakers—even the ones most beholden to the industry—allegorize to some degree the political content of daily life. It is, then, the critic's job to tease out the allegory embedded in the movies they make. That is, in essence, what I set out to do in this book.

Sources

As the above comments render obvious, the approach adopted in this book is indebted to Kracauer's allegorical approach to film criticism and Jameson's pioneering work on culture, politics, and economics. The study has also benefitted from the model that literary critic and film scholar Phillip Wegner provides in *Life between Two Deaths, 1989–2001: U.S. Culture in the Long Nineties* (2009).[35] Through bold interpretations of cinematic, televisual, and literary works made during the long decade of the 1990s, Wegner demonstrates that the period between the fall of the Berlin Wall in 1989 and the terrorist attacks of September 11, 2001, constitutes a pivotal moment in US history. Wegner's virtuoso readings of the *Terminator* films and the movies *Fight Club, Ghost Dog, Independence Day,* and *Cape Fear* are breathtaking in their razor-sharp precision and their ability to generalize their conclusions. Although the present book is more narrowly focused on the particular phenomenon of global capitalism than Wegner's more broad-ranging study of US culture during the long nineties, it owes a great debt to Wegner's book in both its methodology and its overall structure. In many ways, the current project constitutes an attempt to extend Wegner's important work on films of the 1990s into the context of the twenty-first century.

The investigation has also benefitted from cultural theorist Mark Fisher's trenchant study of "capitalist realism" in his 2009 book of that title.[36] Fisher's short and powerful work persuasively makes the case that global capitalism has saturated the cultural landscape to such an extent in the twenty-first century that it is no longer possible even to imagine an alternative to it. The book evokes numerous examples from contemporary films in order to demonstrate this argument. However, although he frequently refers to movies in order to illustrate his points, Fisher does not analyze the films themselves. The methodology adopted in this book is the inverse of Fisher's. Whereas he refers to films in order to advance an argument about capitalism, I bring in theory and context in order to shed light on the films. I would make the same distinction between the approach here and the one adopted in numerous works by Slavoj Žižek, the Slovenian "culture mulcher" whose name appears in many chapters of this book.[37]

The study has also benefitted from the aforementioned *Cartographies of the Absolute* (2015). Toscano and Kinkle's gripping page-turner draws upon an impressive array of material in its Jameson-inspired construction of a "cognitive map" of global capitalism. A good deal of that material is audio-visual. In addition to its theoretically focused chapters, *Cartographies* dedicates a full chapter to the film *Wolfen* (1981), a second chapter to the TV series *The Wire* (2002–2008), and a third—evoked above—to cinematic representations of the global financial crisis of 2008. However, in their chapter on the 2008 meltdown (the part of their book that engages most directly with the issues addressed in the present book), Toscano and Kinkle examine only films that depict the crisis directly, whereas I analyze allegorical refractions of the financial collapse. Moreover, my conclusions are almost diametrically opposed to theirs. Whereas Toscano and Kinkle see precious little critical potential in the cinematic representations of the meltdown that they analyze, I argue that even Martin Scorsese's seemingly jubilatory celebration of a stockbroker's excesses and Woody Allen's not entirely unsympathetic portrayal of a smug New York socialite offer sharply critical perspectives on the debacle of 2008.

Another title that deserves mention in relation to the current project is Kirk Boyle and Daniel Mrozowski's edited volume, *The Great Recession in Fiction, Film, and Television: Twenty-First Century Bust Culture* (2013).[38] The volume's twelve contributors examine a wide variety of popular movies, TV shows, radio programs, literary works, and graphic novels made in the wake of the crash of 2008. The book offers diverse perspectives on what the editors call the "bust culture" of the early twenty-first century. However, the volume's strength, which lies in the diversity of both the material examined and the critical perspectives adopted by the individual authors, also accounts for its limitation. One wonders, in reading, how the various authors would develop their arguments in a book-length study on their topic. The current project proposes precisely the sort of sustained analysis of a tightly circumscribed topic that one craves when reading the individual chapters that comprise Boyle and Mrozowski's wide-ranging volume.

In addition to the interdisciplinary studies mentioned above, numerous monographs have recently appeared on the films or the directors analyzed in this book. Notable titles include David Sterritt's *Spike Lee's America* (2013), Todd McGowan's *Spike Lee* (2014), and Clint Burnham's *Fredric Jameson and "The Wolf of Wall Street"* (2016).[39] The current project has benefitted inestimably from the work presented in those books, but it is distinct from all of them. By organizing the study around a common theme that unites a wide variety of films, as opposed to examining one specific film or a particular director's oeuvre, this book enables the reader to grasp a cultural trend that transcends the work of a single filmmaker and to appreciate the ways that a heterogeneous group of films symptomatically reflects a common problem.

Special mention should be made here of Todd McGowan's analysis of Fernando Meirelles's *The Constant Gardener* in "The Temporality of the Real: The Path to Politics in *The Constant Gardener*." The essay appeared originally as an article in *Film-Philosophy* and then, with very minor revisions, as a chapter in McGowan's fascinating book on "atemporal cinema."[40] McGowan's penetrating insights into Meirelles's strategies of deception, his brilliant interpretation of the heroine's political stance, and his fine analysis of the main male character's "path to politics" strongly influence my reading of the film.

Finally, in addition to these sundry studies of directors, films, and culture more broadly, a wide array of social, political, and economic research has enriched this study. David Harvey's important work on contemporary capitalism informs my overall appreciation of recent global economic developments. I cite his work, in this book, more than I do that of any other author. Without his keen insights into the dynamics of capitalism, the analyses that follow would have been significantly poorer. Walter Benjamin's highly original theory of allegory and Giorgio Agamben's provocative writings on the "state of exception" figure prominently in the analysis of *Children of Men*. Naomi Klein's critique of the so-called "model" theory for the Middle East and Harvey's interpretation of the US-led invasion of Iraq in 2003 shape the interpretation of the film narrative in *Syriana*. Marcia Angell's illuminating study of the ways that multinational pharmaceutical companies operate in the developing world and Joel Bakan's documentary work on the corporation as an institution undergird the analysis of *The Constant Gardener*. Žižek's writings on violence and Giovanni Arrighi's reading of "the long twentieth century," along with Harvey's vital research on neoliberalism, shed light on the socioeconomic subtext of *Inside Man*. Michael Lewis's eye-opening account of the collapse of the US subprime mortgage bond market in 2007 provides a "master code" for the readings of *Blue Jasmine* and *The Wolf of Wall Street*. I also have recourse to Wendy Brown's incisive interpretation of neoliberalism and David Graeber's monumental study of debt in my analysis of *Jasmine*, and to Karl Marx's elaboration of "fictitious capital" in my reading of *Wolf*.

Chapter Outlines

Selecting the individual films for this study posed a formidable challenge. This challenge arose not due to a scarcity of films on the topic but, on the contrary, due to their abundance. Numerous apocalyptic and post-apocalyptic narratives present themselves openly. Jameson's famous dictum that "it is easier to imagine the end of the world than to imagine the end of capitalism" implicitly casts all such contemporary narratives as allegories of the demise of capitalism.[41] In relation to another popular genre of the early twenty-first century, Chris Harman's *Zombie Capitalism* encourages us to perceive the numerous zombie movies and TV shows of the past few decades as allegories of an "undead" system, "seemingly dead when it comes to achieving goals and responding to human feelings, but capable of sudden spurts of activity that cause chaos all around."[42] Similarly, the vampire fad of the 2000s can be interpreted as a mass cultural symptom of a living-dead economic system that, as Karl Marx famously said a century and a half ago, "vampire-like, lives only by sucking living labour."[43] Otherwise, films about upwardly mobile capitalists by day who are serial killers by night clearly allegorize an economic system that subjects the poor and the vulnerable to the whims of the rich and powerful. The latter category would include such movies as Mary Harron's *American Psycho* (2000), Bruce Evans's *Mr. Brooks* (2007), and both Niels Arden Oplev's (2009) and David Fincher's (2011) adaptations of Stieg Larsson's *The Girl with the Dragon Tattoo* (2008). These and countless other films could have found a central place in this book. The reader will undoubtedly have his or her own ideas about other films that would fit neatly in a study of this sort. I hope that this book stimulates readers to develop some of those ideas. The present investigation far from exhausts the subject.

The films examined in this book were selected for the light that they shed on a particular historical sequence, which runs from the immediate post-9/11 period to the global financial crisis of 2008. The thesis of the book is that the particular films chosen, in their chronological ordering, show an arc of popular resistance to global capitalism occurring indirectly in mass culture over the course of roughly a decade. The book develops this overarching argument through a series of detailed analyses of individual films. Each chapter takes as its point of departure a central insight into how a particular film encodes a moment in this historical sequence. In the final pages of this introduction, I propose to enumerate briefly the key insight at the core of each chapter and to sketch in broad strokes the book's overall trajectory.

The first chapter takes as its point of departure the hypothesis that Alfonso Cuarón's *Children of Men* is a contemporary *Trauerspiel*. The latter term refers to a genre of German drama that came into existence during the tumultuous years of the Thirty Years' War that ravaged Europe during the first half of the seventeenth century. In his great study of this theatrical genre, philosopher and cultural critic Walter Benjamin (1892–1940) argues that these tragic dramas, which return obsessively to imagery of skulls and bones, remnants and ruins, fragments and shards, reflect the turbulent historical climate of their time. The *Trauerspiel*'s fixation on images of death and destruction represents one important commonality with Cuarón's bleak depiction of a near-future England—a depiction that, as many critics have argued, very much reflects the misery of our own time. However, a second characteristic of the *Trauerspiel* is equally pertinent to the analysis of Cuarón's film. In contrast to Fletcher, for whom allegory "says one thing and means another," for Benjamin, the allegorical figures that appear in the *Trauerspiel* can mean "absolutely anything."[44] This chapter argues that the movie's central metaphor—that of human infertility and the imminent extinction of the human race—is precisely such a multiplicitous trope. It conjures as much the death of democracy, the breakdown of social solidarity, the destruction of nature, and the manufactured redundancy of human labor as it does the end of humanity. Above all, I argue, it evokes the prospective extinction of the political left as a vibrant counterforce to the destructive forces of globalization.

The disheartened reader will be relieved to learn at this point that Cuarón's pessimistic vision of a society on the verge of total collapse is not typical of the films studied in this book. The *Children of Men* chapter represents the first episode in a grand narrative sketched over the course of six chapters. The subsequent chapters generally become more hopeful (although "less hopeless" might be a better way to put it) as they progress. The disconsolate reader can therefore take comfort in the thought that, by beginning with the grimmest, most depressing, and least uplifting of the movies on the filmography, we can now progress only in the direction of more nuanced appraisals of the contemporary situation.

That being said, the second chapter is hardly cheerier than the first. It examines Stephen Gahgan's notoriously complex geopolitical thriller *Syriana*. The film interweaves narratives of a corporate merger in the US oil and gas sector, a political rivalry in an oil-rich state in the Persian Gulf, a CIA field operative trying to locate a US missile that went missing in the Middle East, and two unemployed migrant workers who use the missing warhead in a suicide attack on a Liquefied Natural Gas carrier stationed in the Persian Gulf. Part of what this chapter does is examine the ways that this film narrative allegorizes global developments at the beginning of the twenty-first century. The central allegorical figure around which the investigation is organized is the one that gives the movie its title. "Syriana," a word never uttered in the film, is an actual term used within right-wing political action groups during the early years of the twenty-first century, designating a hypothetical reconfiguration of the Middle East in ways that would further US interests in the region. According to Klein and Harvey, this conception of a reconfigured Middle East provided a strong impetus for the Bush administration's decision to invade Iraq in 2003. I argue that the movie's ambiguous ending suggests two radically different visions of the map that might emerge from the chaos in the Middle East. One anticipates the conversion of the region into the "Syriana" of the film's title, while the other allegorically prefigures the creation of the Islamic State of Iraq and Syria.

The third chapter shifts from East-West conflicts between the United States and the Middle East to North-South relations between the United Kingdom and sub-Saharan Africa, and from Big Oil to Big Pharma. The title of this chapter, "Corporate Murder," comes from a remark that a British spy stationed in Nairobi makes toward the end of Meirelles's *The Constant Gardener*. The spy uses this evocative expression to describe the assassination of a social activist who had uncovered how a multinational pharmaceutical company was using unwitting patients from the slums of Nairobi as human guinea pigs for a new drug it was testing, but the phrase applies equally to the way that the corporation operates more generally in Africa. As the muckraking activist whose murder at the beginning of the film sets the plot in motion discovered, the drug company has been dumping the bodies of test patients who responded adversely to the drug into unmarked graves and covering them in quicklime. This chapter explores the various "corporate murders" that the movie's fictional pharmaceutical company carries out, and the successive attempts to bring the murderers to justice.

The fourth chapter examines yet another corporate sector: the financial sector. This is the sector that, since the 1980s, has become the predominant force in the global economy. The central insight that animates the argument in this chapter is the revelation that the title character of Spike Lee's *Inside Man* is neither of the film's two main characters but their common enemy, a Wall Street banker who made his fortune in the vilest of circumstances. This chapter argues that this unsavory character represents the type of wealth accumulation that Harvey calls "accumulation by dispossession." Taking my lead from the presence, in one of Lee's famous "signature shots," of a photograph of the Wall Street tycoon with President George H.W. Bush, I examine the three forms of "accumulation by dispossession" that the movie evokes. The first is the type of wealth accumulation associated with Bush's father Prescott Bush, a man who allegedly made his fortune during the Second World War in circumstances not at all dissimilar to those in which the film's eponymous "inside man" made his. The second is the recrudescence of "accumulation by dispossession" that the turn to financialization enabled during the political career of George H.W. Bush (first in his role as vice president under Ronald Reagan, then as president) in the long decade of the 1980s. The third is the profit that political and economic insiders reap from the systemic crisis that, according to sociologist Giovanni Arrighi, the switch from manufacturing to financialization invariably heralds. It is precisely such a crisis that the United States was undergoing when the film premiered in 2006, during the administration of the second President Bush.

Chapter 5 continues the line of inquiry begun in the preceding chapter. It reads Martin Scorsese's *The Wolf of Wall Street* as an allegory of the financial shenanigans that, in 2008, produced the worst global financial crisis since the Great Crash of 1929. However, I argue, the film's allegorical dimensions are as much a matter of form as they are of content. The movie plays us for a chump, I argue, even as it exposes how the wolves of Wall Street rip us off. In order to bring this self-reflexive dimension of the movie into relief from the outset, the chapter begins with an examination of the film's duplicitous narrative strategy, which I then extrapolate first to the eponymous wolf's particular financial schemes and finally to finance capitalism more broadly.

The sixth chapter examines the financial collapse of 2008 from a different angle. The central insight that guides the reading of Woody Allen's *Blue Jasmine* is the homology between the title character's personal itinerary and macroeconomic developments that unfolded on a national scale in the United States during the late 2000s. In the film, Jasmine, a former New York socialite who finds herself suddenly reduced to poverty, suffers a mental breakdown and is then rescued from immediate ruin by her estranged working-class sister. However, despite her best efforts and the support she receives from her sister, Jasmine recovers neither her mental stability nor her financial standing. When the last of her attempts to regain her lost status fails and she suffers her final breakdown at the end of the movie, Jasmine goes into freefall. In sum, replicating in miniature economic developments in the late 2000s, the movie depicts a meltdown and a bailout, but—in contrast to the national narrative spun by media pundits following the crash of 2008—the bailout, in Allen's film, does not lead to a recovery. This chapter analyzes the ways that Allen's story of a woman's collapse, fragile recovery, and ultimate demise recasts and implicitly interprets the socioeconomic macro-narrative of the United States in the early twenty-first century.

1

Exceptions and Rules

States of Emergency in *Children of Men*

IN *THE ORIGIN OF GERMAN TRAGIC DRAMA* (1928), philosopher and cultural critic Walter Benjamin proposes that "the allegorical way of seeing . . . is meaningful only in periods of decline."[1] Benjamin offers the examples of the Middle Ages, when "the impermanence of things was inescapably derived from observation," and the turbulent period of the Thirty Years' War (1618–1648), when "the same knowledge stared European humanity in the face."[2] Commenting on these passages, Susan Buck-Morss, in her magisterial book on Benjamin's *Arcades Project*, concludes that, for Benjamin, "certain experiences (and thus certain epochs) were allegorical, not certain poets."[3] This idea that certain epochs are allegorical is thought-provoking. It suggests that there is something about particular historical periods that lends itself to the allegorical transfigurations that Benjamin finds in the German baroque tragic drama. The overarching argument of the present book is that our own era constitutes such a moment. There is something about the early twenty-first century that calls forth the allegorical mode of representation.

Not all the movies examined in the pages that follow function according to Benjamin's idiosyncratic conception of allegory, but one of them very much does. Alfonso Cuarón's *Children of Men* (2006) exhibits many of the features that Benjamin attributes to the German tragic drama (*Trauerspiel*, lit. "mourning play"). Benjamin's famous statement that "allegories are, in the realm of thoughts, what ruins are in the realm of things" seems tailor-made for a film like *Children of Men*.[4] His assertion that "in allegory the observer is confronted with the *facies hippocratica* [the change produced in the face by impending death] of history, as a petrified, primordial landscape" reads like a poetic commentary on the film narrative.[5] Cuarón's movie shares with the *Trauerspiel* an obsession with fragments, ruins, and remnants. Moreover, if, as Benjamin asserts, in the allegorical *Trauerspiel* of the seventeenth century, "any person, any object, any relationship can mean absolutely anything else," similarly, in *Children of Men*, the various characters, settings, and situations lend themselves to diverse interpretations.[6]

Foremost among the film's polysemous tropes is the one that drives the plot. In the movie, set in England during the year 2027, women have stopped giving birth. The last baby was born in 2009, making the youngest person in the world eighteen years old. When the generation that came of age in the 2020s eventually dies, the human race will be extinct. However, what Cuarón encourages us to think about while watching the movie is less the future of human reproduction per se than the myriad problems of contemporary globalization that the film details as it recounts the story of a cynical middle-aged Brit escorting an inexplicably pregnant African refugee across the barren countryside of a hyper-militarized and rigorously segregated England. This chapter argues that the movie's infertility metaphor transcodes as much the death of politics as it does the degradation of the planet, the ruin of society, or the destruction of humanity itself. Foremost among the problems that the film beckons us to consider, I argue, is the lack of effective resistance to the deleterious effects of globalization that the movie brings into stark relief over the course of nearly two hours.

The interpretation begins with an analysis of the film's opening scenes, which set the movie's tone while communicating with alarming clarity its vision of a society unraveling as people go about their daily routines. I contrast these scenes depicting a neoliberal Britain in a perpetual state of emergency, where citizens go about their business with little regard for the disaster unfolding around them, with our first glimpse inside a miniature hippy commune. The visual information on the screen in the latter scene gives vital clues to the film's conception of history and its nostalgia for the 1960s, which the movie presents as the heyday of social activism. The legacy of the radical sixties lived on, the film implies, up until the 2000s, when it died in the latter years of the decade. I then explore the form of resistance that comes into being when older forms of political contestation perish. The film offers a particularly graphic representation of this new type of resistance in its depiction of an armed uprising inside a refugee camp at the end of the movie. I liken this uprising sequence to the insurrectionary violence that

Benjamin provocatively calls the "real state of emergency" in the *Theses on the Philosophy of History*, his last major work. I then conclude with an analysis of the film's final scene, in which a boat hopefully called the *Tomorrow* arrives to take a miraculously fertile refugee and her newborn baby to a mythical outpost on the Azores islands. Unlike the majority of critics who have written on the film, I do not see the movie's ending as offering an optimistic, redemptive, or hopeful vision of the future. Whatever hope the film offers lies not in the narrative, I argue, but in its unflinching depiction of the horrors of the present. It is the hope that by showing us those horrors, we might see them for what they are and organize an effective resistance to them.

States of Exception

Let us begin with the film's opening words, read by a pair of news announcers over a black screen.

> TV VOICE 1: Day one thousand of the siege of Seattle.
>
> TV VOICE 2: The Muslim community demands an end to the Army's occupation of mosques.
>
> TV VOICE 1: The Homeland Security bill is ratified. After eight years, British borders will remain closed. The deportation of illegal immigrants will continue. Good morning. Our lead story.
>
> TV VOICE 2: The world was stunned today by the death of Diego Ricardo, the youngest person on the planet.

The film's opening line here explicitly calls to mind the anti-globalization movement that came prominently into view during the 1999 protests in Seattle, Washington. Those protests brought together roughly 40,000 demonstrators ranging from rank-and-file union members to anarchists, environmentalists, and anti-poverty activists united in common cause against the World Trade Organization (WTO), which was gathering at the Seattle Convention Center for a scheduled meeting. Protestors considered the newly formed WTO (created in 1995) to be "a secretive tool of ruthless multinational corporations" that enabled "sneaker companies to exploit Asian workers, timber companies to clear-cut rain forests, shrimpers to kill sea turtles and a world of other offenses" by transferring market regulatory responsibility from national governments to an intergovernmental organization that favored business interests over workers' rights, environmental concerns, indigenous ways of life, the livelihood of local populations, and any other concern that might impede the free flow of capital, goods, and services across borders.[7] Unsurprisingly, the protestors clashed with police, leading columnists and reporters to dub the 1999 confrontation "the battle of Seattle" or (as in the film) "the siege of Seattle."

By recasting this one-day confrontation as an ongoing standoff now in its thousandth day, the film situates us, in 2027, in a future where contemporary problems persist in intensified form. The protracted length of the standoff also bodes poorly for the protestors. Unlike the forces of order, which can hold out virtually indefinitely in a clash of this sort, street protestors face myriad logistical challenges, which compromise their ability to continue the struggle even if they do not weaken the demonstrators' resolve. Although the film gives us no details about the Seattle confrontation other than its length, this single piece of information serves to tilt the balance of power in the government's favor in the viewer's imagination.

The second headline takes a similar approach, amplifying the magnitude of a current social conflict, in this case by recasting tensions between Muslims and the British government as a confrontation that has escalated to the point where government troops now occupy mosques. The third headline, which, once again, sounds like an exaggerated version of what could easily be a current news headline, dashes whatever hopes we may have had that the Muslim community might succeed in their efforts to expel the soldiers from their mosques: "The Homeland Security bill is ratified. After eight years, British borders will remain closed. The deportation of illegal immigrants will continue." The latter headline, which transfers the US Department of Homeland Security, created in 2002 by President George W. Bush in the wake of the 9/11 attacks, to Britain, condenses a rich historical reference into a few short sentences. Let us take a moment to unpack this reference.

The US Homeland Security Act (HSA) of 2002 consolidated diverse governmental agencies into a single umbrella organization with a mandate "to ensure a homeland that is safe, secure, and resilient against terrorism and other hazards."[8] The HSA was the culmination of a series of efforts designed to thwart or diminish the severity of threats to national security, threats that the act defines broadly to include anything that menaces "American interests, aspirations, and ways of life."[9] Among the measures leading up to the creation of the Department of Homeland Security is the USA Patriot Act of October 2001, which "allowed the attorney general to 'take into custody' any alien suspected of activities that endangered 'the national security of the United States.'"[10] The Patriot Act was followed, in November of the same year, by President Bush's "military order" authorizing the "indefinite detention" of "noncitizens suspected in terrorist activities."[11] As Italian philosopher Giorgio Agamben demonstrates in *State of Exception*, Bush's order "radically erases any legal status of the individual, thus producing a legally unnamable and unclassifiable being."[12] The only thing to which the legal condition of these people deprived of the most basic human rights could possibly be compared, Agamben argues, "is the legal situation of the Jews in the Nazi *Lager* [camps]."[13] Like Hitler's 1933 Decree for the Protection of People and State, which stripped German Jews of their citizenship, thereby creating a class of beings with no legal status, Bush's 2001 decree authorizing the indefinite detention of suspected terrorists had the effect of creating a class of juridically nonhuman bipeds that it reduced to the minimal condition of existence that Agamben elsewhere calls "bare life": the pure, naked, unqualified existence of a biological entity with no legal status as a human being.[14]

Agamben argues in *State of Exception* that the legal status of detainees in the "new" prison facilities like the US-run Guantánamo Bay detention camp (a status shared by prisoners in the Abu Ghraib facility, which had not yet gained notoriety when Agamben was writing his book) is homologous to that of people interned in the Nazi concentration camps of the 1940s. In both cases, the inmates were stripped of the most basic rights that human beings enjoy. In a previous book, Agamben famously named this figure *homo sacer*, in reference to an archaic Roman law that deprived certain criminals of legal protections.[15] Anyone could kill *homo sacer* with impunity. Killing a "sacred man" was not considered an act of murder. Such, according to Agamben, was the position of Jews under the Third Reich. They had no rights whatsoever, up to and including the right to live. As philosopher and cultural critic Slavoj Žižek points out in his book on the Iraq War (and Agamben will agree with him), the status of the prisoners held in Guantánamo Bay "is directly that of *Homo sacer*: there are no legal rules regulating their imprisonment; they find themselves literally in a legal void, reduced to basic subsistence."[16] It is they who became, in Judith Butler's formulation, "humans who are not humans."[17]

Numerous scenes in Cuarón's film depict this sort of reduction of a class of people to the abject state of bare life that Agamben associates with *homo sacer*. The tracking shot that follows Theo (Clive Owen), the film's antihero, when he arrives at the Alresford train station and walks along the platform on his way to meet his friend Jasper (Michael Caine) shows a group of people of different ethnic backgrounds quarantined in a steel cage in the left of the frame. The camera tracks past an expressionless British guard with a submachine gun and a caged woman who informs the impassive guard in Serbo-Croatian that there must be some mistake.[18] The camera follows Theo from behind as he walks past the woman and a half-dozen other detainees (five European, one African) without taking notice of them. When Theo saunters past a second cage of detainees, also guarded by an armed soldier, the camera pans to an indignant old woman protesting in German to the unresponsive guard. Like the detainees in the previous cage, the refugees quarantined in this second cage are a diverse group, including two sub-Saharan African men, a South Asian woman in a hijab, and a motley group of Europeans of different ages and social classes. The broad racial, ethnic, and social diversity of the prisoners we see quarantined along the platform here calls to mind Žižek's remark, made in the context of the Bush administration's "war on terror," that "we are all *Homo sacer*."[19]

Cuarón's stroke of genius in this scene is to show Theo not caring about the plight of the people quarantined like animals in cages. In her analysis of the movie in *The Promise of Happiness*, social theorist Sara Ahmed criticizes the film for not taking a clearer position on the horrors taking place in the background of the film. "Theo does not see [the] suffering," she writes; "indeed, if we adopt his gaze, then our 'becoming active' also allows us not to see the suffering."[20] Although it is true that if we adopted Theo's gaze we would not see the suffering, the film does not encourage us to adopt his point of view. Cuarón's frequent use of wide tracking shots that include Theo in the frame—instead of eyeline matches (in which a first shot shows a person looking at something and a second shows what she sees), cutaway shots (which interrupt a continuously filmed action by inserting a view of something else), and other editing techniques—makes Theo the object more than the subject of our gaze. What the film depicts is as much Theo's blindness to what is going on around him as it is those goings-on.

Theo is not the only character who ignores the suffering around him. None of the passengers at the Alresford station pays any mind to the caged refugees. The clever inclusion at the end of the scene of a commuter in a tweed cap rushing past Jasper and Theo to catch the train, walking stick in one hand and briefcase in the other, shows how normal this horrifying world has become to some of its inhabitants. Their disregard—their refusal to see—what is happening around them and their indifference to the "sacred men" in their midst are essential components of the mise-en-scène. Central to the film's biting critique of society is the nonchalance of people not directly in the position of *homo sacer*. Their indifference or apathy is in large part the subject of the movie's critique.

Figure 1.1. Theo strolls past refugees quarantined like animals in cages (*Children of Men*, Universal, 2006).

Neoliberal Nightmares

The fourth news headline that we hear at the beginning of the film ("The world was stunned today by the death of Diego Ricardo, the youngest person on the planet") sets up Cuarón's depiction of a politically myopic

Figure 1.2. The inclusion in the frame of a commuter rushing to catch the train at the end of the Alresford station scene shows how normal the state of exception has become (*Children of Men*, Universal, 2006).

British population. As the newscaster starts recounting the circumstances of "Baby Diego's" death, the film cuts from a black screen to the movie's first image, a group of several dozen people crowded into a London coffee shop staring at a television screen situated above our head. A maudlin violin score provides tear-jerking theme music for the news report. Theo enters the café, makes his way through the crowd, orders a coffee, glances up at the TV screen while waiting for his order, then turns and walks out the door as the sound of people sobbing mixes with the cloying TV theme music. These opening shots, which juxtapose an emotionless Theo and a roomful of people engaged in an act of collective mourning, depict the protagonist's isolation from his compatriots. Ahmed aptly characterizes Theo as the film's "affect alien," a person cut off from his peers by his inability to share their feelings.[21] However, significantly, the story that moves the crowd to tears is the human-interest story, not the reports on social conflict or the news of the mass deportation of immigrants. As Ahmed notes, "The death of an individual person is the lead story, individual grief taking precedence over collective grievance."[22] The announcement that "the world was stunned" by the death of the youngest person on the planet operates almost like a performative speech act, creating the reaction it ostensibly reports.

The following sequence, which depicts Theo arriving for work at the Ministry of Energy, sharpens the contrast between the film's affect alien and his compatriots. We hear again the cloying "Baby Diego" TV theme music as Theo walks past his coworkers, who sit at their cubicle desks crying into tissues as they watch the news report on their computer screens. Theo makes his way past his sobbing colleagues, sits at his desk, and looks around the open-concept office with a look of disgust. His gaze comes to rest on the woman in the cubicle facing his. The deep-focus shot of Theo staring at his office mate juxtaposes three images in the frame. In the foreground, we see the woman's desk, decorated with personalizing knick-knacks including a miniature teddy bear, porcelain figurines of mothers and babies, a little statuette of a Dalmatian puppy in a shoe, a miniature British flag, and oodles of baby-themed trinkets. In the middle ground Theo stares indiscreetly at his coworker, and in the background a sheet of plastic covers an upside-down office chair sitting on an empty desk.

The plastic sheet covering the inverted chair on the desk in the background conjures an image of death, the plastic tarp functioning visually like a blanket covering a corpse and the abandoned desk evoking a metaphorical grave. The image leads us to wonder whether the desk is empty because the person who worked there died and, given the film's human-extinction theme, whether the employee has not been replaced

Figure 1.3. The fate of labor. A plastic sheet covering an inverted chair on a desk at the Ministry of Energy evokes layoffs and redundancies more than the prospect of human extinction (*Children of Men*, Universal, 2006).

because there are no more people to hire. But the film clearly tells us later that the infertility crisis occurred all at once. Women got pregnant and gave birth at a normal rate until they suddenly started miscarrying en masse. All things being equal, the number of living adults (those born before 2009, when the infertility epidemic struck, who therefore would be eighteen or older in 2027) should be constant. The applicant pool for a post at the Ministry of Energy would logically be unaffected by the sudden population decline. The inverted chair must therefore represent something other than the imminent extinction of the human race.

Unfortunately, the thinning out of workplaces is a reality with which we have become all too familiar in recent years. As political economist David Harvey notes in *Seventeen Contradictions and the End of Capitalism*, the recent recessions in the United States and Europe (from the 1990s onward) have been followed by so-called "jobless recoveries."[23] In other words, economies have rebounded in those regions even though employment levels have not. According to Harvey, the recession of 2008–2009, dubbed the "Great Recession" in reference to the Great Depression of the 1930s, "has led to the creation of long-term unemployment on a scale not seen . . . since the 1930s."[24] The empty desk covered in plastic in *Children of Men* conjures an image of such a circumstance. It reflects not a decline in the workforce but a reduction of the number of people actually working, which is something entirely different. In short, Theo's workplace is downsizing, as are the majority of workplaces in the real world that can figure out how to get by with fewer employees. In an effort to reduce costs while simultaneously disempowering organized labor, employers have looked for ways to replace human resources with technological resources. Their efforts have been quite successful, resulting in an ever-increasing number of structurally unemployable former workers. "Most of the world's population is becoming disposable and irrelevant from the standpoint of capital," Harvey dispassionately observes.[25] It is evidence of such a state of affairs that we see in the background behind Theo. The inverted chair summons an image of the redundancy of work more than a diminution of the working population.

The contrast between Theo and the woman in the cubicle opposite his reflects two distinct ways of not engaging with the world: one by not caring, the other by caring about something irrelevant. The counter-shot to Theo's gaze reinforces the opposition between Theo's nihilism and his coworker's emotional investment in the personal at the implicit expense of the political. The racking-focus shot shifts definition from a row of trinkets and cute baby toys decorating the horizontal metal bar that separates the two office spaces to the woman bawling unselfconsciously as she watches the report on Baby Diego on her computer. The row of trinkets that demarcates the woman's workspace functions visually like a collection of dime-store talismans protecting the civil servant from both the "affect alien" across from her and the world in general. As she comes into focus in the shot, we see clearly behind her a row of additional office chairs turned upside-down on desks and covered in plastic. One can only imagine that among the things that the woman's fixation on all things baby helps her ward off are unpleasant thoughts about those vacant desks.

The subsequent twenty-second scene, a testament to Cuarón's gift for understated tongue-in-cheek social commentary, shows Theo asking his boss if he can take the rest of the day off (or "finish [his] day's work at home," as he says). Theo stands in a medium long shot at the threshold of his boss's office. He is unshaven with his hair uncombed, a shirttail hanging out of his pants, his collar unbuttoned, and his tie loose around his neck. He has just survived a bomb attack, which could explain his disheveled appearance (although not his three or four days' worth of razor stubble), but Clive Owen plays the scene like a workplace comedy, not a development in an unfolding action-adventure drama. Standing just off center in the fame, with his body at a slight angle to the camera, his head cocked slightly to the side, and one hand dangling at his side several inches lower than the other, Theo informs his boss (Michael Haughey) why he has come to see him: "Mr. Griffiths, I seem to be more affected by Baby Diego's death than I realized, sir. If you wouldn't mind, I'd appreciate it if I could finish my day's work at home." As he explains the emotional effect that Baby Diego's death has had on him, the clownish-looking Theo looks earnestly at Mr. Griffiths, furrowing his brow in an expression of sincerity and indistinctly nodding his head in a gesture that looks more like an unconscious effort of self-encouragement than a conscious attempt to solicit an affirmative response from his boss. At the same time, he inadvertently clenches and unclenches his fists. This nervous tic, which counters the effect of the furrowed brow, subtly communicates to us, and probably to Mr. Griffiths, that Theo is making up a sham excuse to get the rest of the day off. We do not need to wait for the affect alien's subsequent divulgation to Jasper—"Baby Diego, come on. That guy was a wanker"—to appreciate just how deeply the celebrity's death affected him.

The counter-shot to the shot of Theo standing awkwardly in his boss's doorway is one of the great satiric moments in the film. Combining elements of Terry Gilliam's *Brazil* (1985) and Mike Judge's *Office Space* (1999), it shows a skeptical Mr. Griffiths sitting at his desk in his tiny windowless office. Like the woman in the cubicle across from Theo, Mr. Griffiths has decorated his workspace with personalizing items (cricket-themed instead of baby-themed). But the remarkable characteristic of Mr. Griffiths's office is its size. If we were to imagine the poor Griffiths trying to stand up from his desk, we would realize that there

Figure 1.4. If we were to imagine Mr. Griffiths trying to stand up from his desk, we would realize that there is no room for him to pull out his chair (*Children of Men*, Universal, 2006).

is no room for him to pull out his chair. He is trapped between the shelves of binders behind him and the cluttered desk in front of him. One is reminded of Sam Lowry's office at the Ministry of Information in Gilliam's *Brazil*, where the hero shares a desk table with the person in the neighboring office. The only way for the neighbor to enlarge his diminutive worktable is to pull Lowry's miniscule desktop through the wall and into his own workroom. Griffiths's office is like the low-level-management equivalent of Milton's final workstation in *Office Space*, a film in which the cantankerous Milton (Stephen Root) is moved from one dehumanizing office space to another until he finally ends up in a caged-off area of the basement, where his boss, the odious Lumburgh (Gary Cole), asks him if he would mind taking care of the cockroach problem while he is down there.

Mr. Griffiths's response to his subordinate's request completes the portrait of the manager. Without taking his eyes off Theo, Griffiths ritualistically lifts a hand to his face, puts a pill in his mouth, moves the pill to the back of his tongue with a mechanical jaw movement, and then washes it down with a swig of tea from a vanity cup. His only audible response to Theo is a loud gulp. Griffiths of course knows that Theo is making up a bogus excuse, but what can he say? He cannot refuse to let a worker go home on this tragic day, when "the world was stunned by the death of Diego Ricardo." The following shot, depicting Theo on the train to the Alresford station on his way to visit Jasper, confirms that Theo has found the perfect pretext for taking the day off.

In summary, the first few minutes of *Children of Men*, from the opening news headlines through the café scene and the sequence in the Ministry of Energy to Theo's arrival at the Alresford station, present a stark image of a society at loose ends. On the one hand, illegal immigrants are rounded up in mass and quarantined in cages in preparation for their expulsion from the homeland. On the other hand, within the protected zones, life drearily continues for a shrinking number of employees working in soul-destroying conditions, while sensational newscasts distract them from the misery around them. If this scenario sounds all too familiar, it is because it resembles all too much a reality we already know. Žižek pithily characterizes this resemblance in an interview included on the DVD: "Hegel in his *Aesthetics* says somewhere that a good portrait looks more like the person who is portrayed than the person itself, like a good portrait is more you than you are yourself. And I think this is what the film does with our reality."[26] In the spirit of Gilliam's remark that *Brazil*, a dystopian science fiction film that is explicitly about fantasy, "is really a documentary," *Children of Men* invents very little of its imagery in its grim depiction of an apocalyptic future.[27] Much of what we see in the film can be observed in the world around us. As Žižek suggests, the changes that the movie makes to empirical reality "do not point towards alternate reality; they simply make reality more what it already is."[28]

The same strategy applies to the film's depiction of the environment. The first shot of the English countryside, a fifteen-second pan that follows Jasper's car as it drives past mounds of charred animal carcasses burning on piles of dirt, provides an example. In his insightful article on the movie, Zahid Chaudhary notes the resemblance of this shot to iconic photos of the 2001 outbreak of foot-and-mouth disease in the United Kingdom, when ten million sheep and cattle were killed and burnt to ashes in an attempt to halt the disease.[29] While the shot of Jasper's car driving past the heaps of smoldering animal remains evokes a specific historical circumstance, a shot later in the film, which uses the same technique (a pan from left to right that follows a moving car), offers a more general image of environmental degradation. Dead cows, an oil drum on its side, and other debris lie in a pool of stagnant water in the foreground while factories belch smoke and flames out of chimneys in the background. As the camera pans across the desolate landscape, it reveals additional factories polluting the air in the background, a dead pig lying in a ditch beside drain pipes that spew yellowish-green liquid in the foreground, and an array of household trash littering the middle ground. Cuarón's inclusion of the animal carcasses in this shot

Figure 1.5. Dead cows, an oil drum on its side, and scattered debris lie in a pool of stagnant water while factories belch flames and smoke (*Children of Men*, Universal, 2006).

has the effect of visually linking cause and effect (industrial pollution and death), making reality "more what it already is." With the exception of those dead animals, the shot could be right out of Avi Lewis's *This Changes Everything* (2015, coproduced by Cuarón), based on Naomi Klein's book of the same title. Lewis's documentary, like Klein's book, makes a strong case that climate change is a direct result of capitalist globalization and that consequently the environmentalist movement must become anti-capitalist if environmental catastrophe on a global scale is to be averted.

The End of the Sixties

Environmental degradation, dehumanizing working conditions, the manufactured redundancy of social labor, and the forced migration of masses of people are examples of the developments that demonstrators were protesting in Seattle in 1999. Although *Children of Men* does not develop the Seattle reference that it makes at the outset of the movie, it does contain other images of social protest. A striking set of such images appears in our first glimpse inside Janice and Jasper Palmer's house. The scene begins with a slow tracking shot of a collage of photos that move forward in time, from the historical past to the fictional present, as the camera scans a wall in the Palmers' living room. Photographs of Rosa Parks (the African American civil rights activist who refused to give up her seat on a bus to a white passenger in 1955), Angela Davis (a leader of the Black Panthers and an iconic 1960s radical), and John Lennon (the most politically engaged member of the Beatles) circa 1970 lead to a photo of Naomi Klein at a podium. Next to the picture of Klein is a "Don't Attack Iraq" bumper sticker tucked behind a photomontage that places the iconic hooded Abu Ghraib prisoner with electrodes attached to his hands on the Statue of Liberty's pedestal in New York Harbor. These images give way to pictures of Janice (Philippa Urquhart) receiving the 2015 Photojournalist of the Year award and Jasper winning the 2010 Political Cartoonist of the Year award. The camera continues to track along the wall past newspaper headlines documenting the onset of the infertility epidemic, a wave of migrations to England (one front-page article bearing the heading: "Janice Palmer Questions Britain's Ethical Response to the Refugee Situation"), and the passage of a law declaring all immigrants illegal. It comes to rest on a close-up of a magazine with a picture of Janice looking out from behind her camera on the cover. "MI5 [the British intelligence agency] Deny Involvement in Torture of Photojournalist," reads the headline.

Figure 1.6. The wall of heroes in the Palmers' house commemorates half a century of social protest. Photographs of Rosa Parks, Angela Davis, John Lennon, Rigoberta Menchú, Aung San Suu Kyi, and Naomi Klein lead to a photomontage that sets the iconic hooded Abu Ghraib prisoner on the Statue of Liberty's pedestal (*Children of Men*, Universal, 2006).

This wall commemorates half a century of political activism and social change, from the civil rights movement of the 1960s to the antiwar protests of the early twenty-first century and beyond, up to a refugee crisis that eerily anticipates the plight of millions of Syrians in the mid-2010s. The commemorative wall also functions as a mini-biography of Janice and Jasper, documenting their past lives as a celebrated photojournalist and an award-winning political cartoonist. The past images of Janice and Jasper stand in stark contrast to the couple's present state. Janice now lives in a condition of virtual comatose. She is able to breathe and eat but is unable to speak, walk, feed herself, focus her eyes on anything in her field of vision, or register any emotion, let alone take photographs or question Britain's ethical response to the refugee situation. Jasper, by contrast, remains mobile and active, but his primary occupation is now cultivating (and smoking) the marijuana that we see thriving under grow lights in his greenhouse. Although he can get around without any problem, he too is a hollow shell of his former self.

The counter-shot to the shot of the commemorative wall shows Jasper and Theo putting a ruby-colored scarf around Janice's shoulders as a cover version of the Rolling Stones' 1967 hit "Ruby Tuesday," performed by Franco Battiato, plays in the background. The camera tracks slowly forward and pans gently to the right, reframing Janice and Theo as he turns his gaze from her to the wall of memorabilia. An eyeline match reveals that Theo is looking at a snapshot of himself, his ex-wife Julian (Julianne Moore), and their son Dylan. The family photo is the centerpiece of a little shrine, which includes a drawing of Jamaican reggae legend Bob Marley and diverse memorabilia from the 2003 protests against the war in Iraq. We later learn that Julian and Theo met at a demonstration against the Iraq War, that they subsequently married and had Dylan, and that Dylan died in the flu pandemic of 2008. It is following Dylan's death, which led to the couple's divorce, that Theo became the "affect alien" we see in the film. In the early years of the twenty-first century, the film suggests, he was a political activist. Although Theo downplays his earlier political commitments ("You were the activist, I just wanted to get laid," he says to Julian in response to her assertion that "in the old days . . . he was a real activist"), the fact that the couple met at an antiwar rally attests to his activist past. Surely there are easier ways to get laid than attending antiwar demonstrations.

The couple's son's name, Dylan, also suggests Julian and Theo's attachment, in the early 2000s, to a tradition of political activism that the film roots in the 1960s. This name, which none of the characters glosses in the film (and which does not appear in the P. D. James novel *The Children of Men*, on which Cuarón's film is loosely based), gains relevance in light of the movie's sixties-inspired sound track. In addition to photos of John Lennon and the drawing of Bob Marley that adorn the wall of heroes, and the rendition of "Ruby Tuesday" that accompanies the shot of the commemorative wall, the film makes numerous references to the music of the late 1960s and early 1970s. The sound track includes songs by Deep Purple ("Hush," 1968), King Crimson ("The Court of the Crimson King," 1969), Donovan ("There Is an Ocean," 1973), and John Lennon ("Freeda People," 1973), as well as a cover version of the Beatles' "Tomorrow Never Knows" (Lennon and McCartney, 1966). Moreover, due to the striking similarity of the two men's appearance, it is virtually impossible to tell which photos on the commemorative wall are of John Lennon and which are of Michael Caine in the role of Jasper. The physical resemblance between the two figures may be coincidental, but Cuarón and especially Caine, who modeled his performance of Jasper on the late Beatle, play it up.[30] We could include on this list of musical references the iconic inflatable pig floating above the Battersea power station (the film set for the Ark of the Arts), an image that directly references the cover of Pink Floyd's *Animals* (1977). In the context of this multiplication of references to the music of a bygone era, the naming of Dylan (not "Dillon," as some critics write the name) starts to take on a heavy symbolic weight. Although he would be the only US-born artist on the film's roster of iconic musicians, Bob Dylan shares Lennon's status as emblematic pop icon of the times that were a-changin' in the 1960s.[31]

As Fredric Jameson insists, the period generally known as "the sixties"—a period that, according to Jameson, "may be said to have begun (slowly) in 1963, with the Beatles and the Vietnam War, and to have ended dramatically somewhere around 1973–75"—was passionately political.[32] It is the period that saw the emergence of not only the Vietnam War protest movement, which "defined and constituted" the politics of the sixties, according to Jameson.[33] It was also the culmination of the civil rights movement, the heyday of the women's movement, and the apex of radical student engagement. It is the period that saw what, in retrospect, we now know to be the last heroic triumphs of the labor movement, nowhere more apparent than in the streets of Paris in May 1968, when some 11 million workers (more than 22 percent of the total population of France at the time) went on strike, joining ranks with student protestors and nearly bringing the de Gaulle government to its knees.

Everything about Janice and Jasper—their professions and how they practiced them, her "Ruby Tuesday" scarf, his "John Lennon" hair and glasses, the fibers of his bulky wool cardigan, the grain of the wood panels in their living room, their wood-burning stove, the stir-fried vegetables he serves from his wok—code them as 1960s icons. Interpreted metaphorically, their current conditions convey what remains of their heroic generation in an era, such as ours, when rabble-rousing lefties are hollow shells of their former selves—in the imagery of the film, when they have been turned into lifeless automata (such as Janice) or reduced to the state of an "old, obscene, impotent retired hippy person" (as Žižek's memorable characterization of Jasper would have it).[34]

With Janice and Jasper no longer carrying on the legacy of their generation, political activism in the film falls to a group of anti-government militants called the Fishes. This underground revolutionary organization, whose motto is "The Fishes are at war with the British government until they recognize equal rights for every immigrant in Britain," is like a latter-day version of the Weather Underground, the Black Panthers, and the Baader-Meinhof Group rolled into one, with elements of the Irish Republican Army and the Palestine Liberation Organization thrown in for good measure. The group is diverse. The organization's leader, Julian (Theo's ex-wife), who has remained true to the spirit of the sixties, is attempting to persuade the group to abandon the armed struggle and to broaden its base of support by engaging in dialogue with citizens and immigrants alike. She is the only character whose politics the film unequivocally endorses. Other members of the Fishes, by contrast, including Luke (a shrewd opportunist played by Chiwetel Ejiofor), Ian (Luke's loyal adjunct, played by Paul Sharma), and Patric (a foot soldier more interested in shooting people than changing the world, chillingly portrayed by Charlie Hunnam), are planning an armed uprising. When a group of Luke's henchmen disguised as highway robbers suddenly kill Julian early in the film, in a scene that is as shocking in its implications as it is stunning in its technical virtuosity, the hope she incarnates dies with her.

The Real State of Emergency

Luke and his acolytes kill Julian in order to prevent her from escorting Kee (Clare-Hope Ashity), a miraculously pregnant African refugee, to the Human Project, an organization of mythic proportions that is rumored to control an outpost on the Azores islands in the North Atlantic. Rather than delivering Kee to the Human Project, Luke and his faction plan to use Kee's baby to rally people to their cause. Suspecting that her comrades might be planning a coup of this sort, Julian had warned Kee not to trust anyone other than Theo if she should die. Following this advice, Kee puts herself in Theo's hands after Julian's death. Theo initially wants to have nothing more to do with the pregnant refugee, with whom he became embroiled only in view of the £5,000 reward that Julian had promised him for his help in getting her to the Fishes' safe house. He quickly changes his mind when he overhears Luke debriefing his colleagues on Julian's murder, giving the order to have Theo himself killed, and laying out the Fishes' plan to take custody of Kee's child once it is born.

For the remainder of the film, Theo is on the run with Kee and Miriam (Pam Ferris), Kee's devoted midwife. In one hair-raising chase scene after another, the three fugitives flee the Fishes, who track them from one location to the next. The hunted trio's plan is to make their way to the *Tomorrow*, a boat scheduled to pass by a weather buoy at Bexhill-on-Sea en route to the Human Project's fabled encampment on the Azores. However, because Bexhill is now a refugee camp, the trio sees no way of meeting the boat. Jasper then comes up with a plan that sets up the film's climactic final sequence. He convinces his acquaintance Syd (Peter Mullan), a border guard who deals Jasper's homegrown pot, to pick up Kee, Miriam, and Theo and to take them to Bexhill as though they were refugees he had captured.

The sequence at Bexhill is harrowing from the moment the threesome get out of Syd's patrol car, are escorted at baton-point past cages full of wailing refugees, and board the bus that takes them past a gate marked "Homeland Security" and into the heart of the camp. As many critics have remarked, the scene at the bus depot, where guards do an initial triage of the detainees, derives its imagery from the infamous photographs, circulated on the internet in early spring 2004, of tortures conducted at the US-run Abu Ghraib prison during the "war on terror."[35] The bus-depot scene also gives narrative form to Žižek's insightful analysis of the confusion of means and ends in the dehumanization of Jews under the Third Reich: the Nazis "first brutally reduced the Jews to the subhuman level and then presented this image as the proof of their subhumanity."[36] The scene at the depot, which depicts guards performing Abu Ghraib-like atrocities through the bus window while other guards perform the triage inside the bus, depicts both the reduction of detainees to a subhuman level and the guards' disgust with the abject creatures they are in the process of creating.

Once the bus has come to a halt, a guard boards the bus to conduct the selection process. When he turns his attention to Kee, who is going into labor, Miriam rises to her feet, extends her arms outward, looks up to the heavens, and loudly recites a prayer to Saint Gabriel in order to draw attention away from Kee. The guard grabs Miriam by the hair and throws her to the front of the bus to join the group of inmates being tortured outside. The last image we see of Miriam shows

Figure 1.7. The scene of the arrival at the Bexhill refugee camp derives its imagery from the infamous photographs of tortures conducted at the US-run Abu Ghraib prison (*Children of Men*, Universal, 2006).

her being forced to her knees and having a bag like the ones used at Abu Ghraib placed over her head. When the guard again focuses his attention on Kee, Theo intervenes by pointing to Kee's broken waters and yelling "Caca! Caca! Piss. Piss. Caca. Smell." "You smell it yourself," the repulsed guard responds. "You fucking people disgust me," he says, then he turns and walks away. The disdainful guard enacts here a confusion of cause and effect similar to the one described above by Žižek. He does not say "You disgust me" in reference to Theo or Kee and her caca-piss, but *you people*, referring to refugees as a group. The whole lot of them disgust him, and not without reason: they are a disgusting lot, precisely because of the dehumanizing treatment they have received at the hands of guards like the one here recoiling in disgust. By stripping the refugees of human dignity, the government has, in effect, reduced them to a species unworthy of dignity.

In his book on the remnants of Auschwitz, Agamben uncovers a specific application of the word "dignity" to Jews during the Third Reich: "When referring to the legal status of Jews after the racial laws, the Nazis . . . used a term that implied a kind of dignity: *entwürdigen*, literally to 'deprive of dignity.' The Jew is a human being who has been deprived of all *Würde*, all dignity: he is merely human—and, for this reason, non-human."[37] This operation of *entwürdigen*, which the film depicts on countless occasions, lends support to Luke's justification for fomenting the uprising. "Julian was wrong!" he says to Theo near the end of the film. "She thought it could be peaceful! But how can it be peaceful when they try to take away your dignity?" The condition of immigrants in the film has deteriorated to the point that peaceful negotiation with the government seems beyond hope. The political nonentities produced by the government are in no position to fight for their rights. By reducing immigrants to a subhuman level, the British government has created a species of being deemed unworthy of human rights while at the same time denying these rightless people the possibility of contesting their less-than-human status.

The measure that has historically enabled this sort of reduction of a category of people to a class of juridical nonentities, in modern states, is the declaration of a state of emergency. As Agamben's *State of Exception* makes clear, a wide array of governments has had recourse to such a measure. When, upon coming to power in 1933, Hitler suspended the articles of the Weimar Constitution protecting personal liberties, he was following a long tradition of political leaders, in both authoritarian-totalitarian and democratic-parliamentary regimes, who took it upon themselves to suspend constitutional rights in the name of national security.[38] From the French Constituent Assembly's proclamation, in 1791, of the *état de siège*, to George W. Bush's "military order," in 2001, to detain suspected terrorists without trial, many governments have declared martial law, emergency decrees, states of emergency, states of siege, or, as Agamben prefers to call them, states of exception. What made Hitler's Decree for the Protection of People and State unique at the time was the fact that it was never repealed, making of the Third Reich a "Night of St. Bartholomew that lasted twelve years."[39] The exception became the rule under Hitler. What had previously been understood as an exceptional measure, used only in extraordinary circumstances, became the norm for the duration of the twelve-year *tausendjährige Reich*.

This "normalization" of the exception has itself in turn become something of a norm. Since Hitler's permanent institution of what had hitherto been a temporary measure, the "normalized" state of exception has become a paradigm of governance. As Agamben remarks, "The voluntary creation of a permanent state of emergency," first instituted by Hitler, "has become one of the essential practices of contemporary states, including so-called democratic ones."[40] Agamben's prime example of such a "so-called democratic" state is the United States during the war on terror.

Agamben derives his theory of the state of exception from two principle sources: the German Jew Walter Benjamin and the Prussian jurist and political theorist Carl Schmitt, who joined the Nazi Party in 1933 and rose through the ranks under Hitler to become the crown jurist of the Third Reich. The two men engaged in a long-running debate over the nature of the state of emergency. Benjamin's first overt reference to such emergency measures appears in *The Origin of German Tragic Drama*. It constitutes less a critique of Schmitt than a disassociation of the seventeenth-century sovereign from Schmitt's theory of sovereignty. As Schmitt claimed in the notorious opening sentence of *Political Theology*: "Sovereign is he who decides on the exception."[41] Referencing this definition of sovereignty, Benjamin writes: "Whereas the modern concept of sovereignty amounts to a supreme executive power on the part of the prince, the baroque concept emerges from a discussion of the state of emergency, and makes it the most important function of the prince to avert this."[42] This reluctance on the baroque prince's part to declare a state of emergency constitutes an essential difference between the *Trauerspiel*, as Benjamin conceives of it, and the film narrative of *Children of Men*. As we have seen, in Cuarón's movie, Britain now lives in a permanent state of emergency. The exception has become the rule in *Children of Men*.

Nearly twenty years after Benjamin wrote his *Trauerspiel* book, the author offered a very different sort of disassociation between his thoughts on the state of emergency and Schmitt's theory of the sovereign exception. In the *Theses on the Philosophy of History*—Benjamin's last major work, written in 1940, shortly before he killed himself on the French-Spanish border while fleeing the Nazis—he affirmed: "The tradition of the oppressed teaches us that the 'state of emergency' in which we live is not the exception but the rule. We must attain to a conception of history that is in keeping with this insight. Then we shall clearly realize that it is our task to bring about a real state of emergency."[43] This text constitutes Benjamin's last word in the debate with Schmitt. As Agamben argues in his penetrating analysis of the Schmitt-Benjamin exchange, Benjamin's affirmation here that "the 'state of emergency' in which we live is not the exception but the rule" directly puts into check Schmitt's formal disassociation of the rule and its exception. "What Schmitt could in no way accept," Agamben writes, "was that the state of exception be wholly confused with the rule."[44] From Schmitt's perspective, "when the exception becomes the rule, the machine can no longer function."[45] However, Agamben observes, "this confusion between the exception and the rule was precisely what the Third Reich had concretely brought about."[46] The merging of the rule and its exception, which was occurring before his eyes in the 1930s, constitutes Schmitt's blind spot. In contrast to Benjamin, who clearly perceived that the exception had become the rule in Nazi Germany, Schmitt refused to accept the conflation of the two.

Benjamin's "real state of emergency" is both the revelation that the exception had become the rule and the response that stems from this realization. It is not just the lesson to be learned from the tradition of the oppressed—to wit, the recognition that "the 'state of emergency' in which we live is not the exception but the rule"—but a situation that, under such conditions, the oppressed must *bring about*. Benjamin's "real state of emergency" is, in sum, the instigation of a state of emergency directed against a regime that has instituted the exception as the rule: a civil war in response to martial law, acts of terror responding to State terrorism, illegal violence in reaction to the violence of the law. If we wanted to imagine what such a "real state of emergency" might look like, we need look no further than the harrowing depiction of the Bexhill uprising at the end of *Children of Men*.

In the climactic scene of the uprising in Bexhill, the Fishes join forces with Islamic militants inside the camp. As Chaudhary notes in his enlightening analysis of the uprising scene, "The dull landscape of Bexhill has the word *Uprising* written in English and misspelled in Arabic (*Intifada*) on every available window and wall."[47] As Theo, Kee, and Marichka (the duo's Romani contact inside the camp, played by Oana Pellea) try

Figure 1.8. The Bexhill uprising visualizes what the "real state of emergency" evoked by Walter Benjamin might look like (*Children of Men*, Universal, 2006).

to make their way through the chaos to a rowboat in order to meet the *Tomorrow*, the threesome crosses paths with a group of demonstrators marching in the street chanting "Allah akbar!" (God is great) and waving AK-47s in the air. The image is "lifted from news imagery of a Palestinian or possibly Iranian march," Chaudhary comments, "complete with a dead body being carried."[48] The convergence of the two insurgent groups in the uprising scene forges audio-visual, thematic, and ideological links between two heterogeneous "terrorist" organizations: the homegrown radicals represented by the Fishes and the Islamic militants waving their guns in the air. Together, they connote the form of contestation that corresponds to the state of exception, the counterforce that comes into being when segments of the population have been stripped of their humanity and reduced to the abject condition of bare life.

The film does not valorize the uprising. On the contrary, it presents the Fishes as the negative mirror image of the government it is combatting. The "real state of emergency" is an inverted form of the state of emergency *tout court*. It is the form of resistance that emerges when other means of contestation have been rendered powerless or anachronistic. Yet even this last desperate form of rebellion is annihilated in the film's final scene. In this scene, Theo, Kee, and her newborn baby, having made their way through the battle zone of Bexhill to a rowboat docked in an underground tunnel, row out to the buoy, where they wait for the *Tomorrow* to arrive. While they sit waiting in the undulating waves, a squadron of jets flies overhead toward the besieged city they just left. Flashes of light through the clouds accompanied by the sound of bombs exploding in the distance indicate that the government has quashed the uprising by destroying the city and killing its inhabitants in a tactical air raid. With this bombing, all the major characters (other than Kee and Theo) and many of the minor characters that we have met in the film are dead. Whichever ones may have survived up until this point are incinerated in this final air strike. Whatever hope we may have retained up to this point about the possibility of resistance, even in the ambiguous form of the uprising, dissipates in this unremarkable shot of flashes of light reflected in the clouds. The film leaves us with a vast hecatomb, littered with the corpses of all who struggle against the indomitable forces of oppression.

No Hope for Tomorrow

The film's last two minutes contain three major plot developments: (1) Kee, who previously considered naming her baby Froley or Bazooka, tells Theo that she will name her daughter Dylan after his late son; (2) Theo, who, we learn at this point, was hit by a bullet during the uprising, dies; and (3) in the film's last shots, the *Tomorrow* arrives. Sara Ahmed offers a dialectical reading of the first two of these developments: "Although Theo dies, the child becomes his child, replacing the dead child through the gift of a name."[49] Theo's legacy lives on, Ahmed suggests, in the name of the baby girl who bears the name of his dead son. "As a utopic moment, this is far from ambitious," Ahmed writes, understating the case.[50] Indeed, this "utopic" moment is particularly inauspicious due to the loss of the name's sociocultural resonance in the transfer from Theo's son to Kee's daughter. As indicated above, Dylan's name is both a cipher for "the sixties" and an index of Theo's attachment, in the early 2000s, to a tradition of social protest and political activism that the film roots in the 1960s. Nothing in the film indicates that Kee is aware of these associations or shares the cultural references with Theo. What we end up with is "Dylan" as an empty signifier, an homage to Theo shorn of the meaning that the name originally held for him. Theo's legacy lives on in Kee's baby girl, but his son's namesake does not.

Then, in the last thirty seconds of the film, the *Tomorrow* arrives, closing the movie with what Chaudhary calls "a redemptive deus ex machina that promises that wrongs will be corrected, human ills set aright."[51] Chaudhary explicitly reads this redemptive ending as allegorical, in Benjamin's specific sense of the term. "In *The Origin of German Tragic Drama*," Chaudhary writes,

Benjamin explains that the Baroque allegorist's solution to [the] descent into meaninglessness, to the endless casting of meanings on the allegorical sign, was to focus on resurrection, by placing wings on the skull, in the language of their emblematics. Natural death, in other words, is temporary since it is simply a passing over into eternal life. . . . Cuarón's film ends with a similar theological solution to material conflicts, as the ship named *Tomorrow* comes to save the day and to whisk Kee into a promising future.[52]

I have two responses to this thought-provoking interpretation of the ending of Cuarón's film. First, although Benjamin does indeed describe how the German baroque playwrights provided an ultimate "solution" to the seemingly endless accumulation of images of death, ruin, and catastrophe, in Benjamin's opinion this final turn to the Resurrection as a stabilizing moment that retroactively makes sense of worldly chaos represents not the inner truth of the allegorical way of seeing but, rather, its betrayal. As Buck-Morss insists, Benjamin's remarks at the end of his *Trauerspiel* book on the German dramatists' theological "solution" to the antinomy of allegory "must be read not as an affirmation but as a fundamental critique."[53] She cites in this regard the very line (from a play by Daniel Casper von Lohenstein) to which Chaudhary alludes in the passage quoted above, and Benjamin's commentary on it:

> "Yea, when the Highest comes to reap the harvest from the graveyard, then I, a death's head, will be an angel's countenance." This solves the riddle of the most fragmented, the most defunct, the most dispersed. Allegory, of course, thereby loses everything that was most peculiar to it: the secret, privileged knowledge, the arbitrary rule in the realm of dead objects, the supposed infinity of a world without hope. All this vanishes with this *one* about-turn.[54]

"In order to remain true to God," Buck-Morss concludes, citing Benjamin, "the German allegoricists abandon both nature and politics: '[Their . . .] intention ultimately does not remain true [*treu*] to the spectacle of the skeleton, but, treacherously [*treulos*] leaps over to the Resurrection.' "[55] In sum, Buck-Morss argues, in Benjamin's view the baroque poets' theological "solution" to the tragic drama of the seventeenth century represents not the culmination of the allegorical way of seeing but, on the contrary, "its negation."[56]

Second, I would argue that Cuarón's film does not end with the redemptive vision of a hopeful future that Chaudhary discerns in the arrival of the *Tomorrow*. In my view, the movie's last half-minute does not present the sort of "about-turn" that Benjamin denounces in the closing pages of his *Trauerspiel* book. Although the film can be read, and has been read, as a tale of redemption, with Theo playing a Christ-like role in which he redeems both himself and humanity in an ultimate act of self-sacrifice, the film narrative as a whole undermines whatever hope the final shots of the *Tomorrow* piercing through the fog might promise.[57] *Children of Men* is finally more uncompromising in its allegorical vision of the present than were the tragic allegories of the seventeenth century. It remains true (*treu*, in Benjamin's German) to the allegorical way of seeing to the end.

Chaudhary is not the only critic to interpret the boat's arrival as a hopeful sign of a bright future. Žižek, for example, elliptically suggests that the boat represents "the solution": "What I like is that the solution is the boat. It doesn't have roots. It's rootless. It floats around. This is, for me, the meaning of this wonderful metaphor, *boat*. The condition of the renewal means you cut your roots. That's the solution."[58] Ahmed, for her part, who argues that Žižek's reading "prematurely fills the boat with a meaning, as a kind of optimism," nonetheless proposes that "the boat signifies the possibility of tomorrow, of a tomorrow whose arrival might save us from today."[59] Implicitly evoking the Human Project's legendary colony on the Azores, she describes this possibility as a hope "that a new world might be created somewhere, out of the ruins of what has been left behind."[60]

I find these interpretations unconvincing for several reasons. First, although the film does not deny the existence of the Human Project's colony on the Azores, it does not confirm it, either. We do not know, at the end of the movie, whether this mythical organization and its fabled outpost exist or not. Kirk Boyle brings this uncertainty into relief in a brilliant comparative analysis of *Children of Men* and Francis Lawrence's *I Am Legend* (2007). In the latter film, Robert Neville (Will Smith), the sole survivor in New York of an epidemic that killed 90 percent of the world's population and turned the vast majority of the remaining people into zombie-like creatures that feed on the few uninfected survivors, sacrifices himself so that Anna and Ethan, the only other healthy human beings we see (besides the ones who appear in flashbacks) in the first eighty-seven minutes of this eighty-eight-minute film narrative, can survive. Like in *Children of Men*, where rumors of the Human Project's outpost on the Azores offer people a glimmer of hope, Anna holds out hope that a colony of people exists somewhere, from which the human race might be regenerated. Unlike *Children*, however, *Legend* shows us that Anna's faith is well founded. The film ends with Anna and Ethan arriving at the mythical colony of Bethel, Vermont. Boyle's description of *Legend*'s final scene brings into relief precisely the kind of ending we do *not* get in *Children of Men*: "The gates open to two armed soldiers guarding an idyllic Small Town, U.S.A. The bells of a traditional white-steepled Protestant church ring while the stars and bars wave in the wind. A bird's-eye shot reveals that this privatized security state is a self-sustaining farm powered by wind turbines."[61] The contrast between this depiction of an idyllic Green Zone, USA, and the open-ended conclusion of *Children of Men* is striking. By cutting to the closing credits at the moment the *Tomorrow* appears through the fog, Cuarón withholds a vision of "tomorrow," leaving us to wonder what might happen next.

Over the course of its nearly two hours of running time, the film has primed us to anticipate the worst. Both narratively and audio-visually, the movie is constructed to create a constant sense of imminent danger. From the bomb that unexpectedly explodes in the film's opening scene, destroying the café where Theo bought his morning coffee, to the violent uprising and its brutal repression in the climactic Bexhill sequence, Theo and his entourage survive (or don't, in the cases of Julian, Janice, Jasper, Miriam, and ultimately Theo himself) one life-threatening encounter after another. The visceral experience of watching the movie creates a sense of heightened anxiety in which the spectator comes to anticipate danger at every turn.

One of the ways the movie creates this pervasive sense of danger is by systematically eliminating all the people, places, and organizations that promised to offer help. Julian's sudden murder puts Kee and Theo in the hands of the Fishes; when the Fishes turn out to pose a threat rather than offering succor, their "safe house" suddenly becomes anything but safe; subsequently, when, after escaping from the Fishes' "safe house," Kee, Miriam, and Theo find refuge in Jasper's secluded abode in the woods, the Fishes find them and kill Jasper before moving on to hunt the fleeing trio. By the time Kee and Theo make it out of Bexhill and to the buoy, we have become so alert to omnipresent danger that the arrival of a boat through the fog is as ominous as it is promising. The film has prepared us to wonder whether the Human Project is any more trustworthy than the Fishes. One half expects the *Tomorrow*'s crew to open fire on Kee or throw her in a cage.

Moreover, assuming for the sake of argument that the Human Project is indeed dedicated to reviving the human race and that the organization commands an impenetrable space suited to that purpose, what sort of future humanity would develop from a single fertile woman and her offspring? Are we to imagine that this miraculously fecund woman might potentially repopulate the planet? The permutations of such a scenario and what it would inevitably entail for Kee and her children are too sordid to imagine. And even if we are ready to accept Kee's conversion into human livestock for the sake of saving the human race, the unavoidable interbreeding of her progeny would result in a population with a severely limited gene pool. Within one generation every potential breeder would be a blood relative of all prospective mating partners.

Finally, assuming that we are prepared to accept all these suppositions and conditions, what sort of future does the film promise? All the problems depicted in the film, with the possible exception of the one pertaining directly to human reproduction, remain unresolved. The hope that the film offers is the dim prospect that humanity might continue to exist in its current bleak form. Theo forcefully makes this point to Jasper early in the film: "Even if they discovered the cure for infertility, it doesn't matter. Too late. The world went to shit. You know what? It was too late before the infertility thing happened." Nothing in the movie leads us to believe that Theo is incorrect in his diagnosis here. On the contrary, the strong resemblance between the film's vision of the world in 2027 and the present state of the planet suggests that he is exactly right. The striking similarity between Cuarón's dystopian vision of the future and the world in which we live leads us to concur with Theo that "it was too late before the infertility thing happened." The pessimistic conclusion to be drawn from *Children of Men* is that it is already too late.

What *Children of Men* allegorizes is ultimately the current dead-end of history. The arrival of the *Tomorrow* may offer hope that tomorrow will come, but it tells us nothing about what tomorrow might bring. If the future looks anything like it does in *Children of Men*, we have little to look forward to. By showing us a future that looks uncannily like the present, only more so, the movie beckons us to consider our current historical trajectory. If we want to have a tomorrow that is not an exacerbation of the problems of today, we had better look around and see the people quarantined in cages around us, the upside-down office chairs on desks, and the environmental disaster we are in the process of creating. What Cuarón's film does is try to help us see them while offering a vision of what the future might hold if we do not.

2

Mapping *Syriana*

AN EARLY SCENE FROM *SYRIANA*, Stephen Gaghan's 2005 international political thriller, depicts a joint meeting of the boards of Connex and Killen, two US-based oil and gas companies that are in the process of merging into a single energy giant. The scene is set in the Connex boardroom in Houston, Texas. It starts *in medias res*:

> JIMMY: No, I want to talk about the Gulf, and how a goddamn emir . . . What is an emir anyway?
>
> TOMMY: King, it's a king.
>
> JIMMY: A king. Well, how some Podunk king tossed you out on your ass. Every company in the world wanted into Kazakhstan, into the Tengiz, but Killen got it. And then Connex wanted Killen, and here we are.

The speakers here are Jimmy Pope (Chris Cooper), the CEO of Killen, and Tommy Barton (Robert Foxworth), a Connex executive. The situations to which Jimmy cryptically alludes are the ones that set the movie's plot in motion. Connex, a very big company, recently lost a huge natural-gas contract in the Persian Gulf to a Chinese consortium. At the same time, Killen, a smaller company, obtained the rights to the Tengiz Field in Kazakhstan, one of the largest untapped oil fields in the world. In order to take advantage of its rival's success in the Tengiz, Connex is currently in the process of acquiring Killen in view of creating a new corporation, Connex-Killen.

As he alludes to these circumstances, Jimmy picks up a marker and draws the boundary lines of Kazakhstan on a map behind him. The map represents Central Asia, but instead of jagged lines separating the region into countries, it has straight borderlines dividing the territory into color-coded regions belonging to various energy corporations. Alongside such recognizable corporations as Shell and Amoco (spelled "Amaco" in the film) appear the fictional companies of Connex and Killen. As the camera follows Jimmy throughout his speech, we see that the wall behind him is covered with maps of this sort, each dividing a geographical region among various energy companies. This set of maps, which we see only vaguely as the hand-held camera moves to keep Jimmy in the center of the frame, provides a remarkable graphic representation of the geopolitical global present. Individual nation-states no longer control the world's territories. The countries have literally disappeared from the map and have been replaced by the companies that own the world. National sovereignty has given way to corporate dominion. The entirety of the earth's surface now belongs to this or that multinational corporation. If we wanted to imagine what a physical representation of the phenomenon known as "globalization" might look like, we could do worse than this set of maps, in which the multinationals lay claim to every inch of the earth's surface.

The boardroom scene also offers a fine portrait of Jimmy Pope, the CEO of a multinational energy corporation who does not know what an emir is (highly implausible for someone in his line of work) and who cannot understand or accept the fact that the sovereign ruler of a country, "a goddamn emir," as he puts it, can prevent an energy corporation

Figure 2.1. The walls of the Connex boardroom are covered with maps dividing the world into color-coded regions belonging to various energy corporations (*Syriana*, Warner Bros., 2005).

from extracting the country's resources. Jimmy's worldview derives from the maps that surround him, not the anachronistic geographies where national borders still matter.

What is most striking in the scene is the non sequitur between Jimmy's tirade about the "Podunk king" in the Gulf that tossed his colleagues at Connex "out on their ass" and his own company's recent acquisition of oil rights in the Tengiz. The elision in the script creates the impression that he is talking about the same geographical region, as though the Persian Gulf and the Tengiz were the same place. As we will see, this geographical confusion is not isolated to this scene. It is not just Jimmy's speech at the beginning of the movie that conflates these two geographical locations, separated in actuality by thousands of miles; the film as a whole does.

Finally, the fact that we cannot clearly see the maps that cover the walls of the Connex boardroom is also significant. The scene cinematically mimes a challenge that individuals in the real world face in their attempts to perceive the contours of global capital. The planet may be parceled out into multinational corporations, but we do not readily perceive the extent of their dominion. In the film, the maps clearly indicate that corporations own the world, but the camera movement hinders our ability to read them. The scene reproduces on the screen both a clear vision of the extent of corporate power and the experience of being unable to see it. We find ourselves, in watching the scene, in a position analogous to one we occupy in the non-filmic world of global capitalism, unable to grasp the extent of the system's all-encompassing reach.

I have chosen to begin this chapter with the Connex boardroom scene for several reasons. Although not atypical of the movie as a whole, it offers one of the movie's clearest illustrations of the interlocking predicaments that it explores over the course of two hours. While the film is based on a crystalline vision of global developments, it gives us a blurry and confusing image of those developments. That blurriness and that confusion, I argue, are essential components of the phenomenon that the movie explores. *Syriana*'s form is integral to its narrative content. The film depicts a sociopolitical and economic configuration that eludes our ability to conceptualize as a totality. By showing us a clear delineation of the contours of global capital, represented in static form in one of the most straightforward and literal diagrammatic encodings imaginable, and simultaneously obscuring the maps from our view, the boardroom scene nicely conveys both the ubiquity and the elusiveness of global capital. The film is about both of those phenomena.

I also wanted to introduce the notion of mapping from the outset. This notion holds the key to my reading of the film. I use it in three distinct but interrelated ways. First, I argue that Gaghan's film provides a "cognitive map" of globalization in the sense that Fredric Jameson gives to the term in his writings on cultural production in the age of late capitalism. Douglas Kellner makes this connection in his book on the "cinema wars" of the Bush-Cheney years: "A highly complex film, [*Syriana*] sets out to map contemporary global capital and struggle in the Middle East between a myriad of competing forces."[1] The verb that Kellner uses here clearly alludes to Jameson's theory of "cognitive mapping," discussed in my introduction.

The obvious disadvantage of beginning my analysis of Gaghan's cognitive map with an actual map is the prospective reduction of Jameson's evocative metaphor for the process by which subjects might imaginarily represent the world of global capital to something as simple and straightforward as a map on a wall. Jameson argues unequivocally against precisely this sort of literal-mindedness: "Since everyone knows what a map is, it would have been necessary to add that cognitive mapping cannot (at least in our time) involve anything so easy as a map; indeed, once you knew what 'cognitive mapping' was driving at, you were to dismiss all figures of maps and mapping from your mind and try to imagine something else."[2] Echoing this exhortation in *Cartographies of the Absolute*, a tremendous cognitive map in its own right, theorists Alberto Toscano and Jeff Kinkle write, in the context of a survey of a thought-provoking set of maps and globes: "Needless to say, cultural producers, for the most part, do not literally attempt to generate maps of the new interconnected global reality. . . . Rather, it is the task of the critic to tease out the symptoms of . . . the consolidation of a planetary nexus of capitalist power and the multifarious struggles to imagine it."[3] This chapter engages in precisely the sort of activity suggested here by Toscano and Kinkle. If I have begun my analysis of Gaghan's cognitive map with an examination of an actual map, this is due to the importance that configurations of geographical space play in the "map" of global capital that Gaghan constructs. As the movie's title indicates, *Syriana* is a film about cartography in general, and the political partition of the Middle East in particular.

Due both to the movie's narrative complexity and to the importance that the film's basic plotline plays in developing its worldview, I begin my analysis of Gaghan's "cognitive map" with a longish synopsis (six paragraphs) of *Syriana*'s intricate plot. I then engage in a "mapping" exercise in the colloquial sense of transposing plot elements onto real-world events and existing institutions. This is the second sense in which my chapter mobilizes the metaphor of the map.

The latter mapping exercise, an inverse of the operation that the filmmaker undertook in making his film, reveals not one-to-one correspondences but a series of transformations of historical entities and situations into fictional forms. Not least of those entities is the one that gives the movie its title. "Syriana" (a word never pronounced in the film) is an actual term used in Washington think tanks to describe a hypothetical reconfiguration of the Middle East in ways that would further US interests in the region. It is closely related to David Harvey's thesis in *The New Imperialism* that the US invasion of Iraq in 2003 is part of a broader strategy to control the region as a whole; and it is virtually synonymous with the so-called "model" theory, which Naomi Klein dissects with her characteristic precision in *The Shock Doctrine*. The concept of "Syriana" is, in sum, a form of interventionist mapmaking in the literal sense. By a felicitous lexical coincidence, the central metaphor for Gaghan's "cognitive mapping" of the socioeconomic and political situation in the Middle East takes the form of an actual remapping of the region.

With this coincidence in mind, I examine the various maps that appear in *Syriana*. Rather than accurately reproducing existing geographies, these maps reorganize geographical space in revealing ways. Arguing that these maps condense into concrete form the movie's central theme, I then turn to the film's representation of history, paying particularly close attention to the film's portrayal of its two suicide bombers. I conclude with a detailed analysis of a short and seemingly gratuitous shot of a golf course at the end of the film. I argue that this shot, a smooth pan across a putting green, lends itself to two very different interpretations: one anticipating the transformation of the Middle East into the "Syriana" of the film's title, and another allegorically prefiguring the creation of the Islamic State of Iraq and Syria.

Gaghan's Cognitive Map

Syriana is a notoriously complex film. Shot on over 200 locations on four continents and featuring more than seventy speaking parts in six different languages, it weaves together stories of a corporate merger in the United States, a political rivalry in the Middle East, a suicide bombing in the Persian Gulf, and a cat-and-mouse game between a CIA operative and both his counterparts in the field and his bosses back home.[4] Each of these narratives is intricate in its own right, but the film's complexity lies especially in the entanglement of the four stories. Before getting into the film analysis per se, let us begin with an overview of these four principal plotlines.

One of the film's four narrative threads is the one evoked above. It involves the merger of two oil and gas companies, Texas-based Connex, an energy giant that has recently lost drilling rights in the Persian

Gulf, and Killen, which obtained a concession in the lucrative Tengiz oil field in Kazakhstan just prior to the film action. It is those two events—Connex's loss in the Gulf and Killen's gain in the Tengiz—that make the acquisition of Killen, run by Texas oilman Jimmy Pope (the guy who does not know what an emir is), a priority for Connex CEO Leland Janus (Peter Gerety). However, the US Department of Justice (DOJ) suspects that Killen may have bribed Kazakh officials in order to gain access to the Tengiz, and it will only approve the merger if the US attorney general's office can show "due diligence." Dean Whiting (Christopher Plummer), a founding partner of the law firm representing Connex and an influential behind-the-scenes power broker in both Washington and at least one oil-rich state in the Mideast, engages Bennett Holiday (Jeffrey Wright), a consultant at the firm, to smooth things out with the DOJ in order to make sure that the merger goes through. What Justice needs, according to Bennett's reports back to the firm, is "a body": a scapegoat that can take the fall for the Connex-Killen team as a whole. Bennett finds his "body." In the course of his investigations, he discovers that Danny Dalton (Tim Blake Nelson), a Killen executive and a prominent member of the Committee for the Liberation of Iran (CLI), transferred funds to an official in Kazakhstan in violation of the Foreign Corrupt Practices Act. However, the attorney general informs Holiday that "Dalton is not enough," so Holiday offers a second body: his mentor at the firm, Sydney Hewitt (Nicky Henson), the lead lawyer in the Connex-Killen merger, who benefitted from a side deal for excess Iranian pipeline capacity during the merger process. "We're looking for the illusion of due diligence," Holiday explains to Jimmy Pope. "Two criminal acts successfully prosecuted, it gives us that illusion." At the end of the film, the merger goes through, and Lee Janus, formerly CEO of Connex, becomes chief executive officer of the newly formed Connex-Killen Corporation.

Connex's expulsion from the Persian Gulf, which sets the film's plot in motion, is the result of a change in policy in an unnamed oil-rich Middle Eastern state. Hitherto Emir Al-Subbai (Nadim Sawalha) had granted drilling rights to US companies. At the beginning of the film, Prince Nasir (Alexander Siddig), Al-Subbai's shrewd and ambitious older son, has convinced his father to offer the emirate's oil fields to the highest bidder, which in this case is a Chinese consortium. Nasir plans to use the extra money he gets from the Chinese to rebuild his country in line with a set of reforms he envisions addressing problems of corruption, sexual discrimination, and social inequality. However, Nasir's idealistic vision of his country's future runs counter to his father's policies and, toward the end of the film, Emir Al-Subbai reveals to his sons that Meshal

(Akbar Kurtha), the younger brother, who has the political acumen of a kindergartener and no apparent sense of integrity, will succeed him as emir. Refusing to support his father's decision, Nasir organizes a coup d'état, supported by nine of the country's eleven generals, to depose his brother. But Meshal has a powerful ally that his brother does not: the US oil industry, which, through its network of powerbrokers and political action committees—personified in the shadowy figure of Dean Whiting—persuades the US government to intervene on its behalf. As Nasir is driving across the desert to depose his brother and proclaim himself emir, the CIA remotely launches a drone strike from its base in Langley, Virginia, killing Nasir instantly. The film ends with Connex-Killen CEO Lee Janus, recipient of the "Oilman of the Year" award, publicly thanking Meshal, now emir, for his help in getting his company back into the Gulf.

While these first two plotlines portray the inner workings and unsavory behind-the-scenes machinations of energy corporations, political action committees, and royal families, a third narrative thread explores the destabilizing effects of globalization "on the ground," as it were, from the point of view of workers affected by the changes. It is with this third plotline that the movie begins. Following a call to prayer that accompanies the iconic Warner Bros. production logo as it rotates into position on the screen, the film opens with a series of striking images of Pakistani migrant laborers gathered in the desert at dawn. The men stand around smoking, talking, or just waiting silently in loosely formed lines. Muted and set to a haunting harp melody scored by Alexandre Desplat, these images, reminiscent of Sebastião Salgado's documentary photographs of migrant laborers, poetically evoke the individual subjectivity of the men while simultaneously conveying their collective condition. When a foreman starts shoving workers as he selects which ones will have work that day, and another begins beating an old man in the group in order to prevent him from boarding the bus that will transport the laborers to the work site, we immediately appreciate the precariousness of these men's condition. When, ten minutes later, we learn, along with the laborers, that their services are no longer required since the Connex/Al-Salwa oil refinery where they work is now under new ownership, we wonder, with them, what they will do next.

The film then follows two of these migrant workers, Saleem Khan (Sahid Ahmed) and his son Wasim (Mazhar Munir), who no longer have work permits since they are now unemployed. Without work, Saleem and Wasim face deportation back to Pakistan if they do not find another job within two weeks. Hindered from finding a job because he does not speak Arabic, Wasim begins studying Arabic at a local Islamic school, where he and his friend Farooq (Sonell Dadral) are recruited into a terrorist cell that is planning an attack on a US target using a contraband US missile. Although both boys hesitate to complete the mission, Wasim and Farooq nonetheless successfully carry out a suicide assault on a Connex-Killen Liquefied Natural Gas carrier stationed in the Persian Gulf. Having affixed the explosive head of the contraband US missile to the bow of their fishing boat, Wasim and Farooq drive their boat into the side of the tanker.

The story of how Wasim and Farooq came into possession of the explosive device attached to the tip of their boat constitutes the film's fourth narrative thread. The central character in this fourth narrative line is Bob Barnes (George Clooney), based on ex-CIA field operative Robert Baer, whose book, *See No Evil*, served as inspiration and a source of information for the film. This narrative begins with a cryptic sequence in which Barnes sells two anti-tank missiles to a couple of arms dealers in Tehran. One of the missiles goes into the trunk of the arms dealers' car, while the second one is delivered, to Barnes' surprise and consternation, to an Arabic man waiting in the backroom of the deserted restaurant where the transaction takes place. Following the sale, Barnes walks away from the restaurant and toward the camera. He glances up to the top right corner of the frame while advancing into a medium shot as the arms dealers' car explodes in the background. The camera follows Barnes as he continues to walk nonchalantly down the street, ignoring the conflagration behind him. Barnes's nonchalance and his subtle glance up to the corner of the frame are the only visible indications that he has just orchestrated an assassination of the two arms dealers. The shady figure in the back of the restaurant remains a mystery for the next hour of the film. We next see this man, who turns out to be one Mohammed Sheik Agiza (Amr Waked), an Egyptian militant, at the Islamic school where Wasim and Farooq are studying Arabic. It is he who recruits the two boys to the cause and convinces them that they are ready to "flee from the worldly life in order to spread the true faith."

Meanwhile, Barnes, who irritates his superiors by writing embarrassing memos about the missing missile, is pulled out of the field and put behind a desk at Langley, but he turns out to be as much of a nuisance in Washington as he was in the field. Perhaps because Bob proves to be such a pest in Washington, but probably for the more straightforward reason that he is good at his job, his boss arranges for him to be sent to Beirut in order to complete a high-priority mission. This mission turns out to be the assassination of none other than Prince Nasir, whose aspirations for the Middle East threaten US economic and political interests in the region. Unfortunately for Bob, the man he recruits to carry out the hit proves to be a double agent working for Iran who, following orders

Figure 2.2. CIA operative Bob Barnes's nonchalance and his subtle glance up to the corner of the frame are the only indications that he just orchestrated the assassination of two arms dealers (*Syriana*, Warner Bros., 2005).

from *his* superiors, abducts, tortures, and prepares to kill Barnes. It is only thanks to the last-minute intervention of a Hezbollah leader, who has vowed to protect Bob while he is in Beirut, that Barnes escapes with his life. The double agent (played by Mark Strong) then starts broadcasting the news that the CIA is trying to kill Nasir. In response to this accusation, Barnes's superiors at the Agency distance themselves from Bob, claiming that he is a rogue agent working independently. Barnes soon discovers that his access to Agency computers has been blocked, that his passports (in the plural) have been revoked, and that the FBI has launched an investigation into his "rogue" activities in the Middle East. A series of transitions from scene to scene strongly imply that Dean Whiting, head of the law firm orchestrating the Connex-Killen merger and member of the influential Committee for the Liberation of Iran, is behind the decision to blackball Barnes. When Barnes learns of Whiting's shenanigans, he threatens to kill the lawyer if he does not return his passports. Enlightened apparently for the first time to the individual self-interest driving major decisions in Washington (or perhaps just fed up with the mistreatment he has received at the agency), Barnes flies to the Middle East in order to warn Nasir of the plot against his life. But at the moment Barnes intercepts the prince's convoy in the desert, the CIA remotely launches a missile attack on Nasir's vehicle from a circling drone, killing Bob along with Nasir in the blast.

To say that this film narrative is topical strikes me as an understatement. Indeed, some of the plot elements evoke specific world events that made news headlines in the years preceding the film's release. The narrative of the Connex-Killen merger, for example, brings to mind the merger of Exxon and Mobil into Exxon Mobil Corp. (ExxonMobil) in 1999, especially in light of the revelation, shortly after the merger, that J. Bryan Williams, a former Mobil executive, had bribed Kazakh officials in order to obtain drilling rights in the Tengiz. Both Williams and James Giffen, an American consultant based in Kazakhstan who makes a cameo appearance in Baer's *See No Evil*, were indicted in 2003 for violating the Foreign Corrupt Practices Act "in an effort to induce Kazakhstan to close the Tengiz deal."[5] I do not mean to suggest that Connex "is" Exxon or that Dalton and Hewitt are straightforward stand-ins for Williams and Giffen, but the issues addressed in the film do evoke concerns surrounding ExxonMobil around the time of the merger. The facts that "Connex" is almost an anagram of "Exxon" and that Leland Janus ("Lee" to his friends), CEO of Connex before becoming chief executive of Connex-Killen, has the same first name as Lee Raymond, CEO of Exxon (1993–1999) and then of ExxonMobil (1999–2005), only reinforce the association.

Interestingly, the film's characterization of Dalton's involvement in the Tengiz deal recalls the role that Baer attributes to Giffen in his book: "Jim Giffen was Mr. Kazakstan," Baer explains. "If you wanted an oil concession in Kazakstan, you went to Giffen. . . . He was Washington's de facto ambassador to Kazakstan. When Kazak President Nazarbayev wanted to come to Washington, he didn't phone Beth Jones, our ambassador in Alma Ata. He called Giffen."[6] In the film, it is Dalton who is on "the other side" of the Tengiz deal. When Bennett Holiday asks Dalton what he means by "the other side," Jimmy Pope explains: "El Presidente Nazarbayev's best pal in the whole world." This characterization is curious because it implicitly reverses the roles of Dalton and Hewitt, the two fall guys for the Connex-Killen merger in the film, in relation to those of Williams and Giffen, the two men indicted for the ExxonMobil Tengiz deal. In the real world it was Giffen, the "outside" consultant, who was "Nazarbayev's best pal in the whole world," whereas in the fictional world of the film, it is Dalton, the "inside" oilman, who plays the part of "Mr. Kazakstan." In reversing these roles, the film creates a chiasmus, with a fictional oil executive playing the part of the real-life consultant, and a fictional lawyer (a consultant of a different kind) in the place of the actual oilman.

As far as Dean Whiting is concerned, Gaghan says in an interview: "We can probably think of ten of them. It's interesting that men inside one law firm can represent . . . Saudi Arabia and an oil company and a military contractor, and be the private lawyer of a senator."[7] By contrast, the political action committee to which Whiting belongs—as do fellow lawyer Sydney Hewitt and oil executives Dalton and Janus—evokes so forcefully a specific real-world organization that I am almost tempted to call it its referent. How can the fictional Committee for the Liberation of Iran (CLI) not call to mind the empirical organization with the same acronym, the Committee for the Liberation of Iraq (CLI)? Formed in 2002, the real-life CLI was "a short-lived yet influential group of hawkish Beltway think-tankers and politicians who came together at the behest of the George W. Bush administration to support regime change in Iraq."[8] The group played an active role in shaping US foreign policy and in molding public opinion during the period leading up to the invasion of Iraq in March 2003. Composed primarily of men who stood to reap direct or indirect financial benefits from a regime change in Iraq, it represents a fine example of the imbrication of private interest and public policy, not at all dissimilar to the fictional CLI in the film.[9]

"Syriana"

One of the Committee for the Liberation of Iraq's objectives was to justify the war in Iraq and to "sell" the invasion to potentially skeptical populations at home and abroad. A plethora of rationales was proposed for the invasion: Iraqi president Saddam Hussein is linked to the attacks of September 11, 2001 (he was not); he is behind the anthrax attacks that occurred a week after 9/11 (also untrue); he possesses weapons of mass destruction (never found despite an exhaustive search); he is a liar (true of more political leaders than one would care to enumerate) and a brutal dictator (as are innumerable leaders that the United States supports), and so forth. As many critics have pointed out, this multiplication of rationales raised more questions than it answered. Among the numerous attempts to see through the Bush administration's inconsistent arguments and decipher the real impetus behind the invasion, two particularly persuasive hypotheses bear directly on the scenario of *Syriana*.

The first of these theories is succinctly summed up in the title of the first chapter of David Harvey's *The New Imperialism*: "All About Oil." Dismissing "a narrow conspiracy thesis [resting] on the idea that the government in Washington is nothing more than an oil mafia that has usurped the public domain," Harvey proposes that there is "an even grander perspective from which to understand the oil perspective."[10] He summarizes this perspective in the following proposition: "Whoever controls the Middle East controls the global oil spigot and whoever controls the global oil spigot can control the economy."[11] Speculating on the basis of available information that the world's only oil fields likely to last more than fifty years are in Iran, Iraq, Kuwait, Saudi Arabia, and the United

Arab Emirates, Harvey argues that we should not restrict our thinking to Iraq but should consider "the geopolitical condition and significance of the Middle East as a whole in relation to global capitalism."[12] He names Iran and Syria as obvious targets for US-engineered "regime changes" in the future, with Saudi Arabia as a possible third target. Reminding us that the current configuration of the Middle East emerged from the 1919 Versailles Treaty, Harvey comments that "this configuration could be viewed as anachronistic and dysfunctional," favoring the interests of then-dominant powers Britain and France as opposed to the world's current superpower, the United States.[13] As Harvey comments, the Versailles settlement "is generally acknowledged to have betrayed Arab interests."[14] The same would undoubtedly be true of a new map drawn up by the United States, but such a map could be of great benefit to the prospective mapmakers.

The second explanation also has to do with regional mapmaking in the interventionist sense. It is generally known as the "model" theory.

> According to the pundits who advanced this theory, many of them identified as neocons, terrorism was coming from multiple locations in the Arab and Muslim world: the September 11 hijackers were from Saudi Arabia, Egypt, the United Arab Emirates and Lebanon; Iran was funding Hezbollah; Syria was housing Hamas's leadership; Iraq was sending money to the families of Palestinian suicide bombers. For these war advocates, . . . that was enough to qualify the entire region as a potential terrorist breeding ground.[15]

In her incisive book on "disaster capitalism," Naomi Klein asks what it is, according to proponents of the "model" theory, that makes this part of the world such a hotbed of terrorist activity. Rather than considering regional terrorism to be a violent reaction to the forced introduction of neoliberal capitalism and liberal democracy into the region, "model" theorists propose, on the contrary, that this part of the world suffers from a "deficit in free-market democracy."[16] What the Middle East needs is more free-market reform, these theorists suggest, not less of it; fewer trade barriers, not more of them. Conflating free markets with political freedoms and civil liberties, proponents of the "model" theory lump them all together under the generic heading of "freedom," a key dog-whistle term exploited by the US right to gain support for policies that grant anything but freedom. As Klein's book makes crystal clear, only one form of freedom mattered to the Bush administration. When faced with the prospect that free elections in Iraq would likely result in a government hostile to free-market reforms, L. Paul Bremer III, head of the US-led Coalition Provisional Authority in Iraq, cancelled the elections.[17] Actions such as this leave little doubt that the purported "liberation" of Iraq touted by organizations like the CLI pertained primarily if not exclusively to the market.

The keystone of the "model" theory is that one country in the Middle East would serve as a catalyst—a model—for changes throughout the region. Since the United States could not conquer the entire Middle East all at once, the theory goes, it selected a single country to begin the process. Klein explains: "The U.S. would invade that country and turn it into, as [*New York Times* columnist] Thomas Friedman, chief media proselytizer of the theory, put it, 'a different model in the heart of the Arab-Muslim world,' one that in turn would set off a series of democratic/neoliberal waves throughout the region."[18] Described by "model" proponents variously as a "tsunami across the Islamic world" that would sweep from Baghdad to Tehran and "a war to remake the world," the war in Iraq would set the stage for a reconfiguration of the Middle East according to the geopolitical and economic needs of the invader.[19]

Proponents of the "model" theory apparently use a geographically specific name to refer to the reconfigured regional map that they envision. As Robert Baer said in a 2005 interview, "'Syriana' is a think tank term—people want to create this fake country to help our oil interests."[20] Baer traces the term back to the Sykes-Picot Agreement of 1916, when the governments of France and Great Britain secretly met to negotiate their respective spheres of influence in the Middle East in the face of the collapse of the Ottoman Empire. Referencing the same set of circumstances that Harvey recalls in his discussion of the Iraq War, Baer reminds us that Western powers imposed geographical borders in this part of the world a century ago in the aim of furthering their national interests. Sounding very much like Harvey (obvious locutionary differences aside), he cites that founding act of geopolitical violence as the source of current unrest in the region: "Iraq is a fake country. You know, it was three provinces of the Ottoman Empire. It was, you know, melded together. It's why we're having these problems there today."[21] The current use of the term "Syriana" in Washington refers to a similar mapmaking process. The word designates the new configuration—the new "fake country"—that could emerge from the chaos in the Middle East. More precisely, it designates both the map and the act of mapmaking, simultaneously denoting a geographical region and connoting a perspective on US foreign policy.

It is this double sense of the word that writer-director Stephen Gaghan evokes in reference to his film's title: "While 'Syriana' is a very real term used by Washington think-tanks to describe a hypothetical reshaping of the Middle East, as our title it is used more abstractly. 'Syriana,' the concept—the fallacious dream that you can successfully remake nation-states in your own image—is a mirage."[22] Whereas the first of the two meanings of "Syriana" that Gaghan glosses here entails "nation creation" in the literal sense (the process through which nations come into being), the second involves "nation building" in the more abstract sense of forging a sense of national identity and political unity. In both cases, the essential factor is that this "nation," whether geographic entity or abstract idea, is externally imposed in the aim of furthering someone else's interests. Baer's remarks, cited above, helpfully clarify what those interests are: "Our oil interests."

Imaginary Geographies

Although the word "Syriana" does not appear in the film, we can discern the concept during an interview that senior CIA officials conduct with field operative Bob Barnes, the fictional Bob Baer. The scene begins with Bob droning on about the situation in the Middle East. Marilyn, a no-nonsense official with little patience for Bob's vague platitudes, cuts off the interviewee in mid-sentence, summarizes the global situation in a few short sentences, and asks him for the information she needs to know:

> India is now our ally. Russia is our ally. Even China will be an ally. Everybody between Morocco and Pakistan is the problem. Failed states and failed economies. But Iran is a natural cultural ally of the US. . . . And what I'd like to know is, if we keep embargoing them on energy, then someday soon, are we going to have a nice, secular, pro-Western, pro-business government?

Marilyn's synopsis here of contemporary globalization is remarkable for its brevity and acuity. Former enemies of the United States are now allies. Countries once hostile to market capitalism are now partners and competitors in the world market. With the demise of the Soviet Union and the transition of formerly communist countries to free-market systems, the one recalcitrant region in the world—"the problem," as Marilyn calls it—remains the area "between Morocco and Pakistan." Two noteworthy characteristics distinguish this vast region: it is predominantly Muslim and it contains the world's richest oil reserves. Sounding like a good "model" theorist, what Marilyn wants to know is how to convert one regime within this broad territory—Iran, in this case—into "a nice, secular, pro-Western, pro-business government." When Bob expresses his skepticism about such a transition, an off-camera voice informs him that "the reform movement in Iran is one of the president's great hopes for the region and crucial to the petroleum security of the United States." If this voice sounds like it could be coming from the ranks of the CLI, well, it is: the fictional CLI, not the real one. All we need to do is change one letter for the fictional Committee for the Liberation of Iran to appear in its empirical form.

This implicit substitution of an *n* for a *q* raises the question of *where* the film is supposed to be set. *Syriana* never reveals the location of Al-Subbai's kingdom, leading curious viewers to wonder if it corresponds to an existing country. A logical place to look, one might think, would be the map that Bryan Woodman (Matt Damon), Prince Nasir's energy advisor, draws in the sand while describing a shipping strategy to his employer, but this map creates more confusion that it dispels. Although we catch only a few glimpses of Bryan's map as he describes his proposed shipping route to the prince, we can see enough of it to realize that it makes no sense. Bryan illogically places Nasir's kingdom outside of the Eurasian triangle, in a location that would correspond to somewhere in the Indian Ocean. This is clearly not where the film action is meant to take place. Geographically obsessed viewers who rewatch the film, hitting *pause* every time a clue to the location of the unnamed emirate appears on the screen, risk being frustrated by the inconclusive result of their efforts. Production designer Dan Weil and location manager Michael Sharp do a fine job of disguising the country so that it looks like it

Figure 2.3. Bryan Woodman illogically places Prince Nasir's kingdom outside of the Eurasian triangle in the map that he draws in the sand (*Syriana*, Warner Bros., 2005).

could plausibly be any number of states in the Middle East, but is not definitively any of them.

The map evoked at the beginning of this chapter creates only more confusion. As indicated above, the non sequitur from Jimmy's tirade about the "Podunk king" in the Gulf that tossed his colleagues at Connex "out on their ass" and his own company's recent acquisition of oil rights in the Tengiz creates the impression that these two regions are one and the same place. This confusion is sustained throughout the film. *Syriana* never clearly disentangles Connex-Killen's shenanigans in the Tengiz from the company's intervention in the Persian Gulf, leading the viewer to merge the two regions in her mind. It is as if *Syriana* created a virtual geography in the image of its title, where one oil-rich state east of the Mediterranean is interchangeable with another or, even worse, where "everybody between Morocco and Pakistan is the problem."

"*To each film its map*," Tom Conley proposes in the introduction to his exhaustive analyses of movie maps in *Cartographic Cinema*.[23]

> A welter of issues comes forward [when we discern a map in a movie], including perspective, visual style, narrative economy, scale, cinema and history, the stakes of mimesis, and reception. Involved, too, are the vital components of projection and ideology, understood here in the classical sense as the imaginary relation that we hold to real modes of production.[24]

Each of the issues enumerated here by Conley finds expression in Gaghan's film. On the one hand, the maps that appear on the screen, like the one evoked by Marilyn in the dialogue, provide insight into the characters' geo-economic interests or sociopolitical perspectives while proposing a subtle yet insistent critique of those same interests and perspectives. The maps operate, in this sense, much like Saul Steinberg's famous map on the cover of the March 29, 1976, issue of the *New Yorker* magazine, where a few streets in Manhattan occupy fully half of the picture, a small rectangle representing the rest of the United States fills about 20 percent of the image, and way off in the distance are three islands marked "China," "Japan," and "Russia." This map tells us very little about actual geography but a great deal about the point of view of the geographer. The maps in *Syriana* serve a similar function, revealing more about the film's individual mapmakers than they do about the places they map. To the extent that the viewer shares the interests and perspectives of those mapmakers, the film beckons us to reconsider our positions. In this sense, the maps (and the film more generally) function "ideologically," attempting to effect a modification of what Conley, echoing Althusser and Jameson, calls here the "imaginary relation that we hold to real modes of production."

On the other hand, the handheld camerawork, which inhibits our ability to read the maps that appear in the field of the moving image, defies us to discern the contours of a vast and amorphous entity, whose boundaries expand and contract in the viewer's mind over the course of the film. The related fact that some of the maps—like the one drawn in the sand by Bryan Woodman and the one produced imaginarily during Jimmy Pope's tirade in the Connex boardroom—make no cartographic sense further reinforces the geopolitical confusion that the film simultaneously produces and represents. "Surely some films use maps to convey their genre and their style through a seamless relation of narrative space to the film," Conley observes, "while others, *in flagrante delicto* of prevailing mimetic codes, make maps resemble Lautréamont's image of 'an umbrella and a sewing machine on an operating table.'" A third category of films contains maps that "are so heteroclite in form that they lead the viewer 'all over the map.'"[25] The cartographic representations in *Syriana* serve all these functions. Variously coding the film as a geopolitical thriller, juxtaposing incongruous representations of the narrative space, and distorting that space beyond recognition, the maps in *Syriana* alternately serve to ground the film in "the real world" of the Middle East at the beginning of the twenty-first century, to turn that world into a well-nigh surrealist image, and to send the viewer all over the proverbial map.

The movie's imaginary geography does not compromise Gaghan's biting critique of global capitalism. On the contrary, the fanciful world map that the film creates serves as a powerful criticism of the speculators and spies whose interventions around the world serve their own individual or national interests. "Quite often the map [in a film] locates the history of the film within itself," Conley proposes. "It has affinities with a *mise-en-abyme*, but while it may duplicate or mirror the surrounding film, the map can reveal why and how it is made and how its ideology is operating."[26] Conley's pronouncement here pertains directly to a film like *Syriana*—a film in which the heterogeneous regional maps duplicate in miniature the movie in which they appear while revealing, at the same time, how and why those maps are created and the ideologies that subtend them.

If I have placed so much emphasis on the film's creative cartography, it is because so much of the film has to do with reconfiguring the world map. The film's distorted geography serves as a powerful metaphor for the phenomenon it depicts. The actual maps in the movie give graphic form to the film's "cognitive map." They condense into concrete form the fundamental problem that the movie addresses. In view of the film's "cognitive map" of globalization, these fanciful reconfigurations of the world map are consistent with the movie's overall perspective. The maps' inaccuracies and distortions reinforce rather than detract from the film's general message.

Fictional History

Let us turn now from questions of space to the question of time. The film's relationship to history is as nebulous as the borders of Al-Subbai's kingdom. Although the movie is clearly set in a post-9/11 context (as a passing reference to changes in the CIA "after 9-1-1" clarifies), it eschews audio and visual details that would date the narrative to a specific historical moment. There is no incidental picture of President George W. Bush or Secretary of Defense Donald Rumsfeld hanging on a wall, no archival television or radio report that might clue us in to the time period, and, most surprisingly, no overt allusion to the war in Iraq. Given the film's explicit engagement with issues surrounding what was then the ongoing war, the latter omission is particularly striking. We are left wondering whether the action is supposed to be unfolding before, during, or after the Iraq War.

This lack of clarity about the film's diegetic time period leads a critic like Andrew Sarris to wonder in frustration "when all this skullduggery was supposed to be taking place, or if it constituted some timeless allegory on the eternal evil of the oil industry and the politicians, lobbyists and lawyers that do its bidding."[27] I am almost tempted to say: *yes, exactly, the film does constitute an allegory of the evil of the oil industry and the politicians, lobbyists, and lawyers that do its bidding*. But pace Sarris, such an allegory is by no means timeless or eternal. On the contrary, it pertains to a specific politico-economic global configuration at a particular moment in its history—to wit, globalization in its current form. Sarris's exasperation with the film's imprecise relation to historical time amounts to an impatience with the movie's fictional aspects. He essentially faults the film for being a piece of fiction instead of a work of history. I am tempted to cite Aristotle in Gaghan's defense here, recalling that, according to the Greek philosopher, "it is not the function of the poet to relate what has happened, but what may happen."[28] Is this not precisely what Gaghan gives us: not what happened, but what *may* happen? For Aristotle, it is the job of the historian to relate what happened. The poet, by contrast, imagines what *could* happen. According to Aristotle, this difference makes poetry (a category that encompasses fiction in general) "a more philosophical and a higher thing than history: for poetry tends to express the universal, history the particular."[29] Sarris has no patience for this universal dimension; just the facts please, he implicitly demands.

What Gaghan creates in *Syriana* is not historical fiction but a fictional history. It fabricates an imaginary version of contemporary world events, expressing the "universal" dimension of globalization rather than transposing "particular" historical developments onto the screen. In straying from the strictly empirical realm, Gaghan gives himself great leeway in interpreting global developments. What he offers is a hypothetical *explanation*—a "cognitive map"—of current events, as opposed to a representation of what actually occurred.

Emblematic of Gaghan's remapping of current world events is the film's transformation of the *USS Cole*—the US Navy destroyer that an al-Qaeda-affiliated cell attacked on October 12, 2000, while the vessel was harbored in the Yemeni port of Aden—into a Connex-Killen Liquefied Natural Gas carrier. By transforming the vessel from a military ship into an LNG carrier, Gaghan isolates the "origin" of the problem instead of focusing on one of its derivative manifestations. For, in Gaghan's allegorical map, multinational capitalism, especially the energy sector, is the core of the problem. Proposing a hypothetical explanation of current events very much in line with Harvey's thesis that US interventions in the Middle East are "all about oil" (and, by extension, that the *USS Cole* was deployed in the Persian Gulf in order to protect the interests of US multinational energy corporations in the first place), Gaghan displaces the target of the suicide bombing from its empirical ("particular") referent onto its allegorical (or "universal") correlate.

Essential to Gaghan's historical remapping of the suicide bombing is the personal narrative he develops for the two boys who carry out the attack. Numerous reviewers have criticized the film for its sympathetic portrayal of these two suicide bombers. Charles Krauthammer, for example, who proposes, in the pages of the *Washington Post*, that "Osama bin Laden could not have scripted this film with more conviction," argues that "the most pernicious element in the movie is the character at the moral heart of the film: the beautiful, modest, caring, generous Pakistani who becomes a beautiful, modest, caring, generous . . . suicide bomber."[30] Krauthammer is not alone in making this criticism. The most controversial aspect of the movie is its portrayal of the two eminently likable teenage suicide bombers. But what is vital to grasp here is the two boys' itinerary. Farooq and Wasim are motivated not by religious devotion or spiritual conviction, much less by some innate aspect of their culture or ethnicity, but by economic desperation. The problem depicted in the film is socioeconomic, not cultural or religious. There is no "clash of civilizations" at play here. It is the destabilizing effects of globalization that lead Farooq and Wasim to commit their suicidal act of destruction, not religious zeal or an attachment to their cultural identity.

A brief recap of the boys' itinerary brings this social dimension into relief. The first time we see Farooq and Wasim, they are hanging out with a group of friends on an electrical power transmitter in the desert, drinking homemade alcohol out of a recycled plastic bottle, talking about girls, and making fun of each other for being virgins. In case we do not get the message that these kids are not particularly religious, an improvised speech by Farooq clarifies the matter: "If man is made in God's image, then God is deeply messed up." We next see the boys lounging in their trailer at the workers' compound while watching *The Outsiders*—Francis Ford Coppola's 1983 teen classic about tensions between the working-class "greasers" and the upper-class "socs" in Tulsa, Oklahoma—on television. Farooq interrupts two other boys' discussion of *The Outsiders*' plot to announce: "They gave us French fries at the Islamic school." His next contribution to the conversation continues the thought: "And lamb. We got skewers of lamb." A subsequent scene shows Wasim and Farooq kicking around a soccer ball while discussing the source of Spider-Man's powers. When the charming and charismatic Mohammed Sheik Agiza joins their game and invites them to pray together, the boys' attraction to the older man is understandable. He is warm, gregarious, and nonjudgmental, old enough to be a mentor to the boys but young enough to be able to relate to them. Moreover, he makes them feel accepted. The Islamic school also gives them a sense of belonging as well as much-appreciated free food and an opportunity to practice their Arabic. The madrasa is like an oasis in an environment of hardship. It is a place where being a foreigner does not disadvantage the boys, where their employment status is not a source of shame, and where their citizenship status is not an issue.

After Agiza shows the boys the missile head he acquired and tells them that he thinks that they are "ready" to dedicate themselves to a higher cause, both boys show hesitation. First, Wasim confides to Farooq that he does not feel worthy:

WASIM: If I truly lack faith, then I am not the right person.

FAROOQ: The questioning means that you have faith and makes it stronger.

WASIM: That's a lot of shit, I think.

Farooq reflects for a moment before offering the rationale that convinces Wasim: "We'll be able to intervene in the affairs of family members. We'll be able to help them with whatever they need. You'll be able to get your mother here." This exchange clearly suggests that it is socio-economic considerations that persuade the boys—in any case, Wasim—to go through with the mission.

When the time comes to carry out the operation, it is Farooq who hesitates. The hesitation is subtle, but it is unmistakable. The boys are driving their dhow in a small flotilla of fishing boats in the Persian Gulf. Wasim crawls to the front of the boat, programs the missile, and yells back to Farooq, who is looking nervously around him as he mans the rudder. A close-up of Farooq shows him subtly but unquestionably shaking his head *no*. The two boys look at each other in a series of shots and counter-shots, then Farooq gives a tiny head nod, pushes the rudder to the side, opens the boat's throttle, and drives the dhow into the LNG tanker. Reinforcing the relation of cause to effect, the muted audio track plays the same haunting harp melody that accompanied the film's opening images, the ones depicting the scores of anonymous migrant laborers gathered in the desert at dawn. To this musical accompaniment, the screen flashes white as the dhow makes contact with the side of the tanker, then dissolves into a shot that pans slowly across a golf course in the Middle East, where workers silently prepare the turf as massive irrigation sprinklers soak the grass.

The shot of the golf course following the boys' suicide attack serves no diegetic function in the film. The movie contains no other references to this or any other golf course; the shot contains no characters seen elsewhere in the film; and no visual element in the shot (aside from the clear blue sky and the palm trees in the background) appears anywhere else in the movie. The image seems to be gratuitous, but the reprise of the harp melody suggests a connection between the migrant laborers we see at beginning of the film and the workers tending the grounds at the end. Both images imply a class division between the workers we see on the screen and the corporate bosses we do not see. In contrast to the film's opening images, which portray workers who engage directly in creating their corporate masters' wealth, the golf-course shot depicts laborers who facilitate their bosses' leisure activities. Given that golf is not only the traditional sport of choice for the wealthy but also a quintessentially Western sport, the shot of the putting green evokes not just any class division, but a specifically racialized division of classes, where Middle Eastern employees maintain the lifestyle of Western fat cats. The film's representation of "the new imperialism" concludes, in sum, with an image evoking the old one.

How are we to interpret this golf-course shot within the context of the film? On the one hand, the graceful pan creates the impression that "life goes on" (that although Wasim and Farooq have given their lives in a suicide mission to destroy a symbol of their oppression, people go on doing what they were doing). Aesthetically, the gradual fade-in from white to the serene image of the golf course, where sprinklers spray wide arcs of water as they turn on their axes, creates a sense of continuity, reinforcing the feeling that "life goes on." The delicate harp melody further reinforces the calming effect of the smooth pan. On the other hand, the reprise of the harp melody, which the film initially associated with the plight of precarious workers, also serves as a reminder that the conditions that led Farooq and Wasim to undertake their suicidal attack remain unchanged. Wasim's story began as a migrant worker in the desert. Following his descent into abjection, produced by a system over which he has no control, it ends with him lashing out against the system. We are left to wonder whether the workers at the golf course might follow a similar path.

Since the film's premier in 2005, many people in situations similar to Wasim's have indeed followed such a path. If, as Washington think tanks proposed in the months leading up the invasion of Iraq, the 2003–2011 Iraq War established a "model" for the future of the region, this future will be characterized not only by an increased level of ethnic hostility and by an escalation of violence among different religious groups, but also by a surge in anti-Western terrorist activity: the exact opposite of "model" theorists' stated objective. And if the leading terrorist organization in the region succeeds in its endeavors, the new regional map to emerge from the chaos will resemble very little the one envisioned by the "model" theorists. The Islamic State of Iraq and Syria (ISIS), also known as the Islamic State of Iraq and the Levant (ISIL), the proclaimed Sunni caliphate stretching from the Mediterranean Sea to the southern tip of the Arabian Peninsula, is clearly not the sort of map the United States had in mind.

The relation between Syriana and ISIS is one between a US-imagined reshaping of the Middle East and its negation, very much in that order. Although the formation of ISIS predates the Iraq War, the organization's growing power and influence in the region are a direct consequence of the eight-year war. As the group's name suggests, the Islamic State of Iraq and Syria aspires to reconfigure the map of the Middle East and to create thereby a fundamentalist theocracy. Like Syriana, which names both a geographical region and ideological perspective, ISIS is therefore both the name of a geographical entity and the embodiment of a particular ideology. If (quoting *Syriana*'s straight-talking Marilyn) the US objective in the Middle East was to create "a nice, secular, pro-Western, pro-business government," they could hardly have failed more spectacularly. ISIS is the direct and precise negation of Syriana.

The moral of *Syriana*, if there is one, is that the way to combat terrorism originating in the Middle East is not by "liberating" the region, but by addressing the social causes at the root of the problem. Those causes, the film suggests, are the exact opposite of the ones that the "model" theorists propose. If the Krauthammers of the world want to prevent beautiful, modest, caring, generous Pakistanis from becoming beautiful, modest, caring, and generous suicide bombers, the way to do it is by decreasing social inequality and job insecurity, not by introducing a minimally regulated free-market system that exacerbates socioeconomic inequalities and increases workers' precariousness. Unfortunately, history has been moving by and large in the opposite direction, making *Syriana* as timely now as it was when it was released.

3

Corporate Murder in *The Constant Gardener*

During an early scene in Fernando Meirelles's *The Constant Gardener* (2005), British diplomat Justin Quayle (Ralph Fiennes), an impeccably dressed man in his forties, delivers a lecture on behalf of a senior colleague, Sir Bernard Pellegrin, who is unable to present his paper in person. Following the lecture, which concludes that diplomacy is "the very map and marker of civilization," the speaker thanks his audience of several dozen advanced graduate students for their kind attention and begins to pack up his belongings. The auditors give the presenter a perfunctory round of applause and start preparing to leave the lecture hall when Tessa (Rachel Weisz), a young woman seated in the middle of the room, raises her hand and asks the speaker a question: "Excuse me. Sir, I've just got one question. I just wondered, whose map, um, is Britain using when it completely ignores the United Nations and decides to invade Iraq? Or do you . . . do you think it's more *diplomatic* to bend to the will of a superpower and politely take part in Vietnam, the sequel?"

Audience members momentarily stop fussing with their belongings and look at the speaker to see how he will respond to the question. Rather than formulating his own thoughts, Justin speculates how his colleague might address the question: "Well, I think that . . . Sir Bernard would no doubt argue that when, um, peaceful means are exhausted, then . . ." Before he can complete his sentence, the questioner cuts him off to challenge this presupposition. "Exhausted? Mr. Quayle, they're not exactly exhausted, are they? . . . We've taken sixty years to build up this international organization called the United Nations, which is meant to avoid wars, and now we just blow it up because our car's running out of petrol."

As Tessa makes this argument, her colleagues start fidgeting in their seats and continue their interrupted preparations to leave the room. The only audible remark we hear from her peers is a plea for her to *sit down, for Christ's sake*. Tessa continues making her point as her classmates pack their things and start filing out the door. By the time she has completed her speech, Tessa has cleared the room. The only other person remaining in the lecture hall by the time she has finished her diatribe is Justin.

This scene, chronologically the earliest moment in the story, is noteworthy for several reasons. First, it brings into sharp relief the difference between the film's two main characters. The heroine, an impassioned and outspoken young woman who is not afraid to take a firm stance on politically controversial issues, stands in sharp contrast to the older man, who represents, quite literally, the establishment. In contrast to Tessa, who "speaks truth to power," Justin speaks the truth of power. In uncritically conveying Sir Bernard's thoughts, even during the question-and-answer period, Justin defers to his superiors, whether or not he agrees with their position. In fact, when he does start speaking in his own voice (in response to the audience's unsympathetic reaction to Tessa's remarks), he states his general agreement with his interlocutor: "I think the questioner is making a valid point, and that a nation's foreign policy should not be determined by narrow commercial interests." However, rather than eliciting Tessa's sympathy, this comment only fuels her ire: "That's bullshit. You have to take responsibility," she insists, demanding that if he really is critical of British foreign policy, then he should not "apologize for this pathetic country of Britain" that has "burned [its] diplomatic credentials" and is "killing . . . thousands of innocent people just for . . . some barrels of oil and a photo opportunity on the White House lawn."

During the scene, Tessa's peers play a role like that of the chorus in a Greek tragedy, standing in for both the film audience and society as a whole. Their reaction, which changes from curiosity to impatience as Tessa formulates more and more forcefully her criticisms, functions as a proxy for our reaction. Whether or not she is right is almost beside the point. Her tone is enough to turn the crowd against her. Her conviction that what she is saying is important and her stubborn insistence that others take her argument seriously are enough to set people's eyes rolling. By the end of her speech, which increases in pitch and volume in proportion to her colleagues' impatience, she comes across as a hysteric shrieking, rather than speaking, truth to power. The more people ignore her, the louder she yells.

The scene also situates us in the same fictional world as *Syriana*, released the same year as *The Constant Gardener*. Both films are set more or less in the historical present, and both of them examine interrelations between foreign policy and global capitalism. Whereas *Syriana* focuses on East-West conflicts between the United States and the Middle East, *The Constant Gardener* looks at North-South relations between the United Kingdom and sub-Saharan Africa. During the lecture scene, set in a freshly renovated room with floor-to-ceiling windows overlooking the City of London, we do not yet know that much of *The Constant Gardener* will take place in Nairobi, Kenya. Nor do we know that the movie's target will be Big Pharma rather than Big Oil. At this point in the film, we have the impression that *The Constant Gardener* may well be about Britain's oil interests in Iraq. The scene not only situates us in the same general historical and political context as *Syriana*; it leads us to wonder whether the two films deal with the same general topic.

Tessa's speech about Britain's petro-politics does not appear in the John le Carré novel on which the film of *The Constant Gardener* is based. Le Carré's novel was published in 2001, before the Allied forces (the so-called "coalition of the willing," including, most particularly, Britain) invaded Iraq. The comparable scene in the novel revolves around a more theoretical discussion of individual responsibility in relation to the state. Instead of accusing Justin of hypocritically apologizing for Britain's morally bankrupt foreign policy in Iraq, Tessa asks him whether he can imagine "a situation where [he] personally would feel obliged to *undermine* the state."[1] Yet, although le Carré's novel does not contain any references to Britain's petro-politics, the filmmakers' decision to incorporate the oil reference touches the book's genetic core. As le Carré says in an interview included as a special feature on the Alliance DVD: "I was initially going to go for oil. Then I thought, oil was too much on the nose, and I talked to an old Africa hand, and he said: 'Go for the pharmaceutical industry. That's a really delightful metaphor for your purpose.' "[2]

This explanation of *The Constant Gardener*'s genesis speaks volumes about le Carré's approach. The author first had a "purpose," then he selected a metaphor for his purpose. He ultimately decided to use the pharmaceutical industry as his metaphor, but he could equally well have focused on the energy sector had that choice not been so obvious, so "on the nose." Although he clearly undertook meticulous research in order to write his tale of malfeasances in the pharmaceutical industry (more on this point below), the novelist uses drug companies as a metaphor for something more general. That "something" has a name. Le Carré's target is the multinational corporation as such, not this or that particular corporate sector. Big Oil, Big Pharma: same difference, le Carré says in effect. They both obey the same logic. One thing that Tessa's post-lecture rebuttal to Justin accomplishes in the film is to suggest this equivalence of one corporate sector with another. But unlike le Carré, who *replaces* the oil metaphor with the pharmaceutical metaphor, screenwriter Jeffrey Caine *includes* the oil reference in his adaptation of the novel, leading the viewer to wonder if the film is about goings-on in the energy sector. As indicated above, unless the viewer knows beforehand what the movie is about, she could easily think, while watching this early scene, that it is about Britain's petro-politics.

In summary, the lecture hall scene at the beginning of *The Constant Gardener* introduces several overlapping narrative and thematic elements. First, it sets up the relationship between Tessa and Justin, which forms the basis for the film's love story. In juxtaposing his quiet conservatism and her unabashed radicalism, it anticipates future tensions within the couple while simultaneously preparing the viewer for the political intrigue that drives the plot. Second, it introduces the idea of a symbiotic relationship between international affairs and multinational capitalism, which the scene misleadingly presents in relation to petro-politics when the film in fact examines multinational "pharma-politics." This sort of confusion between corporate sectors is not isolated to this scene. On the contrary, the film repeatedly misleads us about *which* corporate sector it is exposing, thereby creating a generalized skepticism about potentially *all* corporate sectors. Finally, by including a proxy audience, the lecture hall scene incorporates a figure of the spectator within the film. As we will see, the narrative of *The Constant Gardener* is designed to convince us that Tessa is right and that we should listen to her. If the film begins with a surrogate film audience walking out in exasperation at Tessa's antics, its task is to bring us around not only to endorsing her point of view, but to adopting it.

What the lecture hall scene does not touch on is the murder mystery that makes up the film's third subplot, along with the love story and the political narrative. Following a cryptic shot of Justin seeing off Tessa and her friend Arnold Bluhm (Hubert Koundé) as they board a plane, the film begins with the murder of Tessa and Arnold. The rest of the narrative, which shifts back and forth between time periods before and after the murder, revolves around the characters trying to solve the central enigma at the core of the various subplots. The film tightly interweaves these three subplots. Part of what makes the adaptation of *The Constant Gardener* so compelling as a work of narrative fiction and so powerful as a piece of anti-corporate propaganda is the extent to which it integrates these three subplots into a cohesive whole, where each subplot reflects and refracts the other two.

This chapter examines the ways the film's three subplots work together to expose the ways that multinational corporations function, to denounce those corporations' motives, and ultimately to inculpate them for heinous acts. Rather than transmitting its critique via depictions of backroom dealings and corporate meetings (as *Syriana* does), the film attempts to win over the viewer by putting us in the position of Westerners who do not understand at the outset what the multinationals are doing in Africa.[3] We then follow the characters as they unravel the various mysteries. I begin my analysis, following a brief overview of the film's backstory, with an examination of the false leads that the film creates in order to put the spectator in a position similar to that of the characters. Taking inspiration from film scholar Todd McGowan's observation that the movie's love story misleads the viewer twice over—once by suggesting that Tessa is having an affair with her friend Arnold, again by using the romance narrative to deflect the film's denunciation of multinational corporations—I explore the ways the film misleads us into thinking that it is exposing one corporate sector and then another, when it in fact sets out to expose yet another. By the time the film narrows the scope of its focus from an array of corporate sectors to one particular sector, the movie has already led the viewer to extend the film's vision of one sector to numerous others. Marcia Angell, former editor-in-chief of the prestigious *New England Journal of Medicine* and senior lecturer in the Department of Global Health and Social Medicine at Harvard Medical School, criticizes the film for clouding le Carré's crystalline description of the way pharmaceutical companies work. However, what the film loses in sectoral specificity, I argue, it gains in its power to generalize its conclusions. In the spirit of le Carré's comment, cited above, about the genesis of his novel, the filmmakers transmit a generalized critique of the corporation as such. That critique ultimately amounts to an accusation that the corporation is a pathological murderer. In the vein of author and documentarian Joel Bakan's thesis, in *The Corporation*, that the corporation is a "pathological institution" driven only by self-interest, *The Constant Gardener* portrays the corporation as a pathological organization willing to kill people in the aim of making a profit and to eliminate anyone who impedes its ability to generate revenue.[4] The chapter concludes with an examination of the various murders that the movie's fictional corporations orchestrate and the ways that the film proposes to deal with murderers of this sort.

Strategies of Deception

The political narrative that drives *The Constant Gardener*'s plot revolves around Tessa's discovery that a British company by the name of ThreeBees is testing a tuberculosis drug on residents of Kibera, Nairobi's sprawling slum, home to an estimated 700,000 to 8000,000 people. The drug, Dypraxa, manufactured by a multinational pharmaceutical company called KDH (for Karel Delacourt Hudson), has been responsible for the death of an unknown number of test patients (numbering sixty-three by the end of the film), but the pharmaceutical company does not want to pull the drug and redevelop it for fear of losing market share. KDH anticipates a worldwide TB epidemic and wants its product to be on the market by the time the outbreak occurs. Instead of publicizing the fatalities, ThreeBees, in collusion with the British High Commission in Nairobi, buries the Dypraxa victims in an unmarked mass grave and erases their medical records. Tessa and her friend Arnold, an Afro-European doctor at Médecins dans l'univers (a fictional version of Médecins sans frontières), begin to piece together the evidence against ThreeBees. Tessa writes up a report of their findings, which she submits to the British Foreign & Commonwealth Office (FCO) and the CEO of ThreeBees. When neither the FCO nor ThreeBees responds to her report, Tessa and Arnold fly from Nairobi to Loki, in northwest Kenya, in order to give a copy of the report to Grace Makanga, an African public health activist, for her to take to the United Nations. The first shot in the film is of Tessa and Arnold boarding their flight to Loki.

Superimposed on this political narrative is a love story, which begins with a fiery Tessa interrogating a hapless Justin following the latter's presentation of Sir Bernard's dull lecture to a group of uninspired students in a London lecture hall. The central tension developed in Meirelles's depiction of the love story is the contrast between Justin's devotion to Tessa, who becomes Mrs. Quayle shortly after the two meet in London, and her commitment to something other than him.

For roughly the first third of the film, we are led to wonder whether that something that draws Tessa's attention away from her husband is Arnold Bluhm. In his insightful analysis of the film's temporality, Todd McGowan patiently details how the film creates the impression that Tessa and Arnold are having an affair. Doubts are raised from the film's opening shot, McGowan remarks, where Tessa and Arnold leave Justin on the tarmac as they walk to their plane.[5] "Sweetheart, don't bother to see us off. It could be ages," she tells Justin before she walks off with Arnold, reaching out and caressing her friend's arm as she turns to wave goodbye to her husband. McGowan goes through the numerous examples that reinforce the suspicion cast in this opening scene that Tessa may be having an affair with Arnold.[6] His fine analysis of how the film's screenplay, editing, and mise-en-scène create this suspicion culminates in an interpretation of a particularly deceptive scene set in the maternity ward of Nairobi's Uhuru Hospital. For about fifteen minutes, we have been seeing Tessa traipsing around Nairobi while pregnant, often in the company of Arnold. The post-childbirth scene begins, following a tracking shot that takes us inside the hospital, with an extreme close-up of an African baby sucking a European breast. This shot is quickly followed by a medium close-up of Tessa nursing the newborn and then by a static medium long shot, held for eight seconds, of Arnold sitting at Tessa's bedside as he watches her nurse the infant. A fifth shot shows Justin in profile with a frown on his face, alone in the frame, observing the offscreen triad formed by Tessa, Arnold, and the baby. The fact that Justin is literally "out of the picture" with the infant leads us to assume that he is figuratively external to the mother-father-baby triad as well. The explanation for the situation comes thirty or forty seconds later, when Tessa tells Sandy Woodrow (Danny Huston), Justin's boss at the High Commission, who is visiting Tessa in the hospital, that her baby was stillborn but that this one, whose mother died, is alive. We then understand that the infant in Tessa's arms is not hers, but for about a minute we were convinced that she had given birth to Arnold's child.

McGowan's interpretation of this deception on the filmmaker's part shows how virtually every scene that calls Tessa's fidelity into question has a political subtext. Scenes that begin by hinting at Tessa and Arnold's romantic involvement end by refocusing our attention on the political drama, or vice-versa. The infant's dead mother in the hospital scene, for

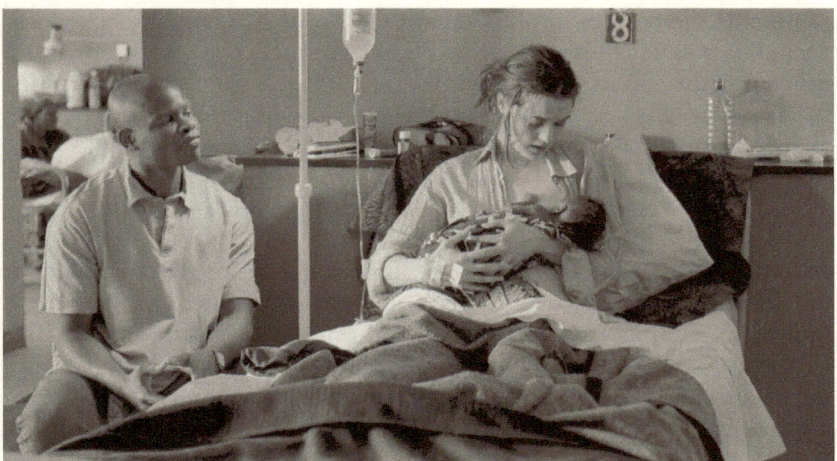

Figure 3.1. An eight-second static shot of Arnold Bluhm watching Tessa Quayle nurse a newborn infant leads the spectator to believe that Tessa has given birth to Arnold's child (*The Constant Gardener*, Focus Features, 2005).

example, is the first Dypraxa victim that Tessa discovers. Wanza Kiluhu (Jacqueline Maribe), the fifteen-year-old mother, died from an adverse reaction to the drug that ThreeBees is testing, not from childbirth. McGowan comments: "The film misleads the spectator here in order locate us within the romance narrative and then reveal how the question of Tessa's fidelity merely obscures the political problem of Western capital's exploitation of Africa as a territory for experimental and dangerous drug testing."[7] Proposing that the infant in Tessa's arms functions as "an objective correlative for two different—and even opposed—responses" in the spectator, McGowan argues that "what begins as a standard romantic storyline about the wrongdoing of a lover becomes a political storyline about the wrongdoing of an entire continent."[8]

In sum, McGowan brings to light a double deception at play in the representations of Tessa's infidelity. On the one hand, these representations are actually misrepresentations. Our suspicions that Tessa may be having an affair are finally laid to rest, along with Justin's, in a post-murder scene about a third of the way into the film, when Tessa and Arnold's mutual friend Ghita Pearson (Archie Panjabi) reveals to Justin that Arnold was gay. On the other hand, the misrepresentations of Tessa's infidelity serve to obscure the corporate misdoings that Tessa and Arnold are investigating. What misleadingly appears to be a development in the love story is in fact a deflected representation of Western corporations' exploitation of the local population. Continuing the line of inquiry opened here by McGowan, I would add that the film also misrepresents the political problem that the love story misleadingly deflects. Meirelles transmits his critique of Western capital's exploitation of Africa using narrative strategies as deceiving as those he employs in narrating the romance. Let us briefly recap the ways the film misleads the viewer about the subject of its critique.

Meirelles's Protean Corporation

For the first half-hour or so of the film, the humanitarian problem at the core of the narrative is the HIV-AIDS epidemic in Nairobi and the limited local availability of antiretroviral drugs to treat the disease. The first scene set in Kibera, for example, shows the street performance of an AIDS-awareness play put on by a popular theater troupe. During a break in the performance, Arnold calls out to Tessa, the only white person in the crowd, and then walks over to see her. As he squeezes past a group of onlookers and leaves the frame, the camera lingers for a moment, shifting focus slightly in order to sharpen the definition of an HIV and AIDS prevention poster in the background. Tessa and Arnold then leave the theater site and walk through Kibera, where Arnold gives nevirapine, an antiretroviral drug, to a resident because, as he explains to Tessa, "the government clinic didn't have any again." An explanation for the nevirapine shortage comes in a subsequent scene, at a party hosted by the British High Commission in Nairobi, where Tessa, "speaking truth to power," undiplomatically asks Dr. Joshua Ngaba (John Sibi-Okumu) of the Kenya Health Ministry whether the pills were "converted into the limo that [he] arrived in." A second explanation for the shortage shifts the blame from corrupt local officials to Western governments and pharmaceutical companies. This is the explanation that the film's fictional HIV-AIDS activist Grace Makanga (Mumbi Kaigwa) proposes in a podcast that Tessa watches just before leaving for Loki: "The governments of the USA and Europe, at the behest of the pharmaceutical companies that seem to control them, . . . give us endless reasons why we should buy your branded drugs at five, ten, twenty times the price." A shot of Tessa watching this podcast is the last image we see before the movie replays the scene of her and Arnold boarding their plane. Even as the two investigators leave for Loki, bringing the narrative up to the point where the movie began, the film continues to create the impression that it sets out to expose the complicity of pharmaceutical companies, Western governments, and corrupt local officials in creating the antiretroviral drug shortage in Africa.

The movie first links HIV-AIDS to tuberculosis about thirty minutes into the film, when Tessa asks Arnold why HIV patients waiting in line at a ThreeBees Medical Mobile Unit in Kibera are carrying little jars of saliva. Arnold explains that the company tests for TB when it tests for AIDS. "What, just for free?" Tessa asks skeptically. Arnold's reply—"A small extra service to humanity"—does not convince Tessa. "They're a drug company, Arnold," she says. "No drug company does something for nothing." Here, roughly half an hour into the film, we have our first clue that the ThreeBees company may be conducting unorthodox tuberculosis treatment or testing on unwitting AIDS patients. It is hardly conclusive. At most, it arouses our suspicion that ThreeBees may be up to something fishy.

The next reference to ThreeBees occurs a few minutes later, when Justin is gardening in the yard. The scene starts with a shot of Mustafa (Samuel Otage), the Quayles' gardener, measuring pesticide into a plastic spray bucket. Justin spends a moment helping Mustafa prepare to spray the garden and then walks onto the porch, where Tessa and Arnold are conspiring in hushed tones about "a marriage of convenience" that is "only . . . going to produce . . . dead offspring." Justin mistakenly thinks that Tessa is referring here to her own marriage and stillborn child. He stops at the top of the stairs and aggressively apologizes for interrupting. Rather than acknowledging the apology, Tessa flies into a rage. "What the fuck is that?" she asks Justin in reference to the box of ThreeBees pesticide in his hands. He defensively says that it is just pesticide, but Tessa is beside herself with fury. "It's just unbelievable. Would you just get that thing out of this house?" she says as she bats the box out of the bewildered Justin's hands.

This pesticide reference constitutes the film's third clue to the nature of the mysterious investigation that Tessa and Arnold are conducting. It is a false lead, but it is a convincing one. In light of the widespread concerns raised in recent decades about the nefarious effects of pesticides on the environment, it would come as no surprise if an activist like Tessa were hostile to a pesticide manufacturer. The name of ThreeBees also conveniently conjures the species most readily associated with the deleterious effects of pesticide. Since around 2005, the year of *The Constant Gardener*'s release, beekeepers have been reporting a rapid decline in bee populations. In 2006, scientists coined the phrase "colony-collapse disorder" to describe the phenomenon that had reduced the number of bee colonies by roughly one-third.[9] The predominant theory among researchers is that pesticides are the primary cause of the collapse. Due to the important role that bees play in pollinating plants, including fruits and vegetables that people and livestock eat, food scientists see the decline in the bee population as a harbinger of coming food shortages. According to an apocalyptic quote attributed (inaccurately, apparently) to Albert Einstein that has become a rallying slogan in recent years, "If the bee disappears from the surface of the globe, man would have no more than four years to live."[10] In this context, the name of ThreeBees comes across as a not-so-subtle preemptive disassociation of their product from the plight of the insects they are inadvertently exterminating. In keeping with the time-tested marketing strategy of coining product names and advertising slogans that connote the opposite of what a company does (such as the Weyerhaeuser timber company's self-branding as "the tree-growing company" in an effort to allay concerns about its clear-cutting techniques), "ThreeBees" comes across as a cagily counterintuitive name for a bee-killing agrochemical company.

The title of *The Constant Gardener* further reinforces the association of ThreeBees with pesticides. This title refers to Justin's gardening hobby, which serves as a metaphor for his retreat from politics into the reclusive world of horticulture. As McGowan suggests in his interpretation of the scene where Tessa asks Justin to take her to Africa (and by extension, to make her his wife), the choice Justin faces is "between apolitical gardening and the political commitment of Tessa."[11] The opposition that

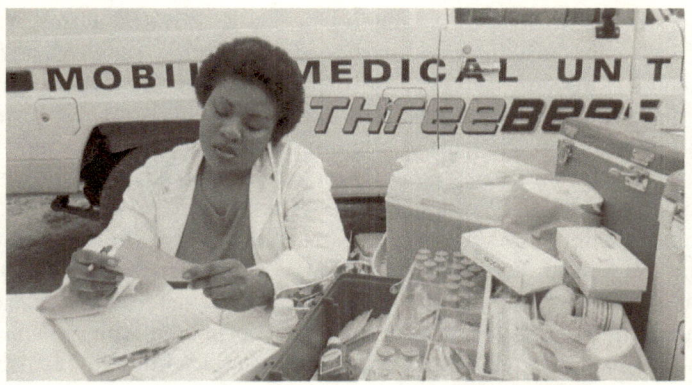

Figure 3.2. By successively depicting ThreeBees as a drug company, an agrochemical corporation, and a multinational food company, Meirelles disperses the image of the corporation across numerous sectors (*The Constant Gardener*, Focus Features, 2005).

McGowan identifies here, which he brilliantly locates within a single deep-focus shot, is conveyed in the editing of the scene that follows Tessa and Justin's confrontation on the porch, after she chastises him for using the ThreeBees pesticide. The scene intercuts shots of Justin and Mustafa working in the garden, digging in the dirt and planting flowers in the yard, with shots of Tessa at her computer, talking online with her contact at Hippo, a German pharma-watch group that monitors drug companies' actions. We later come to realize that the shots of Justin and Mustafa gardening, which the film previously associated with pesticides, present a false lead and that the online conversation about pharmaceutical companies is the real lead. Tessa flies off the handle when she sees the ThreeBees pesticide in Justin's hands because, we infer in retrospect, it is manufactured by the corporation that is responsible for the Dypraxa deaths, not because it is noxious in and of itself. However, when watching the sequence for the first time, an uninformed viewer may logically conjecture that the film is about the counterintuitively named bee-killing pesticide that the unsuspecting constant gardener holds in his hands.

The film's next reference to ThreeBees shows that the company works in yet another corporate sector. The reference goes by in the length of time it takes for a commercial van to turn a street corner in downtown Nairobi. As the van turns the corner, we see that it has an advertisement on its side for "Maziwa" (which means *milk* in Swahili). The ad shows a smiling, healthy, affluent African family in Western dress superimposed on an open field where cows graze. "ThreeBees: Buzzy for Your Health," reads the tagline above a carton of *maziwa*. Of all the commodities Meirelles could have chosen to represent ThreeBees, why milk?

On the one hand, the Maziwa ad vaguely conjures, by way of its association of a multinational agrochemical corporation with milk, the controversial use of bovine growth hormone (BGH) to increase dairy cows' yield. The fact that Monsanto, the first company to receive a patent for BGH, figures on numerous lists of *worst corporations*, often in the top spot, may help to explain why Meirelles chose to represent ThreeBees as a purveyor of corporate milk.[12]

On the other hand, the Maziwa advertisement also calls to mind one of the most famous cases in recent history of a Western corporation exploiting the developing world. I am thinking here of the Nestlé Corporation's notorious campaign to convince Third World mothers to buy instant milk formula instead of breastfeeding their children. Nestlé's multi-pronged marketing strategy included a massive ad campaign, gifts to doctors and donations to hospitals that promoted the formula, and, most infamously, the deployment of "milk nurses," company representatives dressed like medical professionals who promoted the product directly to mothers in maternity wards. Critics blame Nestlé's massively successful campaign, which targeted women who could least afford to buy the formula and who were least equipped to use the product safely, for having created health problems for millions of children annually. The international outcry against Nestlé's predatory campaign culminated, in 1977, in what was then the largest corporate boycott in world history.[13] Although the film makes no overt reference to any of this history, the conjunction of a multinational corporation preying on the Third World and a company selling milk in Africa calls it to mind without belaboring the point. The shot of the Maziwa ad modifies both retrospectively and prospectively our impression of the ThreeBees employees we see in white coats (including the one attending to Wanza Kiluhu in the Uhuru maternity clinic), who dress like they could be "milk nurses."

By successively portraying ThreeBees as a drug company, an agrochemical corporation, and a multinational food company, Meirelles disperses his image of the corporation across numerous sectors. Le Carré's ThreeBees also works in a variety of sectors. A character lists them for us early in the novel: "Hotels, travel agencies, newspapers, security companies, banks, extractors of gold, coal and copper, importers of cars, boats and trucks—I could go on forever. Plus a fine range of drugs."[14] The narrator adds to this list later in the novel, expanding it to include household foods, detergents, roadside cafeterias, gas stations, car batteries, and

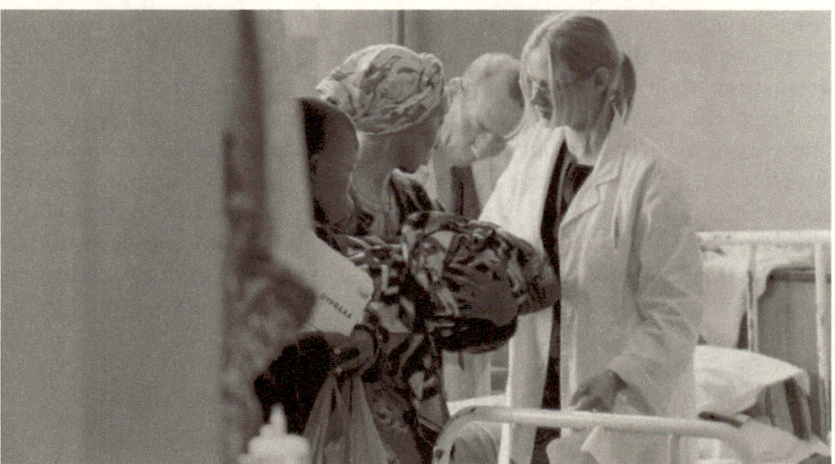

Figure 3.3. ThreeBees employees wear white coats reminiscent of those worn by Nestlé's "milk nurses" during the 1970s (*The Constant Gardener*, Focus Features, 2005).

automotive oils.[15] With the exceptions of pharmaceuticals and household foods, none of the sectors listed here appears in the film. Conversely, the agrochemical industry does not figure in the novel. Moreover, although the book's ThreeBees works in the household food industry, le Carré does not associate it with any particular product. The reference to *maziwa*, like the reference to pesticide, is the filmmakers' invention. What these two references have in common with pharmaceuticals is a strong association with unethical corporate practices. Although some of the sectors enumerated in the novel share this association, Meirelles chooses specific commodities that connote corporate scandal. In contrast to the novel, where the corporation works in a hodgepodge of sectors, in the film, ThreeBees' product line directly evokes corporate misdoings.

This difference, between one set of corporate sectors and another, accounts in part for the contrasting images of the corporation in the book and in the movie, but it is also the different ways that the two works convey this information that account for the dissimilar images. Unlike le Carré's novel, which tells us that ThreeBees operates in an array of corporate sectors and names them for us, Meirelles's film multiplies images of the corporation. The book succinctly tells us that ThreeBees has many divisions; the movie, by contrast, presents one image after another of the corporation, leading us to wonder what sort of company it is. Whereas le Carré condenses a variety of sectors into one corporation, Meirelles disperses the corporation across a variety of sectors. In rhetorical terms, le Carré's ThreeBees is a metonymy (one particular thing standing in for a general thing or class of things) while Meirelles's corporation is a metaphor (one thing related to another by similarity). Meirelles's transformation of le Carré's metonymy into a metaphor alters the way we perceive the corporation. Le Carré controls the image, telling us that the corporation is vast but identifying it for us. Meirelles's corporation, by contrast, has no discernable limit. It could work in innumerable sectors and could correspond to any number of existing corporations. Both the book and the movie generalize their image of the corporation, but whereas one generalizes by concentrating diverse corporate endeavors into one entity, the other multiplies the corporation into a potentially limitless number of sectors.

The Corporation as a Pathological Institution

Meirelles's approach is not without its critics. Marcia Angell, for example, in her important review of *The Constant Gardener* (book and film) in the *New York Review of Books*, finds that the filmmaker fails to communicate adequately the specificity of the corporate sector that the novelist describes clearly and precisely in his book. According to Angell, le Carré's narrative is by no means far-fetched. On the contrary, based on the research she did for her book, *The Truth about Drug Companies*, Angell believes that "most of the background facts about drug company behavior in *The Constant Gardener*, however hard to believe, are correct."[16] She notes particularly strong resemblances between le Carré's story and pharma-giant Pfizer's testing of a new antibiotic called Trovan on uninformed meningitis patients in Kano, Nigeria, in the 1990s. According to her, le Carré's account of a global pharmaceutical company that "distorts [its] research to make [its] drugs look safer," that uses unwitting Third World test subjects as human guinea pigs, and that uses its vast wealth "to influence governments and the medical profession and any other institutions that might interfere with [its] single-minded pursuit of profits" provides "rich [detail] about ordinary drug company practices."[17] In her view, the film fails to provide this rich detail. "Since the film tells us very little about the motives of the drug company," Angell writes, "we are left with a story that . . . is played out in something of a historical vacuum."[18] In contrast to le Carré's novel, which explains in convincing detail why pharmaceutical companies test new drugs in the Third World and how the companies go about conducting their tests, Meirelles's film provides a vague image of corporate misdoings that "most viewers would probably conclude . . . are wildly implausible, in no way representative of real drug company behavior."[19]

Coming from someone of her stature, Angell's assertion that le Carré's novel accurately describes how drug companies work is momentous. Her observation that the film gives less detail than the novel about the pharmaceutical industry's modes of operation (something easier to do in a 492-page book than in a two-hour feature film), and therefore that the movie provides comparatively little insight into how the industry actually functions, is indisputable. However, if our interest in the film goes beyond the specifics of the pharmaceutical industry to the corporation as such—in other words, if our interest in the story extends to what le Carré calls his larger "purpose" in writing the novel—then this observation need not be taken as a criticism. Although Meirelles's film may fail to convey clearly how drug companies work and why they conduct their tests in the ways they do, it is rich in its evocation of corporate behavior more generally. What it lacks in specifics about the pharmaceutical industry, it makes up for in its ability to generalize its image of the corporation. While le Carré provides a limpid description of a specific corporate sector, Meirelles offers an evocative image of the corporation as an institution.

What is a corporation? According to Joel Bakan, author of *The*

Corporation (a book made into a fine documentary film), "the corporation's legally defined mandate is to pursue, relentlessly and without exception, its own self-interest, regardless of the often harmful consequences it might cause to others."[20] For Bakan, the problem with corporations is not that they are run by callous individuals who do not care about the harm they might cause to other people in their pursuit of profit. Rather, the problem lies in the legal mandate of an institution that compels its officers to pursue its self-interest at any cost. As Bakan writes, the mandate of the corporation "compels executives to prioritize the interests of their companies and shareholders above all others and forbids them from being socially responsible."[21] It is worth underling the ramifications of this statement. It not simply the case that corporations are under no legal obligation to be socially responsible. According to the institution's mandate, it is *illegal* for a corporation to act in a socially responsible manner unless the company profits as a result. Bakan could not be clearer on this point. Analyzing the precedent-setting court cases in the United States and Britain that have established the current legal definition of a corporation, Bakan concludes: "Social responsibility is thus illegal—at least when it is genuine."[22] Corporate executives might be caring, considerate, and altruistic people, but they are legally bound to put corporate profit above their ethical concerns. The corporation has, in effect, "a mind of its own," which dictates the scope of action for the actual people that run it. Reminding us that, in the United States, corporations are legally defined as people (by way of a perversion of the Fourteenth Amendment, which was originally written in order to guarantee civil rights to newly freed slaves after the Civil War), Bakan muses what kind of person a corporation would be. He goes through the list of attributes and behaviors associated with pathological personalities (including a propensity for manipulative behavior, a lack of empathy, asocial tendencies, self-aggrandizing tendencies, a refusal to accept responsibility for one's actions, and an inability to feel remorse), and provocatively concludes that the corporate "person" is a psychopath.[23]

The two corporations in *The Constant Gardener*, KDH and Three-Bees, exhibit many of the pathological traits that Bakan enumerates. KDH's motivations seem noble. The company anticipates a worldwide tuberculosis epidemic and is developing a cure for the disease. As a promotional video for KDH that Justin finds late in the film states: "In the twenty-first century, multi-resistant TB will kill one in three. But now there is hope. KDH is developing a revolutionary treatment for TB sufferers. It's global. We call it Dypraxa. You will call it life." Tessa's cousin Ham (Richard McCabe), an attorney specializing in corporate law, who watches the KDH commercial with Justin, interjects: "I call it a blockbuster." Birgit (Anneke Kim Sarnau), Tessa's contact at the German pharma-watch group, translates KDH's motivations into starker terms: "Put into the language that stock exchanges all over the world understand, if the TB market performs as forecast, billions and billions of dollars are waiting to be earned." However, KDH stands to gain those billions of dollars only if the preliminary Dypraxa tests in Africa do not show disturbing side effects. The company therefore needs to make sure that no evidence of the drug's harmful effects becomes public. The film clarifies that Dypraxa is not a bad drug. It is in fact a very good drug, which successfully treats tuberculosis in most cases, but it is lethal in some cases. In order to gain market approval for the drug, the company would have to eliminate those toxic side effects. However, the expense and time delay associated with redeveloping the drug would put the company at a competitive disadvantage relative to other companies in what Birgit calls the burgeoning "TB market," so KDH opts to bury the compromising test results. Although KDH is developing a product designed to save lives, its motivation is profit (as it must be), and it is willing to kill people in the pursuit of this aim.

It is up to ThreeBees, the company that KDH engages to run the clinical trials, to make sure that news of the drug's toxic side effects does not spread. ThreeBees therefore literally buries the evidence of the drug's lethal effects by dumping the Dypraxa victims into an unmarked mass grave and deleting their names from the company's records. When Tessa and Arnold discover what ThreeBees is doing and threaten to go public with the information, the company has them eliminated.

Corporate Murder

The relationship between ThreeBees and its client company is not le Carré's invention. As Angell helpfully clarifies, "A huge new industry has arisen that conducts third-world research for drug companies (like le Carré's fictional research firm, ThreeBees)."[24] These companies, called contract research organizations, or CROs, are essentially subcontractors that independently organize and oversee clinical trials for drug companies. Tactics used by CROs to entice doctors to cooperate (such as offering them monetary gifts that can increase their income tenfold) and to obtain patients' "informed consent" (such as refusing medical treatment if patients do not consent) are not strictly legal, but the drug company remains at an arm's length from the process. By outsourcing the clinical trials, the pharmaceutical companies—KDH, in the film—distance themselves from the legally dubious procedures of recruiting doctors and test patients, and from the messy job of running the trials.

The company knows that the tests are in all likelihood run illegally (for reasons that Angell illuminates in her article), but it needs the tests to be done. Outsourcing provides an ideal solution, enabling the trials to occur while immunizing the drug company from liability.

Subcontracting is an increasingly common corporate practice. The film clearly communicates how it works only once, taking a particularly revealing example. As it happens, this single explanation of subcontracting also contains the film's one and only use of the word "corporate" or any of its cognates (including the word "corporation"). The scene takes place toward the end of the film, after Justin has reconstructed most of Tessa's research following her death. Tim Donohue (Donald Sumpter), a British spy based in Nairobi, catches up with Justin and tries to persuade him to give up his investigation. In the course of their conversation, Tim tells Justin that it was Sandy, Justin's boss at the High Commission, who fingered Tessa:

> He didn't know they'd kill her. Silly sod was besotted with her. But that's the way it works with corporate murder. Boss gets wind of something, calls in his head of security, who talks to someone, who talks to a friend of someone. Finishes up with an answering machine in a rented office, a couple of sensitive gentlemen in a blue pickup truck. They will never know who ordered the hit.

As Tim describes this chain of communication, the various figures he identifies appear on the screen. The "boss" is Sir Bernard Pellegrin (Bill Nighy), head of the British FCO Africa desk; the "head of security" is an anonymous Brit in a suit and tie; the person that the head of security calls is Crick (Nick Reding), the personal bodyguard of ThreeBees' CEO; the "sensitive gentlemen in a blue pickup truck" are two burly white men in their thirties dressed in matching military T-shirts. Each phone call moves the murder further from its point of origin. As is the case with subcontracting more generally, "corporate murder" as described here distances the "boss" from the people who do the work to such a degree that he is immune from liability for their actions. The film gives us to believe that Sir Bernard did not directly order the murder, and yet the murder occurred. "They will never know who ordered the hit," Tim says in summary.

It is curious that in this film about corporations, the one and only time a character uses the term "corporation" (in its adjectival form) describes an organizational matrix for conducting an anonymous murder. What Tim evocatively calls "corporate murder" is usually colloquially referred to as "contract killing," with the added benefit that Tim's description inserts a few extra layers of separation between the criminal in the head office and the crime on the street. One is left wondering whether Tim's curious expression (which does not appear in the book) refers first and foremost to a way of doing a murder or to a corporate procedure.[25] It simultaneously suggests that corporations have a particular protocol for conducting murders and that murder is a standard corporate practice.

In her review article, Angell finds far-fetched the idea that a drug company would kill a whistle blower like Tessa. "It wouldn't have to. Her concerns would have seemed isolated and futile, and the companies would hardly have taken notice of them."[26] Taken as a literal representation of corporate behavior in the pharmaceutical industry, the murder of Tessa and Arnold is undoubtedly unrealistic. But if we think of the murder metaphorically rather than literally, it suddenly appears in a new light. As Tim's explanation clarifies, the orchestration of the hit on Tessa and Arnold mimes a common corporate practice. The "corporate murder" follows the general model of subcontracting. This general operating procedure is in fact the very one that KDH uses when it hires ThreeBees to run its Dypraxa tests in Africa. Both the "corporate murder" and the clinical trials are outsourced to a third party. Moreover, both of them result in death. Tessa and Arnold meet the same fate as the Dypraxa victims. The expression "corporate murder," used in the film to characterize the elimination of Tessa and Arnold, describes the outcome of KDH's endeavors in Africa as well as its standard operating procedure for testing drugs. Although the murder may lack verisimilitude as a representation of empirical drug companies' actual behavior, it serves as a powerful metaphor for what the corporation does. If, as Bakan proposes, the corporation is a "pathological institution" that lacks empathy, refuses to accept responsibility for its actions, and cannot feel remorse, the ones in the film are pathological killers.

It is Justin that makes the connection between one "corporate murder" and the other. The breakthrough linking the two cases comes in the form of a press release announcing the opening of a new KDH facility in Wales. This announcement, which Justin finds while going through Tessa's computer files after her death, is accompanied by a photograph of a group of executives posing in front of the new Wales facility. In the group stands Sir Bernard Pellegrin, Justin's boss's boss. Following up this lead, Justin discovers that Sir Bernard, the link between the public sector and the private sector, the man who oversees British diplomatic operations in Africa and who also presumably sits on the KDH executive board (although the film never explicitly spells out Pellegrin's precise relationship to the pharmaceutical giant), used his considerable power and influence as Britain's top diplomat in Africa to facilitate the Dypraxa tests in Kenya in exchange for the foundation of a KDH facility in Wales. "That plant KDH built in Wales could have gone to France," Sandy Woodrow explains to Justin by way of justification for his complicity in the affair. "Fifteen hundred jobs in a depressed region." We can only speculate what Sir Bernard stood to gain personally from the arrangement in the form of kickbacks, bonuses, increased KDH stock value, or a combination of the three. In sum, Tessa's report threatened innumerable people who stood to gain either directly or indirectly from the drug's approval, including not least of all Sir Bernard himself, so Pellegrin placed a phone call to his head of security, who called someone else, who talked to a friend of somebody else, and so on down the line until the message ended up on the answering machine of a couple of sensitive gentlemen in green T-shirts.

In solving the mystery of Tessa's death, Justin ends up reconstructing the research that led to her murder. He re-solves Tessa and Arnold's Dypraxa case and consequently now poses the same threat that they did. Despite numerous warnings that he should abandon his investigation or "join his wife," Justin doggedly pursues his research until he has both rebuilt the original case against ThreeBees et al. and constructed the new case against Pellegrin and his associates. At the end of the film, Justin does indeed join his wife, becoming the casualty of a "corporate murder" orchestrated by the same people who arranged the hit on Tessa and carried out, moreover, at the same remote location on Lake Tukarna, in northern Kenya, where she lost her life. The end of the film therefore returns to its beginning, with the depiction of a "corporate murder" reminiscent of the one that set the narrative in motion. The movie that started (following an intro shot) with the murder of Tessa and Arnold ends, at the same isolated location, with Justin's murder. The film even uses the same technique—a shot of flamingos taking flight in reaction to the sound of gunfire that we do not hear on the sound track—to convey the two killings.

As it turns out, Sir Bernard had every reason to fear that Justin might create a problem as big as the one his wife caused. The last thing Justin does before going to Lake Tukarna and waiting patiently for the arrival of some sensitive gentlemen in a pickup truck is mail a package, including Tessa's original report on ThreeBees and Sir Bernard's self-incriminating response to it, to Ham, Tessa's devoted cousin. The film's climactic penultimate scene, during which Ham reads Bernard's response aloud to a crowd of fifty or sixty people, including Pellegrin himself, reinforces the movie's cyclical structure.

At the beginning of the film, we recall, Justin delivers Sir Bernard's lecture about the value of diplomacy to a group of students in a London lecture hall; at the end, Ham reads Sir Bernard's response to Tessa's ThreeBees report (a response written in the form of a letter to Sandy Woodrow, who mediated between Tessa and Pellegrin) to scores of people gathered in Westminster Abbey for Justin's funeral. As McGowan, who calls attention to this symmetry, astutely remarks, "The ideological valence of these two events differs dramatically. Whereas Justin's reading places him in the position of an ideological spokesperson, Ham's reading exposes the underside of that ideology."[27] Moreover, in giving the lie to Sir Bernard's earlier remarks on diplomacy, Ham's public reading of Bernard's letter at the end of the film exposes Bernard himself. "The issue here is deniability," Ham reads aloud, citing Pellegrin. "If nobody told us Dypraxa was causing deaths, we can't be held responsible. But, my dear Sandy, should it ever become known that we've closed our eyes to the deaths, none of us would survive the scandal." As Ham reads these lines, the camera alternates between shots of the orator at the podium, close-ups of Sir Bernard's twitching face, and shots of the audience, including members of the press in the back rows who become increasingly animated in each successive shot. Unable to master the situation, Bernard finally storms out of the hall, followed by a train of inquisitive reporters shoving microphones in his face. In sum, the public reading of Sir Bernard's letter performs precisely what the epistle describes. When this letter warning about the consequences of the information going public itself goes public, the letter writer does not survive the scandal. In contrast to the novel, where we learn by way of a news brief that "FO Africa Tsar Sir Bernard Pellegrin . . . sought early retirement in order to take up a senior managerial post with the multinational pharmaceutical giant," in the film, Sir Bernard falls victim to his own words.[28]

Angell criticizes the movie for adding this "Hollywood-style" ending to the story.[29] It is true that the film viewer does have the satisfaction, denied in the novel, of seeing the reptilian Sir Bernard get his comeuppance. Moreover, in contrast to the book, where the disgraced ThreeBees "[rises] from the ashes," in the movie, Tessa and Arnold manage to bring down the embattled firm.[30] Faced with the prospect of embarrassing revelations about their complicity in covering up the Dypraxa deaths, members of the British diplomatic corps sever ties with the company, leading to the downfall of ThreeBees CEO Kenny Curtiss (Gerard McSorley), before they (or, in any case, their ringleader) follow him into ignominy. Likewise, KDH can no longer afford to be affiliated with a company accused of dumping bodies into a mass grave and covering them with quicklime. What do they do? They hire another firm to complete the research. "The highly respectable firm of KDH Pharmaceutical, which has enjoyed record profits this quarter, . . . has now licensed ZimbaMed of Harare to continue testing Dypraxa in Africa," Ham bitterly says in his closing monologue. The latter revelation suggests the efficacy of the drug company's modus operandi. Both the firm that KDH hired to do its dirty work on the one hand and the corrupt officials who facilitated the company's shady endeavors in Africa on the other hand fall from grace. The pharmaceutical giant, by contrast, survives unscathed. These different outcomes for the various people and organizations involved in the "corporate murders" reveal the clear advantages of the subcontracting structure for a firm like KDH.

However, the film's cyclical structure holds out the prospect that the company at the top of the pyramidal structure may be held to account. A comparison of the funeral scene at the end of the movie to the lecture-hall scene at the beginning brings this prospective castigation into relief. In conclusion, I propose to recall briefly the three salient elements I focused on in my gloss of the lecture scene (the relationship between Tessa and Justin, the figure of the spectator, and the image of the corporation), to elaborate them in a bit more depth, and to compare and contrast them with their corresponding elements in the funeral scene.

Becoming Tessa

As mentioned in my introduction, the lecture scene juxtaposes Tessa's unabashed radicalism to Justin's quiet conservatism. The scenes of the couple during the time they lived together in Nairobi develop this opposition, showing (on the one hand) his love and respect for her but also his wish that she would spend less time doing whatever she is doing with Arnold and more time being his wife, while depicting (on the other hand) her deep commitment to her work in addition to her affection for her husband. Following Tessa's death, however, Justin undergoes a radical change of character, resulting in him becoming more and more like his late wife. McGowan offers an ingenious reading of what this conversion entails. Mapping Tessa's and Justin's contrasting approaches to politics (during the couple's time together) onto French psychoanalyst Jacques Lacan's graph of "sexuation," McGowan argues that Tessa falls on the feminine side of the graph, characterized by the "not-all" or "not-whole" (*pas-toute*) and the logic of the exception, while Justin follows the masculine logic of the "all" or "whole" (*tout*).[31] McGowan juxtaposes two examples, which he reads with characteristic bravura, to demonstrate his point. Early in the film, he reminds us, just after Tessa's stillbirth, the Quayles drive past the mother, brother, and son of Wanza Kiluhu, the young woman who died in the Uhuru maternity ward. Knowing that the family faces a forty-kilometer walk to their home in Miluri, Tessa asks Justin to pull over and give the Kiluhus a ride. "Be reasonable," Justin pleads. "There are millions of people. They all need help." Justin embodies the masculine logic of the "all" here, McGowan proposes. Instead of responding to the exceptional case of the Kiluhu family, he sees "the big picture" and knows that helping three people in a sea of millions will have no palpable effect on the overall situation. "Yeah, but these are three people that we can help," Tessa responds. McGowan comments: "For Tessa, as for the feminine logic of the not-all, we need not think of the whole that we can't help but only the exceptions that we can. According to this logic, there is no whole, only exceptions."[32] The direct counterpoint to this scene appears near the end of the film, when Justin finds himself in a group of United Nations aid workers fleeing from a raid on a village in Sudan. As he boards the plane that will take the aid workers to safety, Justin pulls a young Sudanese girl onto the plane with him. Echoing Justin's earlier comment to Tessa about there being "millions of people" who "all need help," the UN pilot informs Justin that he cannot take the girl onto the plane. "There are thousands out there. I can't make an exception for this one child," the pilot explains. As McGowan notes, Justin's reply to the pilot repeats virtually verbatim Tessa's earlier rebuttal to Justin on their drive home from the hospital: "This is one we can help." This scene in the plane, McGowan comments, in which Justin repeats virtually word-for-word his wife's earlier rejoinder to his "masculine" logic of the all, "depicts [Justin's] conversion to Tessa's logic of the not-all."[33]

Justin's conversion is complete by the end of the film. He has, in effect, "become" Tessa by the movie's end. His identification is complete to the point of following her into the grave by going to the very location where she lost her life and waiting for the arrival of some sensitive gentlemen ("same people who did . . . Tessa, I shouldn't wonder," Tim Donahue speculates) in a pickup truck.

Two additional figures follow Justin in "becoming Tessa." The first is Ham. Although his identification with Tessa is not total, like Justin's, Ham's narrative, thematic, and ideological functions in the funeral scene are to continue her legacy after her death. The film's cyclical structure brings these functions into relief. This cyclical pattern does not entail simple repetitions but a series of iterations in which each new cycle includes the previous ones within it. If we were to think of the film's narrative configuration as a set of concentric circles, including (1) the Dypraxa deaths that Tessa and Arnold uncover and (2) the murder of the Tessa and Arnold, which Justin uncovers while simultaneously solving the mystery of the Dypraxa deaths, then (3) Justin's murder, which Ham brings to light along with the double murder of Tessa and Arnold and the Dypraxa case that they originally solved, would represent a larger circle encompassing the other two. Each circle inscribes within it a new crime as well as the old, but it also identifies a new criminal in addition to the previous ones. Tessa and Arnold expose ThreeBees and are instrumental in bringing about the company's downfall; Justin implicates the British government in both the double murder and the Dypraxa deaths. The next ripple outward would include KDH, the remaining culprit. Although Ham does not succeed in bringing down the latter company, if we think of the end of the film as a new beginning, inaugurating the next revolution of the cycle, the helix would logically expand to include KDH as it spirals outward. The film's cyclical structure, which Meirelles renders explicit by ending the film with a series of shots that expressly recall the movie's opening shots, invites us to consider this possibility.

Here the second figure that follows Justin in "becoming Tessa" serves a vital function. That second figure is us, the film audience. The movie has painstakingly brought us around to embracing Tessa's position. In initially casting doubt on Tessa's character by making us suspect that she is cheating on her caring, attentive, and altogether likable husband, and then dispelling our doubts, the film retroactively constructs Tessa as a virtuous character, someone in whom we should have had faith all along. Her fidelity to Justin translates, for the viewer, into her trustworthiness more generally. Like Justin, we feel foolhardy for having ever doubted her. With the elimination of our lingering doubts about Tessa's fidelity to Justin, any reservations we may have had about her integrity, and by extension about the value or legitimacy of her work, vanish. By first casting doubt on Tessa's virtue and then dissipating our doubts, the film (in contrast to the novel) effects a conversion of the spectator, in which we are led to overcome whatever initial doubts we may have had about her, to embrace her fully as a character, and to trust her motivations and actions.

The film's tight focalization on Justin, who appears in virtually every scene set after Tessa's murder, contributes to winning us over to Tessa's position. Unlike the novel, which filters much of the action through the points of view of Sandy Woodrow and his wife, Gloria (a relatively minor character in the movie), the film by and large restricts our knowledge of what is going on to Justin's perspective. This is especially the case in the post-murder scenes, which dominate the last hour of the film. The more the film limits our perspective to Justin's, the more it aligns our position with his. The film puts us cognitively in his position by restricting our understanding of events to what he is able to comprehend. The film thereby forces us to adopt his perspective, whether we want to or not, even as he identifies with her. In this way, the film implicitly includes us, who are forced to identify with the male protagonist, in Justin's conversion to the logic of the not-all.

Finally, the film transcodes our conversion to Tessa's position in its contrasting representations of the spectator at the beginning and the end of the movie. I argued in my introduction that the audience gathered to hear Justin read Sir Bernard's lecture acts like the chorus in a Greek tragedy, standing in for the film audience. I would argue that the crowd gathered at Justin's funeral serves a similar function. In contrast to the lecture hall scene, however, where the auditors walk out in the middle of Tessa's speech from impatience or embarrassment, during the funeral scene audience members rush out of the hall in order to pursue Sir Bernard. It is not boredom, frustration, or impatience that drives the crowd out of Westminster Abbey, but their interest in pursuing a corporate murderer. Whereas the earlier scene depicts members of a proxy film audience rolling their eyes (literally, in the case of a particular audience member) in response to Tessa's antics, the later scene shows a surrogate film audience awakening from its political slumber in the back rows and continuing the work that she began. To the extent that those auditors in the back rows, who follow Ham's lead in following the leads of Tessa and Justin, represent the filmgoer, the movie allegorizes our political awakening. According to the film's logic, we should leave the theater with the idea that we might follow Tessa's path (assuming that we did not walk out of the cinema part way through the picture out of frustration, boredom, or impatience).

What Ham ultimately exposes is the mechanics of corporate murder. Passing without transition from Justin's murder to the Dypraxa deaths, he asks in frustration: "So who has got away with murder? Not, of course, the British government. They merely covered up, as one does, the offensive corpses. Though not literally. That was done by person or persons unknown. So who has committed murder? Not, of course, the highly respectable firm of KDH Pharmaceutical." Ham is proceeding here by antiphrasis, implicating the culprits that have "got away with murder" by saying that they are "of course" innocent. What enables these culprits to maintain their innocence is the subcontracting structure outlined so eloquently by Tim in his description of "corporate murder." In following standard corporate protocols for outsourcing unethical or illegal work, the criminals have in effect washed their hands of the crime.

As Ham names the various people and organizations that have got away with murder, the scene cuts, in a manner reminiscent of the technique used to depict Tessa's "corporate murder," to the various criminals still at large. The British government is represented by a cheerful Sandy

Woodrow kicking around a soccer ball with his son. The reference to the "person or persons unknown" that disposed of the Dypraxa corpses is accompanied by a shot that pans from anonymous workers throwing dead bodies into the back of a pickup truck to Crick, ThreeBees' in-house thug, seen in reflection in his car's rearview mirror as he oversees the disposal of the bodies. Shots of KDH's corporate headquarters and the company logo represent "the highly respectable firm of KDH Pharmaceutical." In identifying these organizations that have got away with murder, Ham beckons his audience to hold them to account. That audience very much includes us, moviegoers who sit as comfortably in our seats as the mourners in Westminster Abbey sit in theirs. Following the leads of Tessa and her husband, Ham has exposed the murders, the murderers, and the corporate structure that protects the killers. It is up to us to follow his lead.

4

Secrets of Primitive Accumulation

Inside Man

Spike Lee's *Inside Man* (2006), a bank-heist thriller based on an original screenplay by Russell Gewirtz, presents a ruthless critique of finance capitalism. The film is as thoroughgoing in its denunciation of the world of high finance as Meirelles's condemnation of corporate capitalism in *The Constant Gardener*. Like the Meirelles film, which casts multinational corporations as pathological murderers, *Inside Man* takes a hyperbolic example of the way capitalism works and generalizes it to typify the system. While the fictional corporations in Meirelles's film metaphorically represent the corporation as such, the unscrupulous Wall Street banker in *Inside Man*, who made his fortune in the vilest of circumstances, personifies the financial sector more broadly. Moreover, as with *The Constant Gardener*, Lee's film presents people from diverse backgrounds working in tandem to hold the movie's fictional financier to account. In so doing, *Inside Man* not only creates a damning image of the corporate banker; it also offers a vision of the unethical tycoon's prospective downfall. To the extent that the movie's fictional banker is emblematic of the sector in which he works—which is a very great extent indeed, I argue—the film constitutes a fantastic allegory of the demise of Wall Street.

I should acknowledge from the outset that my appreciation of *Inside Man* represents a minority position. Rather than viewing it as a potent class allegory, many reviewers welcomed the movie as a refreshingly apolitical piece of genre entertainment from a notoriously provocative filmmaker. David Edelstein's review in *New York* magazine is typical of this sentiment: "The normally subversive Spike Lee takes a rare genial tack in *Inside Man*. . . . This is a leisurely, smoothly made and very pleasant hostage picture." Although he faults the film for being a bit *too* smooth, Edelstein acknowledges that he found himself "savoring a thriller (as well as a Spike Lee 'joint') that wasn't, for a change, in my face."[1] In a similar vein, Peter Rainer, writing in the *Christian Science Monitor*, expresses relief at the film's "absence of any real social or racial bent": "Lee's movies are so overwrought and argumentative . . . that something like *The Inside Man* is welcome."[2] The film's detractors tended to focus on its conformity to the "heist" genre, its superficiality, and the implausibility of the plot: "It's glossy, it's upbeat, it's superficial, and it's wildly implausible," writes Kevin Maher, for example, in *Sight & Sound*.[3] "*Inside Man* is a run-of-the-mill heist film, something that merely fills up time," opines David Walsh, not mincing his words, on the World Socialist Web Site.[4] Reviewers who looked past the gloss and the generic form to try to uncover a deeper sociopolitical significance in the film tended to focus on Lee's depictions of race and racial discrimination. One would think from reading this diverse set of reviews that *Inside Man* is either a toned-down and updated version of *Do the Right Thing*, Lee's critically acclaimed 1989 film on racial tensions in the Bedford-Stuyvesant neighborhood of Brooklyn, or a rehashing of *Dog Day Afternoon*, Sidney Lumet's classic 1975 bank-heist drama, but without the politics. One of the few reviewers to see past both the film's slick veneer and Lee's well-deserved reputation for confronting issues of race was Ali Jaafar, who aptly commented that "where *Do the Right Thing* offered a state-of-the-union address on race, *Inside Man*'s underlying concern is class."[5]

Curiously, the two scholarly articles dedicated to the film, Lori Harrison-Kahan's "*Inside Man*: Spike Lee and Post-9/11 Entertainment" and Hamilton Carroll's "September 11 as Heist," both interpret the movie as a refraction of tensions in New York following the attack on the World Trade Center on September 11, 2001.[6] Each of these articles is interesting in its own right. What I find surprising is that both of the scholarly articles written on the film interpret it as a working-through of post-9/11 anxieties. I suppose this is to be expected, given the context. A movie by a New York filmmaker known for his ability to capture the mood and tone of the city, shot in 2005 largely on location in and around a fifty-seven-story bank located less than a mile from the site of the World Trade Center, is bound to generate this sort of commentary. Both Carroll and Harrison-Kahan make a strong case for the ways that the film's primary location in Lower Manhattan evokes Ground Zero of the 9/11 attacks. But surely the story of a bank heist set in Manhattan's financial district also has something broader to say about finance capitalism. If one were to imagine a location that might represent this form of capitalism, which subordinates processes of production to the accumulation of money profits and which has become the predominant force in the global economy since the 1980s, a bank just off Wall Street would be a fine choice. Before or beyond connoting Ground Zero, "Wall Street" is a metonym for finance capital everywhere and in all its avatars.

The film returns obsessively to imagery of Wall Street. From its opening credit sequence—which intercuts shots of the New York Stock Exchange, the iconic bronze "Charging Bull" sculpture in Bowling Green Park, and a street sign marking the corner of Wall and Broadway with shots of a van driving across Brooklyn and into Manhattan's financial district—to its numerous shots outside the bank that situate us in the heart of the financial district, *Inside Man* insists on the film's location. This chapter explores what the film gains from grounding this "heist" narrative in its Wall Street location.

I also argue that critics universally misidentify the movie's title character. The film's "inside man" is not first and foremost the savvy criminal that pulls off the perfect bank robbery in Lower Manhattan but the wealthy and respected banker who profited from the plight of European Jews during the Second World War and used his ill-gotten gains to build a financial empire on Wall Street. The eponymous "inside man" is the criminal who built the Manhattan Trust Bank in 1948, not the one who robs it in 2005. In the vein of Mack the Knife's suggestion in Bertolt Brecht's *Threepenny Opera*, that founding a bank is a more serious crime than robbing one, *Inside Man* pits a righteous bank robber against the real criminal on Wall Street.[7]

The itinerary of Arthur Case (Christopher Plummer), the founder of the film's fictional Manhattan Trust Bank, is not completely fanciful. Joel Bakan's *The Corporation* recounts how respected US corporations benefitted from working with the Nazis during the Second World War. Archival documents discovered in 2003, the year before Bakan's book appeared in print and three years before *Inside Man* opened in theaters, suggest that Prescott Bush, father of George H.W. Bush (forty-first president of the United Sates) and grandfather of George W. Bush (forty-third president of the United States), also benefitted from working with the Nazis. In contrast to companies like IBM and General Motors, however, which had long-established business operations, Prescott Bush rose from rags (or a prep-school uniform, in his case) to riches in the 1930s and early 1940s. This man from a modest background allegedly founded a formidable financial empire, which in turn helped him to establish the longest political dynasty in US history, on money he made as an executive at two banks that worked closely with Hitler's financial backers. In this context, the film's inclusion of a photo of Arthur Case with the first President Bush and First Lady Barbara Bush takes on more significance than simply connoting what a well-respected guy Case is.

I argue in this chapter that the title character of *Inside Man* represents the form of wealth accumulation that Karl Marx famously called "primitive accumulation" in the first volume of *Capital* and that David Harvey, for reasons explained below, prefers to call "accumulation by dispossession." Following a synopsis of the film's plot, the analysis begins with an examination of the movie's title. Arguing that Arthur Case is the film's quintessential inside man, I examine the movie's portrayal of this war profiteer-turned-philanthropist, paying particularly close attention to the mise-en-scène of a dolly shot in which the banker and his desk seem to detach themselves from the physical space of his office and glide toward the spectator as the wall behind him recedes into the background. Following clues presented in this shot, I elaborate in detail the historical context of the Wall Street banker's continued prosperity during the Reagan-Bush years and beyond. Drawing on a wide array of social and political-economic research, from Harvey's work on neoliberalism to Slavoj Žižek's writings on systemic violence and Giovanni Arrighi's analysis of the rise and fall of the American empire, I argue that the figure of Arthur Case allegorizes three stages of US economic and political hegemony, from its consolidation in the 1940s through its transformation in the 1980s, to its projected demise at the beginning of the twenty-first century. Released in 2006, when George W. Bush was in the middle of his second term as president, *Inside Man* beckons us to consider the origins of capitalist power in the United States, its transformation in the last few decades of the twentieth century, and the consequences of those changes in the twenty-first century. The chapter concludes with an examination of the film's depiction of class antagonism, in which members of the disenfranchised classes work together despite their differences against a cabal of financiers and political insiders who are living through a "wonderful moment" of increased wealth, power, and influence at the expense of their compatriots.

A Film in Which "Things Ain't All They Appear to Be"

The plot of *Inside Man* revolves around a bank robbery that takes place at the fictional Manhattan Trust Bank's flagship branch at 20 Exchange Place, located a block south of Wall Street. Four robbers dressed as painters, wearing coveralls, white face masks, and dark sunglasses, enter the bank in the morning, lock the front door, and take all the bank employees and clients hostage. For the next hour and a half of the film, which corresponds roughly to a 24-hour period, the gang's leader, Dalton Russell (Clive Owen), plays a cat-and-mouse game with Detective Keith Frazier (Denzel Washington), the police's hostage negotiator. Inside the bank, Russell and his fellow bank robbers (played by Carlos Andrés Gómez, Kim Director, and James Ransone), who refer to one another as Steve, Stevie, and Steve-O, dress all the hostages in the same painters' get-up that they are wearing and repeatedly move the hostages from room to room. Shuffling the hostages this way enables the anonymous robbers to slip in and out of the group without the actual hostages knowing. Because the gang members never expose their faces to their captives, except in one scene when Steve-O strategically removes his mask while posing as a hostage, none of the hostages is able to identify the bank robbers when they are later released.

Outside the bank, in a Mobile Command Center (MCC) parked between Exchange Place and Wall Street, Frazier and his partner, Detective Bill Mitchell (Chiwetel Ejiofor), try to figure out the robbers' tactics and motivations, while simultaneously attempting to prevent Captain Darius (Willem Dafoe) from storming the bank before they can negotiate the hostages' release. From the moment we meet Frazier, we are given to understand that he is under tremendous strain. On the personal side, his girlfriend, Sylvia (Cassandra Freeman), a fellow police officer, is pressuring him to marry her, but Frazier believes that their modest salaries are insufficient to start a family. He is trying to earn a promotion to Detective First Grade, which, he believes, would enable the couple to support a family. However, this promotion is in jeopardy because Frazier is currently under investigation for having allegedly stolen $140,000 that disappeared during a drug bust he made prior to the film's action. The only reason he is called to the scene at the bank is because the regular hostage negotiator is on vacation. Moreover, we learn that during his training Frazier botched a previous negotiation with a man in a hospital, who ended up shooting himself and his girlfriend rather than surrendering. These circumstances put enormous pressure on Frazier to achieve a successful outcome to the hostage situation at Manhattan Trust.

When Arthur Case, chairman of the Manhattan Trust Board of Directors, learns of the hostage situation, he immediately contacts Madeleine White (Jodie Foster), a "fixer" who interrupts her meeting with Osama bin Laden's nephew (whom she is helping to buy a co-op apartment on Park Avenue) in order to meet with Case. What the banker wants is for White to obtain the contents of a safe deposit box at the

Exchange Street branch. A series of negotiations results in White managing to enter the bank and meet with Russell: White pressures the mayor (Peter Kybart), over whom she has a great deal of influence, to strong-arm Frazier into letting her speak to the bank robbers; Frazier reluctantly agrees because the mayor warns him that his career will be over if he does not comply with White's request. It is when White meets with Russell inside the bank, more than an hour into the film, that we learn of Case's dark past: "He used his position with the Nazis to enrich himself while all around him people were being stripped of everything they owned. Then he used his blood money to start a bank," Russell recounts to White. This revelation provides a retrospective explanation for a previous scene in which gang members pick the lock of a safety deposit containing pouches of diamonds, a ring case, and a document addressed to Case on Nazi letterhead. Knowing that the "fixer" has no leverage over him, Russell sends her away empty-handed. He uses the conversation as an opportunity to share his knowledge of Case's past with her rather than to negotiate the terms of his release.

The bank robbers stand by their original demands: they want two buses with full gas tanks and a fueled jumbo jet with pilots waiting for them at JFK International Airport. In the course of the negotiation process, Frazier becomes convinced that these demands are in fact ploys for more time. "You don't want a plane. You never did," Frazier says in a face-to-face meeting with the masked gang leader inside the bank. "Who ever heard of bank robbers escaping on a plane with fifty hostages? You saw *Dog Day Afternoon*," he remarks, making one of the film's numerous references to Lumet's classic movie of a bank heist gone awry. On his way out of the bank, Frazier attempts to disarm Russell at the door, leading the robbers to shoot a hostage in retaliation. This murder triggers a police raid. However, the bank robbers, who managed to place a bug inside the police van by attaching a transmitter to a cash box they strapped to a freed hostage, know of the raid in advance. The three "Steves" blend in with the hostages and rush out the door with the rest of the captives. When the SWAT team storms the bank, they find "no bad guys, no booby traps, no tunnels, no damage . . . and nothing missing." What they discover instead are the toy guns that the robbers used during the holdup and the pump that the gang used to squirt imitation blood during their faked execution of a mock hostage. Dalton Russell, the one criminal the police might be able to identify, is nowhere to be found.

The movie's twenty-minute dénouement, which corresponds to roughly a week of diegetic film time, contains five major plot twists. Because these plot twists have generated confusion among critics and fans alike, let us take a moment to look at them each in turn.[8] The first of these twists involves Frazier's career. When, toward the end of the movie, the detective tells his boss, Captain Coughlin (Peter Gerety), that they have no suspects and no robbery, the captain tells him to "bury it." As the two cops part company, Coughlin tells the detective "something that [he] probably did expect. They found that missing Madrugada money" (a reference to the $140,000 that Frazier was accused of having stolen). The conjunction of these two plot developments—the captain's order to bury the case and the news that the Madrugada money mysteriously turned up—confirms our suspicion that Case and White are pulling strings behind the scene by advancing Frazier's career with the tacit understanding that the investigation will go no further. We have seen in previous scenes that this is the way that Case and White work: you do me a favor, I do you a favor. What comes as more of a surprise is the idea that Frazier is subject to this sort of influence. Although the film goes to some length to attribute a motive to the embattled detective, Denzel Washington's charismatic interpretation of Detective Frazier as an easy-going charmer serves to persuade us that he would not steal money or sell his soul in order to advance his career. David Sterritt categorically states that the corruption charges against Frazier are "bogus," but in fact all we have to go on to make such an assessment are the detective's denial and Denzel Washington's sympathetic portrayal of the character.[9] Frazier's response to Coughlin, when the captain asks him if he wants to know where they found the money, does little to exculpate himself: "In my bank account? . . . My summerhouse in Sag Harbor? . . . My wallet?" Moreover, Frazier clearly states at one point that he sold out to White. Following the staged execution of the hostage, as Captain Darius and his team are preparing their assault on the bank, Mitchell warns his partner that "if this goes down wrong, they're going to dump this whole mess in your lap." Frazier responds by saying: "I'm making Detective First Grade. Things ain't all they appear to be." Although it is indeed the case that things are not what they appear to be (the bank robbers are not really robbing the bank, the murder did not actually take place, and so forth), Frazier knows none of this. What he is referring to is not the hostage situation but his own situation, as becomes clear when he explains to his partner what he is talking about. Elucidating why he thinks he is going to make First Grade despite the mounting evidence to the contrary, Frazier tells Mitchell: "Thank the mayor and our mystery guest for that." Two subsequent scenes confirm what Frazier says offhandedly here to Mitchell. In one scene, when White debriefs Case on the follow-up to the hostage situation, she says with regret that "Detective Frazier turned out to be quite sharp," meaning that he figured out more than Case would have wanted him to know. "But I just fast-tracked his career a little and he's under control," she reassures the banker. Finally, in the film's last scene, Frazier lays his newly acquired Detective First Grade certificate on his dresser, confirming that White kept her word. In this film where "things ain't all they appear to be," the upstanding detective proves to be more ethically ambiguous than he appears at first blush to be.

Although Frazier benefits from allowing White to meet with the bank robbers, he does not follow Captain Coughlin's order to bury the case. On the contrary, he obsessively continues to look over the evidence. The second plot twist occurs when Frazier discovers, in going over the bank documents, that there is no record of safety deposit box number 392. Following up this lead, the detective obtains a court order to open the box and finds that it contains a half-empty pack of chewing gum, a Cartier diamond ring, and a handwritten note telling him to "follow the ring." An explanation for the ring is given in a separate scene, in which Case confides to White that it belonged to a wealthy family of French Jews that were deported to a concentration camp during the Holocaust. "We were friends," the opportunist banker confesses to White. "I could have helped them. But the Nazis paid too well." Although Frazier is unaware of this history, he surmises that the person who would be able to explain the enigma of a bank robbery in which thieves stole no money but instead left a cryptic note about a mysterious ring in an unlisted safe deposit box is the man who built the bank in 1948. In a final showdown between the detectives and Case, Frazier and Mitchell confront the banker, who denies knowledge of the safe deposit box. Frazier's parting remark to Case is that he is going to "follow that ring."

Frazier also confronts White, playing back to her a conversation that he surreptitiously recorded of the two of them and the mayor, in which the latter pressures Frazier to "give Miss White whatever she needs, or your career is over. Done. Kaput." In his final scene with White, Frazier gives her the compromising recording in exchange for her implicit promise to contact the War Crimes Issues office in Washington, DC, to pursue Case. The scene anticipates the demise of Case, but it also suggests White's downfall. Madeleine White is a fixer whose success as a behind-the-scenes miracle worker the film attributes both to her ability to influence people and to her reputation for absolute discretion in delicate matters. She is the person to whom rich people turn for help when they cannot go to the police or exert influence through legal channels. Her name does not appear in directories or databases but is passed along by word of mouth from one Fortune 500 CEO to another. "Whoever gave you my number got the same deal," she says to Case when the two first meet. "Clearly, they must have been satisfied." Later, in an effort to allay Frazier's concern that she might double-cross him, she assures the detective that she got where she is "by collecting friends, not enemies." In betraying Case, she is making an enemy that will clearly not be satisfied with her work. In so doing, she is implicitly destroying her career. A fixer that betrays a client by giving his name to the War Crimes Issues office in Washington is not a fixer at all. At the end of the movie, White has a short career ahead of her.

The film's biggest twist occurs when Russell, who has been hiding for a week behind a false wall that the team built in the bank's storage room (hence the gang's stalling tactics), emerges from hiding and strolls out of the bank with a knapsack full of diamonds and the incriminating document on Nazi stationery, leaving the ring for Frazier to find. On his way out of the bank, he bumps into Frazier, who is arriving with his court order to open the safe deposit box. Because Frazier has never seen Russell's face, he does not recognize him. Russell walks out the front door and meets up with his cohorts, who are waiting for him in an SUV parked outside the bank. We recognize the three Steves and a fourth person, Chaim (Bernie Rachelle), an observant Jew who was negotiating a bank loan when the robbers arrived and who, we remember at this point, later told fellow hostages that he teaches courses on genocide, slave labor, and war reparation claims at Columbia Law School. When Russell tells him that he left the ring in the safe deposit box, Chaim expresses his consternation. "Trust me," Russell reassures him. "I left it in good hands."

In the film's final scene, Frazier arrives home, greets Sylvia, and lays down his newly acquired Detective First Grade certificate on his dresser. He then puts down his gun, badge, and cell phone. Reaching into his jacket pockets to see if there is anything else he should remove, he discovers a diamond the size of a small hailstone. A flashback of Russell and Frazier colliding at the bank entrance, which visualizes Frazier's memory of the encounter, explains how the diamond made its way into Frazier's pocket. Russell, who learned over the course of their exchanges that Frazier cannot afford to buy Sylvia a ring and who developed a respect for the detective in the course of their negotiations, slipped it into his pocket when they bumped into each other in the bank lobby. The film that depicted a standoff between a cagey cop and a mastermind bank robber ends with a solidarity between the two men, who together bring down the real criminal on Wall Street.

Who Is the Title Character of *Inside Man*?

As we can glean from this synopsis, both the bank robbery and the film rely on complex strategies of deception. Things are not what they appear to be either inside the bank or on the screen. Numerous critics have called attention to these techniques of deception. Carroll, for example, enumerates the diverse modes of subterfuge and obfuscation that the bank robbers employ:

> The criminals . . . force their hostages to strip down to their underwear and to don dark-blue jumpsuits, white facemasks, and dark sunglasses identical to the ones that they themselves wear; . . . they fake the execution of a hostage; they bug the police command trailer and deliberately mislead the police; and they appear to all leave the bank mingled amongst the hostages when the police storm the building. In their execution of a hostage taking that is in reality a piece of theater designed to enable another criminal act to take place unnoticed (Russell's internment and subsequent theft of the diamonds), the criminals produce a fake or a double of the real event.[10]

In sum, Carroll concludes: "A crime has taken place, but it is not the one that the police believe has been perpetrated or that the film's audience has watched unfold on the screen before them."[11] What I would add to Carroll's catalogue of misleading clues is the one that appears in the film's title.

Every critic who comments on the title of *Inside Man* identifies Dalton Russell as the movie's eponymous hero. The identification is understandable. Russell is one of the film's two main characters (the other being Frazier); his last name is the same as screenwriter Russell Gewirtz's first name, leading us to wonder whether he embodies the film's general perspective and is therefore, logically, its title character; he has "inside" information on Case; and he is literally inside the bank for the week that follows the staged robbery. The film's opening scene, in which Russell directly addresses the camera in a close-up, cryptically alludes to his location inside the bowels of the bank:

> My name is Dalton Russell. Pay strict attention to what I say because I choose my words carefully and I never repeat myself. I've told you my name. That's the "who." The "where" could most readily be described as a prison cell. But there's a vast difference between being stuck in a tiny cell and being in prison. The "what" is easy. Recently I planned and set in motion events to execute the perfect bank robbery. That's also the "when." As for the "why," beyond the obvious financial motivation, it's exceedingly simple. Because I can. Which leaves us only with the "how." And therein, as the Bard would tell us, lies the rub.

Lee films this sharply scripted monologue using one of his signature shots, in which he places the camera and the actor on a dolly and then pulls the dolly back (or in this case, pushes it forward) with both the camera and the actor on it, thereby enabling the actor to move through space without locomoting. It is a technique first developed by French New Wave director Jacques Demy for a scene in *Les Parapluies de Cherbourg* (1964) in which Geneviève (Catherine Deneuve) and Guy (Nino Castelnuovo) float through a street in Cherbourg on the eve of Guy's departure for Algeria. Critics generally attribute the invention of the technique to Lee, who does not, to the best of my knowledge, credit Demy with its innovation, and who uses it in almost all his feature films, sometimes more than once.[12] The shot appears in various forms on four occasions in *Inside Man*. Two of these four uses of the signature "Spike Lee shot" are of Russell in his cell: once at the beginning of the movie and again toward the end, when we see the opening shot in reverse, the camera dollying back instead of forward, as we hear Russell repeat his opening monologue. In the opening scene, the shot gives the impression that the cinderblock wall behind Russell, which is invisible in the blackness surrounding him at the beginning of the shot, emerges from the background and moves into place directly behind him as he delivers his speech. The inverse shot toward the end of the film creates the opposite effect, the wall receding and fading into darkness as Russell repeats the film's opening lines.

The placement of this monologue at the beginning of the movie (before even the opening credit sequence), the fact that Russell conveys the information in a direct address to the film audience and that he uses terse language to communicate precisely with the spectator, and Lee's recourse to his signature dolly shot to film the scene lend credibility to the information conveyed. However, when we hear the monologue repeated near the end of the movie, after we have learned about Case's past and how Russell and his gang plan to bring down the immoral banker, the narrator's explanation of the "why" ("beyond the obvious financial motivation, it's exceedingly simple. Because I can") rings hollow. We realize at this point that Russell is an unreliable narrator and that both he and the film have been misleading us from the beginning. The repetition of the deceptive monologue confirms yet again, from a fresh perspective, that things are not what they appear to be in this movie where appearances are perpetually deceiving.

David Gerstner, in his chapter on *Inside Man* included in Paula Massood's edited volume on Lee's oeuvre, and David Sterritt, in his compulsively readable *Spike Lee's America*, subtly indicate that there is something unsatisfying about the film's identification of Russell as the movie's inside man in their compelling discussions of the way the movie allegorizes the director's relationship to Hollywood. Although Sterritt affirms that "the title character of *Inside Man* is Dalton Russell," he also cagily remarks that "one can't resist seeing [*Inside Man*] as one of Lee's most thinly veiled allegories for his aspirations as a filmmaker—to be an inside man, able to pivot at will between specialized, personal projects that speak primarily to his devotees and smoothly machined mass-audience projects that speak to everyone everywhere."[13] Sterritt's argument here echoes an interpretation advanced by Gerstner, who writes: "It is Lee/Russell who gets away with the heist, perhaps with the help of the other inside man, Detective Frazier. Lee/Russell commits the perfect crime by appearing to do one thing (and in that they have succeeded—make a Hollywood genre film/steal the documents) while unfolding something entirely different."[14] This association between the filmmaker's incursion into Hollywood and Dalton Russell's assault on the bank is compelling and intriguing, but is it accurate to identify either of these figures as an "inside man"? The *Reverso* dictionary defines the pronominal adjective "inside," in the title's colloquial sense, as "arranged or provided by someone within an organization or building, esp. illicitly."[15] The term carries this sense in an expression like *inside job*, whereas the bank heist (or the "Hollywood heist") is accomplished by an outsider who breaks into the system from without. If either Lee was a Hollywood insider or Russell worked at the bank, the appellation would fit them better. As it is, the term applies to them only antiphrastically. They are "outside men" who penetrate the system from without.

The movie presents two hypothetical "inside men," in the colloquial sense of the expression, neither of which is Russell (or Frazier, an even less likely candidate for the title role, whom Gerstner implausibly proposes in passing is "the other inside man"). One of these inside men is Chaim, the Jewish legal scholar who poses as a bank customer and is taken hostage by the bank robbers at the beginning of the movie. Not only does he teach courses on genocide, slave labor, and war reparation claims at Columbia Law. We also learn during an interrogation scene between him and the two detectives that he knows about diamonds: "What do you think a guy like me should pay for a diamond ring?" Frazier asks him at one point. "Depends," Chaim responds. "How many carats? If you'd like, I could give you my nephew's number." Whatever knowledge Russell and his gang have of Case's past implicitly comes from Chaim, who has both familiarity with diamonds and expertise on the type of crimes that Case committed in order to obtain his own cache of diamonds. My reluctance to identify Chaim as the movie's title character stems from the filmmakers' decision to depict him as a mock bank customer rather than a bank employee and their relegation of this diamond aficionado-*cum*-war crimes specialist to the status of a minor character, who has few significant lines and no dedicated shots in the film.

The character whose very essence is that of an inside man is Arthur Case, the American banker stationed in Switzerland during the early 1940s, who "used his position with the Nazis to enrich himself." He is an "insider" in every sense of the term. Not only did he benefit from his close relationship to the Nazis to amass wealth confiscated from European Jews and then use his position at a Swiss bank to hide his spoils. He, in turn, became a pillar of society upon return to the United States, where he presided for more than half a century over a financial empire he founded with his blood money.

A Portrait of the Wall Street Banker as a War Profiteer

The shots that accompany Russell's narration of Case's activities during the Holocaust bring together the "inside man" of the 1940s and the same man's "insider" status in the decades that followed. As the masked bank robber tells White of Case's exploits in Europe sixty years previously, the scene cuts to another "Spike Lee signature shot," this one of Arthur Case seated at his massive mahogany desk in his beautifully furnished and tastefully decorated office in lower Manhattan. As Russell recounts the story of Case's collaboration with the Nazis during World War II, the camera does a reverse dolly shot, pulling Case and his desk forward and thereby creating the effect that the wall behind him is retreating into the background. As the wall recedes, we can barely make out a set of three color photographs on a credenza situated behind the banker. These photos show Case posing with George H.W. Bush (who served as vice president of the United States under Ronald Reagan between 1981 and 1989 and then as president between 1989 and 1993) and his wife Barbara, with Margaret Thatcher (prime minister of Britain between 1979 and 1990), and with Rudy Giuliani (mayor of New York City between 1994 and 2001).[16] Midway through Russell's narration, the scene cuts neatly to a forward tracking shot that advances at the same pace that the previous one receded. This second shot reveals in close-up the objects on the credenza that Case's seated figure obscured from view in the preceding shot. These objects include vintage family photographs of a young Arthur Case and his relatives, a commemorative plate recognizing Case's achievements at Manhattan Trust, a framed letter on White House stationery, and two plaques (one bearing a Star of David, the other adorned with a menorah) recognizing his contributions to the Jewish community and/or Israel.

Figure 4.1. As Dalton Russell recounts the story of Arthur Case's collaboration with the Nazis during World War II, the camera does a reverse dolly shot, pulling Case and his desk forward and thereby creating the effect that the wall behind him is receding into the background. Photos of Case posing with the first President George Bush, with Prime Minister Margaret Thatcher, and with New York's Mayor Rudy Giuliani are visible on the credenza (*Inside Man*, Universal, 2006).

The juxtaposition of the audio track and the image track in these two complementary shots—the juxtaposition of Russell's narration of Case's misdeeds in the 1940s and imagery documenting the banker's good deeds during the following decades—brings together the inside man that made his fortune from the misfortunes of others, on the one

Figure 4.2. Objects on display in Arthur Case's office include a commemorative plate recognizing the banker's achievements at Manhattan Trust, a framed letter on White House stationery, a plaque bearing a Star of David, and a plaque adorned with a menorah (*Inside Man*, Universal, 2006).

hand, and the generous philanthropist and political insider, on the other. Case explains the relationship between his past actions and his subsequent deeds in a scene toward the end of the film, when White recounts to him what Russell told her about his past. "It was 60 years ago," the banker explains. "I was young and ambitious. I saw a short path to success and I took it. I sold my soul. And I've been trying to buy it back ever since." The philanthropist describes his charitable actions here as acts of atonement—attempts to make up for past misdeeds by counterbalancing them with good deeds. The fact that two of Case's awards of recognition come from Jewish organizations suggests that he has been particularly generous to the community he pillaged in order to amass his wealth in the first place. However, as Todd McGowan comments in his analysis of the complementary tracking shots inside Case's office: "This sequence reveals that despite all Case's subsequent humanitarian activity, what defines him as a character—what gives him his singularity—is his act of profiteering on the Holocaust. Nothing can remove this singularity, not simply because of the horror of the act itself but because he continues to enjoy the monetary gains from it."[17]

The contrast between the ambitious banker's inhumane past actions and his subsequent humanitarian deeds shows "the two faces of Arthur Case," analogous to "the two faces of George Soros" that Slavoj Žižek presents in his book on violence: "Soros stands for the most ruthless financial speculative exploitation combined with its counter-agent, humanitarian concern about the catastrophic social consequences of unbridled market economy."[18] Soros, the financier who "[made] billions at the expense of the European governments by betting against their ability to stay within the guidelines of the ERM [the European monetary system's Exchange Rate Mechanism]," is also one of the world's greatest philanthropists, donating billions of dollars to progressive causes over the past few decades.[19] He is a model for the figure that Žižek calls the "liberal communist," a category that includes such figures as Microsoft's Bill Gates and the CEOs of Google, IBM, Intel, and eBay in addition to Soros. These super-rich philanthropists are "true citizens of the world," Žižek admits.[20] They are people who feel that their elevated position in society endows them with a social responsibility to share their riches with the less fortunate. However, Žižek insists, it is only by engaging in ruthless business practices in the first place that these men possess the wealth that they then use to mitigate the catastrophic consequences of their actions: "Charity is the humanitarian mask hiding the face of economic exploitation."[21] The disjunction between Case's two relationships with the Jewish community—profiteering from the Jews' misfortune in the most brutal fashion, on the one hand, and contributing to Jewish causes, on the other—offers a hyperbolic account of the way philanthropic capitalists relate to society by munificently giving with one hand what they stole with the other.[22]

Profiteering during the Second World War may be a hyperbolic example of how capitalism works, but it not anomalous. Joel Bakan recounts in *The Corporation* how in 1937 executives at General Motors transformed their German subsidiary, Adam Opel AG, into an armaments concern that manufactured trucks for the German army.[23] Although GM boasts that the company contributed to the war effort by building vehicles for the Allied forces, they are less forthcoming about their contributions to the Nazi war machine. General Motors is not the only firm to profit from working with Germany during the war. In the film version of *The Corporation*, Michael Moore alleges that the Ford Motor Company and Coca-Cola also found ways to profit in Germany during the war. But it is Edwin Black's detailed account of IBM's business dealings with the Third Reich that receives the most attention in the film. Black, the author of *IBM and the Holocaust*, shows how the Nazis used the IBM punch-card system, the predecessor of the computer, to categorize and keep track of prisoners detained in concentration camps. The fact that IBM technicians had to service the punch-card machines on site on a monthly basis, "even if that was at a concentration camp such as Dachau [or] Buchenwald," belies the claim that the company did not know how the Nazis were using their machines.[24] The tech firm's business relationship with the Third Reich continued at least through June 1942, six months after the United States declared war on Germany. Not only was IBM's collaboration with the Nazis immoral, in other words; it was also illegal, at least for the first six months of 1942. But it was lucrative. "IBM's motivations for working with the Nazis . . . 'was never about Nazism,'" Bakan clarifies in the print version of *The Corporation*, citing Black. "It was about profit."[25] Like Arthur Case, for whom "the Nazis paid too well" to pass up the opportunity to work with them, the executives at IBM were merely taking advantage of a business opportunity.

What separates Arthur Case from executives at firms like GM, IBM, Ford, and Coke is the fact that he founded his financial empire on the gains he made during the Holocaust, whereas they strove to maintain or expand their business operations during the war. Case's actions during the war correspond more closely to those of a man like Prescott Bush than they do to the wartime ventures of GM or IBM. Bush, who was working at a hardware store when he met his future wife in 1917, became fabulously wealthy in the 1930s and 1940s, during which time he was allegedly "a director and shareholder of companies that profited from their involvement with the financial backers of Nazi Germany."[26] In a long and detailed article published in *The Guardian* in 2004, Ben Aris and Duncan Campbell analyze "newly discovered files in the US National Archives [showing] that a firm of which Prescott Bush was a director was involved with the financial architects of Nazism."[27] Building on research that journalist Eva Schweitzer, reporter John Buchanan, and former US attorney John Loftus conducted on the same archival documents, Aris and Campbell conclude that "while there is no suggestion that Prescott Bush was sympathetic to the Nazi cause, the documents reveal that the firm he worked for, Brown Brothers Harriman (BBH), acted as a US base for the German industrialist, Fritz Thyssen, who helped finance Hitler in the 1930s."[28] In addition to being a partner at BBH, Aris and Campbell allege, Bush was also "the director of the New York-based Union Banking Corporation (UBC) that represented Thyssen's US interests and he continued to work for the bank after America entered the war."[29] How much money Mr. Bush personally gained in his roles as executive and stockholder at BBH and UBC is a matter of speculation. Although "some claim that Bush sold his share in UBC after the war for $1.5 million—a huge amount of money at the time"—Aris and Campbell report that "there is no documentary evidence to support this claim."[30] Whatever the sum may be, the homes that Bush maintained during the postwar years in New York City, on Long Island, and in Connecticut, together with his 10,000-acre ranch in Maine, his plantation in South Carolina, and the secluded island he owned off the Connecticut coast, suggest that he did not do too poorly for himself.[31]

Accumulation by Dispossession

One way to think about the difference between the rags-to-riches stories of Arthur Case and Prescott Bush, on the one hand, and the actions of executives at GM, IBM, Ford, and Coke, on the other hand, is via Karl Marx's distinction, in volume one of *Capital*, between two phases of accumulation. The bulk of Marx's book is dedicated to the analysis of the capitalist mode of production. This is the mode of production that came into being during the sixteenth century and was well on its way to becoming the dominant means of wealth accumulation in the mid-nineteenth century, when *Capital* was written. Marx's tome analyzes, for the most part, the way this system works once it is in place and running according to its internal logic. Following his lengthy analysis of this mode of production, Marx adds a concluding set of chapters in which he examines the origins of capitalism. This last part of the book, dedicated to what Marx calls, following Adam Smith, "primitive" (or "original") accumulation, analyzes "an accumulation which is not the result of the capitalistic mode of production but its point of departure."[32] "Here we are forced to confront the thievery, predation, violence and abusive use of power that lay at the historical origins of capitalism," David Harvey writes in his companion to Marx's *Capital*.[33] Countering the idyllic myth that "long, long ago there were two sorts of people; one, the diligent, intelligent, and above all frugal élite; the other, lazy rascals, spending their substance, and more, in riotous living," Marx argues that "in actual history, it is a notorious fact that conquest, enslavement, robbery, murder, in short, force, play the greatest part" in the historical division of the classes.[34] This history "is anything but idyllic," Marx insists.[35] It "is written in the annals of mankind in letters of blood and fire."[36] The account of Arthur Case's wartime activities constitutes an "origin" story reminiscent of the one that Marx traces here to the birth of capitalism. Whereas firms like GM and IBM attempted to conduct business as usual under unusual circumstances, taking advantage of opportunities to maintain or enhance production during the war, Case engages in something more akin to primitive accumulation.

Marx's analyses of primitive accumulation account both for the ways that a class of people confiscated wealth that they then put into circulation as capital, and for the concomitant "proletarianization" of the rest of the population, who were thrown off the land and forced to work for the new class of capitalists in order to survive. Obviously, Case's actions during the Holocaust pertain only to the first of these two processes. Moreover, in Marx's account, "primitive accumulation" is, as the term implies, something that happened once, long ago, in the distant past. However, regarding the latter point, social theorists such as Rosa Luxemburg, Hannah Arendt, and Harvey have insisted that Marx is wrong to relegate this sort of appropriation to the prehistory of capitalism.[37] On the contrary, they argue, what Marx calls "primitive accumulation" is an integral part of the way capitalism works on an ongoing basis. "All the features of primitive accumulation that Marx mentions have remained powerfully present within capitalism's historical geography up until now," Harvey writes.[38] Since he finds it "peculiar to call an ongoing process 'primitive' or 'original,'" Harvey substitutes the term "accumulation by dispossession" for the set of processes that Marx dubbed "primitive accumulation."[39]

Accumulation by dispossession takes many forms. Harvey's examples include the expropriation of peasants in order to extract natural resources from the earth, governments' use of eminent domain to expel indigenous populations from the land in order to create so-called Export Processing Zones, the privatization and commodification of everything from water and public utilities to health care and education, biopiracy, the enforcement of international patent laws that prohibit farmers from saving seeds and thereby impede their ability to live as they have for centuries, the management and manipulation of international financial crises, and so forth.[40] None of these forms of accumulation is on the wane. On the contrary, Harvey insists, appropriations of this sort have become increasingly prevalent in recent decades. Rather than subsiding, let alone occurring only in some far-off prehistory of capitalism, "in our times, the techniques for enriching the ruling classes and diminishing the standard of living of labor through something akin to primitive accumulation have proliferated and multiplied."[41]

One of the essential steps that enabled the resurgence in recent decades of accumulation by dispossession was the deregulation of the financial sector that began in the early 1980s. "Deregulation allowed the financial system to become one of the main centres of redistributive activity through speculation, predation, fraud, and thievery," Harvey writes.[42] "Increasingly freed from the regulatory constraints and barriers that had hitherto confined its field of action, financial activity could flourish as never before, eventually everywhere."[43] Capital in the 1980s "began to live its life in a new context," Fredric Jameson writes in "Culture and Finance Capital": "no longer in the factories and the spaces of extraction and production . . . , but rather in the form of speculation itself."[44]

Jameson offers a brilliant reading of what this turn to financialization entails by way of an application of the two meanings implicit in French philosopher Gilles Deleuze's neologism, "deterritorialization," to the global economic context. "Deterritorialization" in Jameson's reading involves initially a transfer of capital from one sector or site of production to another, often by physically relocating operations from an area where wages and taxes are high and labor laws are strong to a region where wages are low, taxes minimal, and labor protections weak. "Then there is the grimmer conjuncture," he writes, "in which the capital of an entire center or region abandons production altogether in order to seek maximization in nonproductive spaces, which . . . are those of speculation, the money market, and finance capital in general."[45] Whereas in the first of these developments, "deterritorialization" takes the form of capital flight, "the pondered or hasty moving on to the greener pastures of higher rates of investment return and cheaper labor," in the second, "deterritorialization" implies an abandonment of the Earth-bound process of production altogether, with capital attaining its "ultimate dematerialization" on the floor of the stock market.[46] It is the latter of these two developments that is the moment of finance capitalism.

Financial speculation constitutes a different type of "accumulation by dispossession" than the one in which Arthur Case engaged in the

1940s. It is more akin to the type of redistributive activity associated with Prescott Bush's son George than with the elder Bush's ventures during the Second World War. In his roles as vice president under Reagan during the 1980s and then as the forty-first president of the United States in the early 1990s, George H.W. Bush (often called "Bush 41" in order to distinguish him from his son, George W. Bush, the forty-third president) was instrumental in bringing about the so-called "neoliberal revolution" that took place in the 1980s.

Definitions of neoliberalism vary. Whereas a political theorist like Wendy Brown, taking inspiration from Michel Foucault rather than Marx, convincingly argues that neoliberalism represents a "peculiar form of reason that configures all aspects of existence in economic terms," political economists like Harvey study the ways that the introduction of a broad range of policies (including the privatization of virtually everything other than air and sea water, unimpeded free trade, union busting, reductions in government spending, regressive taxation, and austerity budgeting, as well as the wholesale deregulation of the financial sector) have exacerbated class differences to the benefit of the extremely wealthy and the detriment of nearly everyone else.[47]

Proponents of neoliberal economics claim that enhancing the private sector will generate economic growth and therefore will benefit those at the bottom of the social scale as well as those at the top. Using phrases like "a rising tide lifts all boats" and proposing theories such as "trickle-down economics," neoliberal apologists claim that economic policies favoring the wealthy and the privileged ultimately benefit the poor and underprivileged as well. However, as Gérard Duménil and Dominique Lévy conclude after careful reconstruction of the data, neoliberalism was from the start "the expression of the desire of a class of capitalist owners and the institutions in which their power is concentrated, which we collectively call 'finance,' to restore . . . the class's revenues and power."[48] Thomas Piketty's monumental book *Capital in the Twenty-First Century* makes crystal clear what this restoration of class power at one end of the social spectrum has entailed for people at the other end of the social scale. The inequality of wealth is currently at its highest level since 1929, the year of the Wall Street crash. If the current trend continues, the gap between the wealthiest people in the world and the rest of the world's population will soon be wider than at any time in documented economic history. Piketty's study leaves little doubt as to when this trend toward record-level inequality began: 1980, the birth year of the neoliberal revolution.[49]

Key figures in the neoliberal revolution are Margaret Thatcher, who became prime minister of the United Kingdom in 1979, and Ronald Reagan, who was elected president of the United States in 1980. Together, these two leaders embarked on a remarkably successful campaign to "disembed capital" from its social and political constraints.[50] The system's primary beneficiaries are the bankers, hedge fund managers, and corporate executives in the top 0.1 percent of the income-earning bracket, who saw their share of the national income multiplied roughly fivefold in the United States and nearly sixfold in the United Kingdom between 1980 and 2006, when *Inside Man* premiered.[51] One of the great "innovations" of neoliberalism in the United States was to bring these two groups—elected politicians and top executives at big firms—closer together by rolling back laws that restricted the amount of money that corporations could donate to political campaigns. What then emerged was an increasingly symbiotic relationship in which capitalists could make unlimited donations to politicians who promoted their interests; those politicians, who were indebted to the donors that helped put them in office, then passed business-friendly legislation that further enriched the executives, who in turn had more money to contribute to political campaigns, and so forth: a vicious circle that "in effect legalized the financial corruption of politics."[52]

The photographs in Arthur Case's office of the Wall Street banker with Thatcher, Bush 41, and Rudy Giuliani (a Tory and two Republicans) conjure precisely the sort of symbiosis between government and industry that has flourished under neoliberalism. The fact that all the figures who pose with Case in the pictures he displays in his office are on the neoliberal-right side of the political spectrum hardly seems coincidental. The juxtaposition of these photos with Case's array of awards recognizing his humanitarian endeavors leads us, in turn, to wonder what sort of causes the philanthropic banker supports. The idea that these causes may well be the type of humanitarian enterprises called "public-private ventures," which since the 1980s have generally entailed the privatization of hitherto public domains rather than the other way around, does not seem at all far-fetched. If the images of Case with Thatcher et al. offer clues to the type of humanitarian causes the banker supports, even his charitable gifts may be acts of accumulation by dispossession. It is not just his past actions—his "primitive accumulation" of capital during the Second World War—that the film condemns; the movie also beckons us to consider the inside man's role in ongoing processes of accumulation by dispossession.

The Short American Century

The film's inclusion of a photo of Arthur Case with George H.W. Bush as opposed to Ronald Reagan, a more iconic neoliberal figure, makes sense in light of the Bush family history. It invites us to make connections between one form of accumulation by dispossession and another by way of implicit links between Prescott Bush and his son George H.W., between Case's actions in the 1940s and his position in the latter part of the twentieth century, and ultimately between war profiteering and neoliberalism. At the same time, it also points forward to Bush 41's son, George W. Bush, who was in the middle of his second term in office as the forty-third president when the movie opened in theaters. The figure of George H.W. Bush points both back to his father and forward to his son, conjuring a period spanning some sixty years, from the 1940s to the 2000s.

Numerous social historians and political economists have seen fit to divide this sixty-year period into two distinct phases of US social and political history. The thirty-year span between roughly 1945 and 1975 represents a period of remarkable economic growth and financial stability in the United States. During that time, the country's power and influence grew internationally while at home the gap between the rich and the poor was the narrowest it had ever been. I do not mean to romanticize this moment in US history, during which time the United States orchestrated the military overthrow of democratically elected leaders in Latin America and elsewhere, led a savage campaign against the people of North Vietnam, fruitlessly attempted to remove Fidel Castro from office in Cuba while supporting countless US-friendly dictators around the world, and persecuted US citizens accused of harboring communist sympathies. But it is also the period that saw the birth of a broad middle class (albeit a middle class that remained largely white), the rise of trade unionism as a powerful political force, substantial gains in wages and benefits for workers across a wide array of sectors, the institution of progressive taxes that held extreme differences between rich and poor in check, and the development of a welfare state that provided a safety net for the most vulnerable Americans. This is the period during which Keynesian economics flourished in the United States, to the relative benefit of the majority of the country's population. Then, in the late 1970s, faced with the toxic mixture of a high inflation rate and rising unemployment known as "stagflation," US Federal Reserve Board chairman Paul Volcker engineered what Harvey characterizes as "a draconian shift in US monetary policy" designed "to quell inflation no matter what the consequences might be for unemployment."[53] This move, which came to be known as "the Volcker shock," resulted in a consolidation of wealth into the hands of the wealthiest 1 percent (and especially the wealthiest 0.1 percent) of the population and the relative impoverishment of nearly everybody else. With the subsequent electoral victory of the Reagan-Bush ticket in 1980, the class warfare inaugurated by Volcker became unofficial government policy. Through "further deregulation, tax cuts, budget cuts, and attacks on trade union and professional power," Reagan and Bush orchestrated a "momentous shift towards greater social inequality and the restoration of economic power to the upper class."[54]

In *The Long Twentieth Century*, sociologist and world-systems analyst Giovanni Arrighi brings to light a remarkable facet of the shift that occurred in the United States under Reagan and Bush. Tracing the relationship between capital accumulation and state development over of a 700-year period, Arrighi shows how each of the world's capitalist superpowers, from fourteenth-century Florence to nineteenth-century Britain, switched from trade and production to financial intermediation and speculation in the years leading up to its demise.[55] Borrowing an expression from economist Gerhard Mensch, Arrighi designates this shift as a "signal crisis" indicating the moment when a superpower's capitalist class no longer sees investment in the production and trade of commodities as profitable and looks, instead, to high finance as a way to generate revenue.[56] The reversing origins of US corporate profits over the sixty-year period between 1945 and 2005—from roughly 55 percent of corporate profits coming from manufacturing and 8 percent coming from financials in 1945 to approximately 45 percent coming from financials and a measly 3 percent from manufacturing in 2005—indicate the magnitude of the switch that took place in the United States.[57] Arrighi's study brings into relief the macro-economic consequences that this switch from manufacturing to financialization has had for each of the world's historical capitalist superpowers. Examining the changing fortunes of Florentine, Venetian, Genoese, Dutch, English, and finally American capitalism, Arrighi discovers that the switch from productive capitalism to finance capitalism has, in each case, led to a "terminal crisis" marking the end of the power's global reign. However, Arrighi notes, although the switch from production to finance "has never been the expression of a lasting resolution of the underlying systemic crisis," it can transform the final years of a hegemonic power's reign into "a 'wonderful moment' of renewed wealth and power for [the] promoters and organizers [of the switch]."[58] While the financial empire built on production decays, Arrighi suggests, financialization enables the system's proverbial "inside men" to benefit from the collapse while exacerbating the consequences for everybody else.

If the turn to finance capitalism that took place in the 1980s under Reagan and Bush constitutes a "signal crisis" marking the beginning of the end of the US's global hegemony, the "terminal crisis" confirming the systemic nature of that crisis would be the series of financial crises that punctuated the first decade of the twenty-first century, from the bursting of the dot-com bubble in 2000–2001, which reduced the inflated stock of numerous companies to nothing, to the subprime mortgage crisis and the crash of the US housing market in 2007–2008, which created the worst global recession since the Wall Street crash of 1929. In his postscript to the 2010 edition of *The Long Twentieth Century* (a work originally published in 1994), Arrighi cites these two developments, as well as the United States' misguided response to the attacks of 9/11, as confirmation that his earlier conjectures were accurate. "The US *belle époque* came to an end" during the reign of Bush 43, he affirms in his 2010 postscript, "and the US world hegemony entered what in all likelihood is its terminal crisis."[59]

Inside Man as Class Allegory

Inside Man was released in the midst of this terminal crisis. Its story of a bank heist on Wall Street, released at a moment when Wall Street bankers were enjoying a "wonderful moment" of speculative gains at the expense of their compatriots (indeed, at the expense of much of the world's population), offers viewers a fantasy vision of a redistribution of wealth from the rich and powerful 1 percent to the embattled 99 percent. If, as Susan Buck-Morss concludes in a trenchant article on contemporary neoliberalism, "there *is* class warfare being waged, from the top down," *Inside Man* presents the counter-vision of class warfare being waged from the bottom up.[60]

Here the class alignments that take place over the course of the film are instructive. As indicated above, much of the film narrative depicts a standoff between the detectives and Russell's gang. To this narrative opposition between cops and robbers corresponds a set of audio and visual cues that increases the distance between the two groups. Composer Terrence Blanchard creates a distinct musical theme for each of the two main characters, for example. The "Russell theme," a blend of horns and strings that builds in a series of crescendos, contrasts with Frazier's more percussive jazz theme, driven by a punchy bass line. These musical cues complement the different cinematographic strategies that Lee adopts in filming the two protagonists. While he favors smooth Steadicam shots and minimal editing in his depictions of Russell, he uses a hand-held camera and has recourse to more frequent cuts in depicting Frazier's frenzied attempts to gain control of the situation.[61] Clive Owen's and Denzel Washington's very different acting styles further reinforce these audio and visual differences. Washington, a method actor, infuses Detective Frazier with a free-and-easy charm while also creating the impression that the detective is improvising on the spot, whereas Owen's more restrained acting style creates the image of a bank robber in total control of both himself and his environment. The contrasting costumes the two men wear further emphasize the differences between them. Although Frazier generally wears modest business attire, he does sport a flamboyant suit toward the end of the film, and the Panama hat that he wears on numerous occasions offers him the opportunity to run his hand along the brim in a stylized gesture reminiscent of characters in Jean-Pierre Melville's *Le Samouraï* (1967) and the Coen brothers' *Miller's Crossing* (1990). Russell's facemask and dark glasses, by contrast, which he wears throughout much of the film, inhibit self-expression, thereby exaggerating the actor's toned-down portrayal of the character. To these sundry differences the film adds a racial element by juxtaposing the two African American detectives to the four white bank robbers and their Orthodox Jewish cohort. All these differences, which the film accentuates rather than minimizes, make the solidarity that emerges between the two groups all the more remarkable. What the film presents is a miniature version of coalition politics, in which people from dissimilar backgrounds, with different motivations and character traits, working on opposite sides of the legal system, come together in common cause to bring down a common enemy.

That common enemy is, in the first instance, Arthur Case, who represents the most unsavory aspects of capitalist accumulation. He is the target of Russell's precisely orchestrated attack. However, once Russell transfers the diamond ring (and the responsibility for following it up) to Frazier, the target dilates to include a larger grouping of New York's financial and political elite. The movie's penultimate scene, in which Frazier confronts the mayor and Madeleine White at the Four Seasons restaurant in Midtown Manhattan, implicitly enlarges the net to include additional figures. In conclusion, let us take a look at this scene.

The scene in the Four Seasons begins with a hand-held shot that follows Frazier up the stairs and into the restaurant's posh dining room. The maître d'hôtel makes it clear to Frazier that he is out of place in the upscale establishment by asking the detective if he has a reservation in a tone of voice that sounds more like a challenge than a question, and then aggressively asking Frazier if he can take his hat. When Frazier tells the condescending maître d' to get his own hat, the scene cuts to a wide view of the dining room as Frazier crosses the floor and walks toward a table where White sits with the mayor and a third diner. "They're looking to invest $4 billion over the next four years," we hear White say to the mayor as Frazier approaches the table. "And that's all in place," the third diner adds. Frazier interrupts the conversation and informs the group that "there's an old American saying: 'When there's blood on the streets, somebody's got to go to jail.'" As he recites this proverb, the camera pans down from Frazier's face to the Cartier diamond ring that he displays for the seated diners. The mayor then asks Edwin, the hitherto anonymous diner at the table, to excuse them for a moment. The last shot of Edwin, a distinguished looking middle-aged man wearing horn-rimmed glasses and a bow tie, shows him walking toward the camera while looking back at the table he just left, obviously curious about Frazier's cryptic remark. His subtle gesture of buttoning his jacket as he rises from the table and walks away comes across like an unconscious effort to protect himself from whatever unpleasantries are about to take place in his absence.

The conversation that ensues is indeed unpleasant, especially for White, whom Frazier blackmails into delivering Case to the War Crimes Issues office in Washington, DC, in exchange for not pursuing her and the mayor for their unethical and illegal methods of coercion. The fixer communicates her acquiescence by asking Frazier how he would like to appear on the front page of the *New York Times*. In return, the detective gives her his surreptitious recording of White and the mayor strong-arming him into letting her meet with Russell inside the bank. "We got to keep the real criminals off the streets, Your Honor," he explains to the dumbfounded mayor, who responds with a vacant smile. A wide high-angle shot of the dining room shows Frazier leaving the table and walking toward the staircase. The scene concludes with the film's only shot of Madeleine White losing her composure, as she scowls in close-up while watching the detective exit the room.

Frazier's remark about somebody having to go to jail when there is blood on the streets refers back to a previous scene in which White recites an aphorism she credits to the Baron de Rothschild in order to explain her employer's actions in the 1940s: "You know, there's a famous saying by the Baron de Rothschild," she explains to the detective. "'When there's blood on the streets, buy property.' I think Mr. Case really took that sentiment to heart. But he is no different than half the Fortune 500." The film's appropriation of the Baron de Rothschild's saying here is rich and complex. Although Rothschild originally uttered his phrase in the context of actual bloodshed, the saying is now applied metaphorically to investment opportunities more generally. Mortgage and Equity Management expert Craig Garcia translates the Baron's advice into limpid terms for the contemporary investor: "When everyone is selling, it's a great time to buy!"[62] Variously called "contrarian investing" and taking advantage of a "Rothschild moment," the idea of buying (gold, oil, water, property, or whatever) when there is metaphorical "blood on the streets" has become a central principle of smart investing in recent years.⁶³ By associating Rothschild's proverb with Case's activities during the Holocaust, the film reinvests the slogan with all its violence. One is reminded of Marx's affirmation, evoked above, that the history of primitive accumulation "is written in the annals of mankind in letters of blood and fire." Conversely, by proposing the hyperbolic example of war profiteering during the Holocaust as the secret of primitive accumulation, the film takes a particularly horrific historical moment to exemplify capitalism. The movie thereby creates a chiasmus. The Baron's phrase, originally coined in the context of violence and bloodshed but now used to describe "best practices" in the investment community, applies once again, in the film, to actual bloodshed while, conversely, the image of war profiteering during the Holocaust is proffered as the unspeakable inner truth of capitalism. In this context, White's remark to Frazier that Case is "no different than half the Fortune 500" simultaneously points in two directions. On the one hand, Case (like half the Fortune 500) is merely a cagey businessman, taking advantage of a "Rothschild moment" when it arises. On the other hand, they (like him) are potential war profiteers, willing to send their friends to the gas chamber as long as they get a share of the spoils.

Frazier's substitution of "somebody's got to go to jail" for "buy property" in his recasting of the Baron's aphorism renders explicit the movie's critique of capitalists who follow Rothschild's advice. Those who buy property when proverbial blood flows in the streets should be thrown in jail, this reformulation suggests. That group implicitly includes the diners to whom Frazier recites the modified proverb. Although we do not

Figure 4.3. A wide high-angle shot of Detective Frazier crossing the dining room of the Four Seasons restaurant enlarges the field of prospective criminals (*Inside Man*, Universal, 2006).

know the details of their conversation, the threesome is clearly discussing an investment opportunity, with White and Edwin lobbying the mayor for support and undoubtedly offering him an incentive to champion their initiative. Frazier's parting remark to the mayor, "We got to keep the real criminals off the streets, Your Honor," which sums up the movie's overall message, applies to White and the mayor, and by extension to the innocuous-looking Edwin, as well as to Case.

Finally, by including wide shots of the upscale dining room at the beginning and the end of the scene, Lee further broadens the spectrum of potential criminals. These shots situate us in space, but they also multiply images of the rich and powerful. Although shots of well-dressed business people enjoying salmon and asparagus in a fancy restaurant do not in themselves conjure images of corruption, the context of the shots leads us to wonder how these upper-class diners came into their wealth in the first place, and what they do to multiply it. We are left wondering how many Arthur Cases and Madeleine Whites there are in the room.

5

Fictitious Capital and Narrative Spin in *The Wolf of Wall Street*

MARTIN SCORSESE'S *THE WOLF OF WALL STREET* (2013), based on screenwriter Terence Winter's adaptation of Jordan Belfort's 2007 memoir of the same title, recounts the story of a young stockbroker's remarkable success as a salesman of worthless penny stocks in the late 1980s, his subsequent prosperity as the founding director of a brokerage firm that specialized in pump-and-dump schemes in the 1990s, the life of debauchery that the broker led on the proceeds of his scams, and finally the spectacular crash of both the broker and his firm less than a decade after he founded it. Much of what makes this story timely is the implicit superimposition of Belfort's rise and fall onto the boom and bust of the US subprime mortgage market in the 2000s. Released several years after the collapse of dicey mortgage-backed securities that investment firms had been packaging and selling as though they were virtually risk-free, causing the worst global recession since the Great Depression of the 1930s, *The Wolf of Wall Street* beckons us to make connections between the shady trader at the film's core and the bankers, brokers, and hedge fund managers whose schemes crashed the global economy in 2008.

The financial crisis of 2008 is both typical of contemporary capitalism and historically distinct. On the one hand, the proliferation of mortgage bonds in the early to mid-2000s and the sudden collapse of their value in 2007–2008 is just another boom-and-bust cycle in the recent history of global capitalism. Since the 1970s, financial crises have become regular occurrences. One of the things that *The Wolf of Wall Street* does is remind us of this volatility. By beginning the narrative (following a few introductory scenes) on Black Monday, the day in 1987 that saw the biggest one-day drop in the stock market since the crash of 1929, the film reminds us of the cyclical nature of capitalist expansion and contraction in recent decades. On the other hand, unlike most of the crises that have erupted over the past few decades—which have been, for the most part, localized to specific geographical regions or economic sectors—the crash of 2008 was global in its reach and widespread in its effects. Consequently, the subprime mortgage crisis, which, as Keynesian economist Joseph Stiglitz quips in his book on the meltdown, bore the "Made in the USA" label at a time when few manufactured goods could, directly impacted US citizens and Wall Street brokerage firms as well as international investment groups and residents of other countries.[1] Unlike the bursting of the Japanese asset bubble in 1990, the 1994 economic crisis in Mexico, the 1997 Asian Financial Crisis, and the Argentine economic crisis of 1999–2002, the crisis of 2008 hit the global financial center on Wall Street and devastated the world's biggest economy before rippling outward, wreaking havoc throughout the world and bringing the global financial system to the brink of collapse. Like the film's eponymous "wolf" says at the conclusion of his own story, in 2008 "the chickens had come home to roost."

Similarly, the story of the young broker's rise and fall is both biographically specific and emblematic of a larger trend. *The Wolf of Wall Street* belongs to the tradition of "economic confessions" that Mark Hayward analyzes in a recent article—confessions that "are as much about the economy as they are about the subject who confesses."[2] The film's Jordan Belfort (Leonardo DiCaprio) both represents an empirical individual and functions allegorically as an embodiment of contemporary capitalism. In this context, the movie's depictions of Belfort's compulsive infidelity to his wives, the shots of him weaving in and out of traffic as he careens down the freeway at 200 miles per hour, and the numerous scenes (many of them quite funny) showing his diverse reactions to an array of recreational drugs both convey the behavior of a particular person and conjure an image of the capitalist as a reckless and self-centered hedonist.[3] In a similar vein, Belfort's demolition of his Lamborghini while driving in a Quaalude-induced stupor, his crash landing of his helicopter roughly three minutes into the film, and the climactic capsizing of his 170-foot yacht depict events in the life of the young broker while metaphorically evoking the market's crash landing.

This chapter argues that the film's depictions of Belfort's escapades allegorize the movements of contemporary capital. This allegorical dimension is a matter of form as well as content. Part of the film's originality lies in the way it transposes the stockbroker's first-person account into the audio-visual medium of cinema. Belfort, who is both the film's main character and its narrator, is as unreliable in one role as he is in the other. In order to convey this unreliability, Scorsese and Winter devise a narrative strategy in which Belfort the narrator and Belfort the character both come across as untrustworthy sources of information. As a result, we are often unsure how to situate ourselves in relation to the material. If we sometimes feel, while watching the film, as though we were the "mark" in a three-hour Jordan Belfort sales pitch, at other times the camera signals to us that we are being "played" by the narrator and the film as a whole, much like the hapless investors that the first-rate scammer rips off in the narrative proper.

I begin my interpretation of the film with an analysis of its opening scenes, which set up the story while situating the viewer in relation to the material. Arguing that these scenes both mislead the spectator and reveal—sometimes subtly, sometimes overtly—that they have done so, I compare the movie's narrative strategy to its depictions of Belfort's scams. The schemes that Belfort and his team of trained brokers use to make their fortune are simultaneously particular to the way his firm operates and representative of a more general way of doing business on Wall Street. Countering the numerous arguments, many of them advanced by financial insiders, that Belfort's scams are not typical of the way that "legitimate" brokerage firms operate, I insist on the continuities between Belfort's modus operandi and the operations of established Wall Street firms. In sum, I argue, Belfort is not a bad apple in a generally good bushel but a fairly typical apple in a rotten bunch. Like his venerable peers, what Belfort does is create "fictitious capital," which he then converts into cash before it sheds its imaginary value. In recent decades, the fabrication of this sort of artificial capital—"capital without any material basis in commodities or productive activity," Harvey writes, glossing Marx's term—has become an increasingly common way for crafty financiers to make a fortune at the expense of investors.[4] What makes Belfort's story so accessible is the simplicity of the scheme he devises to convert other people's money into fictitious capital and then transform it back into cash before it evaporates. In short, Belfort is a first-class salesman, which is to say, in the context of the film, a first-rate liar. However, Belfort's dishonesty also produces some knotty narrative problems. The movie presents its own version of the liar's paradox, in which what we know about the deceitful stockbroker comes to us from the mouth of that same dodgy broker. In order to bring this paradox into relief from the get-go, I begin my analysis with an examination of the film's duplicitous narrative strategy, which I then extrapolate first to Belfort's sales techniques and finally to finance capitalism more generally.

The Wolf of Wall Street as Mock Infomercial

The movie's complex narrative strategy begins from the moment a sepia shot of a lion sitting in profile in front of a computer-generated jungle landscape appears on the screen following the production logos for Paramount Pictures and Red Granite Pictures. The lion lifts its head and roars in a gesture reminiscent of the MGM production logo. As the beast completes its roar, its head metamorphoses into a contour drawing of a lion's head, set against a diagrammatic representation of a globe, and the words "Stratton Oakmont, Inc." appear beside the icon. Viewers who know that the Stratton Oakmont investment firm, a notorious over-the-counter brokerage house that existed in the suburbs of New York between 1989 and 1996, is the subject of the movie realize at this point that the film narrative has already begun. Those who do not recognize either the name or the corporate logo of Stratton Oakmont have no reason not to think that this third title represents a film studio involved in the production of the movie. The graphic creates the impression that Stratton Oakmont, in conjunction with Paramount and Red Granite, produced

Figure 5.1. The Stratton Oakmont logo at the beginning *The Wolf of Wall Street* creates the impression that the company coproduced the film we are about to watch (Paramount, 2013).

the film we are about to watch. There is nothing that distinguishes the four-second production logo of a lion roaring and then morphing into a corporate emblem from similar graphics that appear at the beginning of other movies.

A rapid montage of Wall Street imagery follows the Stratton Oakmont production logo. In the space of nine seconds, we see in quick succession a street sign marked "Wall St." with a blurry view of the New York Stock Exchange (NYSE) in the background, a street-level shot that pans up to the pillars of the NYSE, black-and-white images of stock prices scrolling by on ticker feeds inside the Stock Exchange, close-ups of Arturo Di Modica's "Charging Bull" in Bowling Green Park and a stuffed bear standing in front of the NYSE, and a series of black-and-white shots of traders yelling on the floor of the Stock Exchange. A man's voice accompanies this rapid-fire montage: "The world of investing can be a jungle," the voice informs us. "Bulls. Bears. Danger at every turn." A soothing piano jingle signals a shift in the presentation as the resonant voice reassures us that there is a way for investors to negotiate their way through this jungle: "That's why we at Stratton Oakmont pride ourselves on being the best. Trained professionals to guide you through the financial wilderness." A smooth tracking shot of a lion sauntering through an open-concept office past rows of conservatively dressed

Figure 5.2. The mock ad for Stratton Oakmont shows rows of confidence-inspiring stockbrokers speaking calmly on the phone (*The Wolf of Wall Street*, Paramount, 2013).

brokers, who speak calmly on the phone or to one another, accompanies this encouraging news. Additional shots of the "king of the jungle" strolling through the well-managed office, and of confidence-inspiring traders conducting business on the telephone, reinforce our sense of calm and stability. When the lion passes a distinguished-looking middle-aged man reviewing a stock portfolio with an ethnically mixed group of young trainees, the speaker delivers his tagline: "Stratton Oakmont. Stability. Integrity. Pride." Over the last few words of this tagline, the Stratton Oakmont production logo of the roaring lion reappears on the screen.

Both the fabricated Stratton Oakmont production logo at the beginning of the movie and the mock Stratton Oakmont ad that follows lure us into thinking that they are presenting one thing, when in fact they present something else. The production logo that at first appears to represent a film studio involved in the making of the movie turns out to be an emblem for a brokerage firm advertised within the film. The mock commercial, in turn, initially presents itself as part of the film narrative proper. When we first hear in voiceover that the world of investing can be a jungle as we see shots of Wall Street, we assume that the film's narrator is setting up the story for us. It is only when the piano music kicks in and the voice changes registers that we begin to sense that we may be watching a mock TV commercial. Our suspicions are then confirmed with the reappearance of the Stratton Oakmont logo. With this second occurrence of the corporate logo, we realize that the film has duped us twice: once into thinking that a company called Stratton Oakmont coproduced the movie, and again into believing that the narrative proper had begun with the film's opening lines, when in fact we were watching a mock advertisement.

With these two misleading presentations, the film has subtly introduced twice, within the space of about half a minute, one of its principal themes: the disjunction between appearance and reality, in particular as they pertain to the stock market and most especially as they relate to the brokerage firm at the movie's core. This disjunction, which we only half-register as the audio-visual information whizzes by, begins to emerge as a bona fide theme in the shot that immediately follows the Stratton Oakmont commercial. This open-frame shot shows a large group of exuberant young urban professionals gathered around a massive target with a dollar sign in the middle. The rambunctious crowd, composed entirely of white men, counts in unison up from one to three, at which point a dwarf wearing a padded Velcro suit, a helmet, and goggles flies into the frame from the left and sticks to the target on the right. The crowd goes wild, with people cheering and waving around wads of cash. The contrast between this shot of the Stratton Oakmont trading room and the firm's

Figure 5.3. The first shot inside the Stratton Oakmont investment firm presents the company as an outlandish fraternity house (*The Wolf of Wall Street*, Paramount, 2013).

self-presentation in the mock ad could hardly be starker. Whereas the ad is designed to convince investors that they are in good hands with the "trained professionals" at Stratton Oakmont, our first glimpse inside the firm shows a bunch of testosterone-imbalanced yuppies placing bets on a dwarf-tossing contest. In contrast to the advertisement, which conjures a sense of calm and stability, the shot of the brokerage floor creates an impression of exuberance and excess. An informed investor would never trust this pack of wolves to offer sound financial advice or to make wise investments on her behalf.

In his book on Fredric Jameson and *The Wolf of Wall Street*, Clint Burnham proposes that the cut from the mock commercial at the beginning of the movie to the shot of the mayhem on the Stratton Oakmont trading floor communicates to the viewer what Wall Street "is really about": "*This is what Wall Street* is really about, the cut tells us: not those respectable, honest, suit-clad brokers helping you make money. Rather, they get together in obscene cabals."[5] Although I entirely agree with this interpretation, I would want to insert an intermediate step between "Wall Street" and the "obscene cabal" on the brokerage floor.

In addition to deceiving us about us about what happens on the trading floor of Stratton Oakmont, the ad at the beginning of the movie misleads us in another way as well. This mock advertisement, which bears striking resemblance to a Dreyfus Money Market Funds commercial from 1992, creates the impression that the firm is located on Wall Street, whereas the real Stratton Oakmont was located on Long Island.[6] Due to the ad's liminal position, neither completely outside the narrative nor entirely within it, it is not just the implicit TV viewers targeted by the ad that are led to think that the firm is located on Wall Street, but the film spectator as well. Our initial impression that the narrator is setting up the story at the outset of the movie, and the conclusion that we unconsciously draw from this impression (to wit, that the movie is about Wall Street), remain with us as the narrative unfolds. The movie never clearly disabuses us of this miscomprehension. In contrast to Ben Younger's *Boiler Room* (2000), a film also based on Stratton Oakmont, which clearly situates the firm in a suburban corporate plaza similar to the actual brokerage's location on Long Island, Scorsese's film takes no pains to clarify that the firm is located outside New York City. Although we see a clear view of Stratton's modest first location in a converted automotive garage somewhere in the outskirts of the city, and we do catch a glimpse, in the background of a brief shot toward the beginning of the movie, of an anonymous suburban office building resembling the actual firm's headquarters, the film's numerous shots of iconic locations in Manhattan's financial district lead us to place the brokerage imaginarily on Wall Street. This false impression, which the movie's title does little to dispel, enables the film to generalize its image of the investment manager and his firm as though they represented finance capitalism more broadly.

On the one hand, then, what the cut from the Stratton Oakmont ad to the firm's trading floor accomplishes is a revelation of the jarring discrepancy between the brokerage's glossy image and what goes on behind the scenes. The relation between the ad and the scene that follows is roughly comparable to the effect that would be achieved by juxtaposing a fast-food commercial and the gruesome scene from Rainer Werner Fassbinder's *In a Year with Thirteen Moons* (1978) shot inside a slaughterhouse. On the other hand, the ad creates the impression that the firm is a bona fide Wall Street brokerage as opposed to a fly-by-night boiler room located in a nondescript corporate plaza somewhere on Long Island. The latter impression, in turn, works simultaneously on two levels. First, within the context of the narrative, the ad serves to convince investors that Stratton Oakmont is a brokerage house on par with established firms like Goldman Sachs, Merrill Lynch, Lehman Brothers, and so forth. Second, due to the ambiguous status of the film's opening words and images, the ad simultaneously leads moviegoers to believe that Stratton Oakmont is representative of Wall Street. The first two of these three roles that the ad plays in the movie have to do with the different ways that the firm misrepresents itself in order to woo investors. The third serves the very different function of suggesting that the firm, and by extension the various ways it misrepresents itself and its services, are representative of Wall Street firms more generally.

The multilayered narrative strategy that the mock advertisement sets in motion at the outset of the movie continues as the scene on the brokerage floor progresses and the narrator begins telling his story. Following the shot of the dwarf hitting the target, we see the DiCaprio character (still anonymous at this point) and a fellow broker suit up another dwarf, whom they pick up and hurl at the target to the enthusiastic cheers of the crowd. A head-on shot of the dwarf flying directly toward the camera freezes just as the human dart's face fills the frame prior to his impact with the target. Over an extreme close-up of the airborne dwarf's contorted face, we hear the narrator start to tell his story. "My name is Jordan Belfort," he recounts over the freeze-frame shot of the dwarf's face. "Not him," the narrator clarifies. "Me," he says, as the scene cuts to a freeze-frame medium close-up of Belfort with his mouth open in an inaudible roar and his arms outstretched in our direction, as though he had just released the dwarf.

This short film segment is noteworthy for several reasons. In addition to embellishing the image of the Stratton Oakmont trading floor as an outlandish fraternity party, where self-designated masters of the universe treat little people as playthings, it also gives important information about the film's narrative technique. In it we learn not only that Belfort is the film's narrator, but also that his narration entertains a dynamic relationship with the imagery on the screen. This relation is conveyed explicitly in the freeze-frames, when Belfort clarifies that he is the guy throwing the dwarf, not the flying dwarf that we see on the screen. In contrast to the innumerable examples of movies in which the audio-visual information presents itself as a translation into sounds and pictures of a verbal account, here the narrator shows an awareness of the imagery on the screen and responds to it. Belfort is not just the narrator of a story that a filmmaker comes along and transposes into sounds and images after the fact, the freeze-frame shots imply, but an active agent involved in the creation of the audio-visual document.

This wink to the film audience at the outset of Belfort's narrative reinforces the idea that the Stratton Oakmont production logo wordlessly suggests at the beginning of the movie. Both the Stratton logo, which initially appears under the guise of a film studio emblem, and the infusion of Belfort's subjectivity into the imaginary filmmaking process when he starts telling his story, cleverly conjure an image of the broker and his firm's presence behind the camera as well as in front of it. The viewer begins to entertain the idea that within the fictional context of the movie, the entire film is a huge infomercial for Belfort and his firm. With the freeze-frames, the idea begins to emerge that two different film narratives, identical in content, are unfolding simultaneously on the screen: one written by Terence Winter, directed by Martin Scorsese, starring Leonardo DiCaprio, and coproduced by Paramount and Red Granite Pictures; and another put together by the fictional Belfort and his associates, and promoted by Stratton Oakmont in conjunction with the two films studios.

As Belfort continues his opening monologue, the film aesthetic explicitly mimics that of an infomercial. In the first of several shots in the movie that track Jordan from the front as he walks toward us while addressing the camera, the well-dressed broker descends a curved oak staircase in his picture-perfect mansion and walks out the front door to his waiting limousine. The scripted monologue, in which Belfort details his daily drug intake, could be an excerpt from a memoir, which it is, more or less, but the way Scorsese shoots the scene evokes the self-promotional infomercial genre. The director depicts Belfort as the self-promoting salesman would want to be portrayed; he shoots the scene the way Belfort would want it filmed. The suggestion is that DiCaprio's Belfort is not only crafting the words that we hear but that, behind the scenes of the virtual film we are watching, he is participating in decisions over mise-en-scène, camera angles, and the like.

The Wolf of Wall Street does not consistently maintain the fiction that Belfort is co-directing or co-producing the film—an exercise that could become cumbersome for the director, tiresome for the spectator, or both—but it does return recurrently to the idea, reinforcing our sense that the narrative unfolding on the screen doubles as an imaginary self-promotional video coproduced by Stratton Oakmont. This suggestion that the real film that we are watching dissimulates a fictive infomercial just below its surface takes a particularly droll form toward the end of the movie, when an actual mock infomercial appears on the screen.[7] This commercial, set to music reminiscent of the upbeat "Lifestyles of the Rich

Figure 5.4. Scorsese uses an aesthetic borrowed from infomercials to film Jordan Belfort's opening monologue (*The Wolf of Wall Street*, Paramount, 2013).

and Famous" theme, starts with Jordan walking toward us as the camera dollies back. "Do you dream of becoming financially independent but struggle every month just to pay your bills?" the dapper Belfort asks us as he strolls from the front door of a pristine mansion to a Rolls Royce parked in front of the house. "Would you like to own a home like this," he continues, gesturing to the enormous house behind him, "but can barely afford to pay your rent? My name is Jordan Belfort," he says, repeating the first sentence he uttered in the movie, before launching into a self-promotional sales spiel about how he can make anyone a millionaire. The mise-en-scène and the reframing of Belfort as he addresses the camera here hark back to the earlier scene of the broker at home in his mansion, thereby suggesting a homology between the mock infomercial and the larger film of which it is a part. The scene comes across like an audio-visual mise-en-abyme of the movie as a whole, a sort of infomercial-within-the-infomercial.

This mock infomercial does not divulge Belfort's secret to wealth creation. A caption at the bottom of the virtual television screen urges viewers to call a toll-free number in order to enroll in "Jordan Belfort's

Figure 5.5. The infomercial for "Jordan Belfort's Straight Line" seminar is an audio-visual mise-en-abyme of the movie as a whole (*The Wolf of Wall Street*, Paramount, 2013).

Straight Line" seminar, where they can learn how to make their fortune. Unlike the imputed TV viewer, however, the moviegoer is privy to Belfort's wealth-creation techniques. Included in the price of admission to *The Wolf of Wall Street* is a get-rich-quick scheme, which the film lays out for us in broad strokes.

How to Make a Fortune in Three Easy Steps

Several key sequences in the movie depict the secret to Belfort's success. All of them have to do with obfuscation and deceit. The first of these sequences occurs about fifteen minutes into the film, after Jordan has lost his job at the Wall Street investment firm of L. F. Rothschild when the company collapsed following the 1987 stock market crash. Responding to an ad in a newspaper for stockbrokers, Jordan arrives at a grungy storefront in a desolate Long Island strip mall. The sound of a toilet flushing punctuates our first glimpse inside the Investor's Center, where a dozen men in jeans and sneakers bark into the phone at customers. "They're up and comers. That's what that means," one broker yells into the phone. "It's three cents a share. That's three dollars, you cheap fuck!" another hollers. Dwayne (played by an uncredited Spike Jonze), the Investor's Center office manager, conducts an impromptu interview with the former Wall Street broker and hires him on the spot. During the interview, Dwayne explains to the interviewee that the Investor's Center sells penny stocks: "You know, uh, companies that can't get listed on NASDAQ, they don't have enough capital? Their shares trade here," he elucidates. The interviewer further explains that, in contrast to the blue-chip stocks traded at firms like Rothschild, which pay traders a commission of 1 percent per trade, penny stocks offer brokers a 50 percent commission. Seeing the tremendous potential profit to be made from peddling this low-grade stock, Belfort sets immediately to work.

The interview scene cuts directly to a shot of Jordan on the phone with a prospective investor. Seated in the middle of the Investor's Center office, surrounded by his fellow brokers, he delivers a pitch-perfect sales call to his mark, and makes a $4,000 trade. "The other guys looked at me like I'd just discovered fire," the narrator says in voiceover. The key to Belfort's success here is that he uses Wall Street sales tactics to sell strip-mall grade stock. Everything that he says to the sucker on the other end of the line could plausibly apply to an actual investment opportunity, which, if it had any basis in fact, could potentially make an investor a lot of money. Since no such opportunity exists in this case, Belfort makes one up. Seemingly without blinking, he creates an imaginary scenario ("Something just came across my desk, John. It is perhaps the best thing

I've seen in the last six months") and fabricates a company history that suits his purpose: "The name of the company, Aerotyne International. It is a cutting-edge high-tech firm out of the Midwest awaiting imminent patent approval on the next generation of radar detectors that have both huge military and civilian applications." We know from the interview scene that the information on file at the Investor's Center gives no such detail about the company. All Dwayne knows about Aerotyne is that it is run by a couple of brothers in Dubuque, Iowa, whose mom answers the company phone. He is pretty sure that the company makes radar detectors or microwaves or something like that. Just to make sure that we understand that Jordan's characterization of the company is hogwash, Scorsese inserts a shot of the Aerotyne International building into the scene of the smooth-talking salesman pitching the stock. This shot of an eight-by-twelve-foot ramshackle garage with a weatherworn "Aerotyne Ind. [sic]" plaque nailed above the padlocked doors serves a narrative function roughly analogous to the first shot inside the Stratton Oakmont trading room at the beginning of the movie. It reveals that Belfort's characterization of the stock he is selling has no more basis in reality than the Stratton commercial has in relation to the brokerage it advertises.

Jordan excels at his job at the Investor's Center. "I was selling garbage to garbage men and making cash hand over fist," he says, summing up his time at the penny-stock firm. However, the problem with penny stocks, from the ambitious broker's point of view, is that the trades tend to be small. Unlike major investment firms, which target wealthy investors and money managers, penny-stock firms like the Investor's Center sell modest bundles of stock to smalltime investors. The originality of the scheme that Belfort devises to overcome this limitation lies in its combination of the advantages of high-commission penny stocks with the benefits of large-sum trades. Having discovered how effectively Wall Street sales tactics work for selling strip-mall grade stock to low-stake investors, he now takes the next logical step, peddling large quantities of penny shares to millionaires. In order to pull off this coup, the cagey con man needs to be able to present the company, as well as the stock, as something it is not. It is in this context that he comes up with the idea for Stratton Oakmont.

At this point in the story, Belfort and his buddy Donnie (Jonah Hill) have struck out on their own. The two of them now run their own penny-stock firm out of a converted commercial garage in an anonymous New York suburb. The sequence in which Belfort lays out his plan to his small group of employees begins with the crafty salesman revealing the company's new name and insignia. "Gentlemen, welcome to Stratton Oakmont," he tells his band of a dozen or so brokers as he unveils the logo of the lion's head in profile set against a globe. The company name and logo are strokes of marketing genius. Both the Anglo-Saxon-sounding name of the brokerage house, which conjures a nonexistent pedigree (and which has no referent in the movie, "Stratton" and "Oakmont" having no meaning beyond their connotative value), and the majestic lion's head framed by the globe, which gives the firm the allure of an industry leader, are integral elements of Belfort's sales strategy. They function as components of a sales pitch that begins before the clients even pick up the phone. As Belfort says to his band of dim-witted brokers, the firm's new name and logo are designed to create the image of "a firm whose roots are so deeply embedded into Wall Street that our very founders sailed over on the Mayflower and chiseled the name *Stratton Oakmont* right into Plymouth fucking Rock." Belfort then lays out the sales strategy that he wants each of his brokers to follow: "What we're going to do is this. First we pitch them Disney, AT&T, IBM, blue-chip stocks exclusively. Companies these people know. Once we've suckered them in, we unload the dog shit. The pink sheets, the penny stocks, where we make the money." Donnie, the smart one in the group, immediately grasps the wisdom of this tactic. His approving nods as Jordan unveils the strategy contrast with the confused look on the face of Chester Ming (Kenneth Choi). When the camera pans from Chester to Nicky Koskoff, aka "Rugrat" (P. J. Byrne), and Alden Kupferberg, aka "Sea Otter" (Henry Zebrowski), who chuckle in recognition of the technique's sly logic, we see that the brokers are starting to understand how the system works.

The scene then cuts without transition to a shot that zooms quickly into a close-up of Jordan's face as he explains "the key to making money in a situation like this": "Now the key to making money in a situation like this is to position yourself now, before the settlement. Because by the time you read about it in the *Wall Street Journal*, it's already too late." By the time we come to the end of the second sentence here, we realize that Belfort is pitching a stock to a prospective investor, not elaborating his system to his band of brokers, but it takes us a few seconds to come to this realization. The clean cut from shot to shot, the similarity of Belfort's costume in the two scenes (same suit and shirt, different tie), the audio continuity from one shot to the next, the smooth transition in the dialogue from one money-making scheme to another, and the fact that we do not see the phone in the second shot lead us initially to process the information on the screen as a continuation of the preceding scene.

The sales-call scene then shifts back without transition to the scene of Belfort explaining his system. "Then you wait," he tells his group of brokers, directly referencing the moment depicted in the preceding shot. The sequence continues in this vein, shifting back and forth between

Figure 5.6. Continuities in editing, costume, dialogue, sound, and mise-en-scène lead the viewer initially to perceive the sales-call scene as a continuation of the sales-training scene (*The Wolf of Wall Street*, Paramount, 2013).

Jordan's description of his sales technique and a depiction of the system in action. When the sales trainer asks his group of trainees, who are hanging on his every word at this point, what they should say when a customer waffles, the camera cuts to a shot of Sea Otter on the phone reading directly from a typewritten script that his trainer has provided: "You mean to tell me that if I put you in at Union Carbide at seven and took you out at 32," Otter confidently says, sounding like a seasoned Wall Streeter, while Jordan, gesticulating beside him, lip-syncs every word that should be coming out of his trainee's mouth. A shot returning to the original sales call shows Belfort miming the act of reeling in the investor like a fish and then bending him over and sodomizing him as he brings the sale to a close. The scene then segues into a whirlwind montage of the brokerage's first few years of operation, where we see the firm grow in size and move from its modest garage location to a massive office

Figure 5.7. Alden Kupferberg reads from a typewritten script while Jordan lip-syncs every word that should be coming out of his trainee's mouth (*The Wolf of Wall Street*, Paramount, 2013).

space as we hear a continuous sales pitch spliced together from the phone calls of half a dozen different brokers. This fast-paced montage of the firm's auspicious beginnings incorporates a brief conclusion to the original sales-call scene, in which Jordan sums up his thoughts on the sale he just made: "What a fucking idiot," he says after hanging up the phone on the investor.

Belfort is by no means the only person to develop a system for ripping people off and pocketing their money. He is not even a particularly rare breed. Economics professors George Akerlof and Robert Schiller dedicate a recent book, *Phishing for Phools: The Economics of Manipulation and Deception*, to examining the widespread phenomenon.[8] Using the metaphor of *phishing*—a neologism coined in the 1990s to describe internet fraud—to characterize a wide range of activities, most of them perfectly legal, Akerlof and Schiller examine how investment bankers, commercial lenders, credit card companies, advertisers, auto dealers, elected politicians, the food and pharmaceutical industries, cigarette manufacturers, and liquor companies successfully "phish" unsuspecting consumers, whom the authors dub "phools." Akerlof and Schiller do not mean for "phool" to be a derogatory term. Virtually everyone is a phool at some point, they argue. It is the "phishermen," and especially the lax regulations that enable their scams to flourish, that the authors criticize in their book, not the phished phools.

The shots of Belfort reeling in his phish and pronouncing him a phool (or "a fucking idiot," in his lexicon) provide a fine illustration of the phenomenon that Akerlof and Schiller study in their book. However, we too fall prey to Belfort's scheme. For the brief moment after the sales-training scene cuts to the sales-call scene but before we have fully assimilated the scene change, we are in the position of the gullible investor. The long silence in the phone call, as the investor processes the information he has just received from the cold-calling broker, gives audio form to our own momentary confusion, as we try to make sense of what we have just seen and heard in the film. We are in a momentary cognitive limbo while we work out what is going on in the sequence. Then, once we have established what is happening on the screen, the sequence sweeps us back off our feet with a lightning-speed montage held together by a single continuous sales pitch spoken in half a dozen voices at different times and in different locations. The sequence plays us for a phool even as it reveals how the phishing scheme works.

The third leap forward in the development of Belfort's scam entails the launch of new issues. The film returns to the infomercial aesthetic to explain how these launches work at Stratton Oakmont. As the genial salesman walks through the animated Stratton trading room, the camera tracks him from the front while he offers an informal mini-tutorial on IPOs: "An IPO is an initial public offering. It's the first time a stock is offered for sale to the general population. Now, as the firm taking the company public, we set the initial sales price, then sold those shares right back to our friends. The . . ." At this point in the exposition the good-humored narrator breaks off his explanation. "Look," he says with a chuckle. "I know you're not following what I'm saying anyway, right? That's okay. That doesn't matter. The real question is this: 'Was all this legal?' Absolutely fucking not. But we were making more money than we knew what to do with." Here the broker plays us for a different sort of fool from the one the film plays us for in the combined sales-call and sales-training scenes: one too dumb to understand how his pump-and-dump scheme works. In fact, the scheme is relatively straightforward. Here is how it works.[9]

Belfort first buys shares of a company that his brokerage is taking public. In order to circumvent laws prohibiting him from purchasing more than 5 percent of a stock that his firm launches, he recruits someone outside his organization—a person called a "rat hole"—to buy additional shares, which the rat hole holds in his or her name. Belfort then uses the power of his brokerage to drive up the price of the stock. The more shares his traders sell, the higher the price goes. As brokers in other firms see the price rise, they join in the action by advising their own clients to purchase some of the stock. A scene in the film shows stock for Steve Madden shoes rise from $4.50 per share at 1:00, when Stratton opens the stock for sale, to $18 a share at 1:03, netting Jordan $13.5 million in three minutes. In addition to driving up the stock price, the purchase orders that other brokerage houses process also obscure the stock manipulation going on inside Stratton Oakmont. To an outside observer, the spike in price looks like the result of a widespread buying frenzy, as opposed to a manipulation orchestrated by a particular firm. Once the stock value peaks, Belfort and his rat holes sell off their shares. Because the broker and his rat holes own so much of the stock, this rapid sell-off (which has to be done all at once in order to maximize profit) causes the stock to plummet. In the end, the investors are left holding worthless claims. In the process Belfort has made millions for himself, while all the traders involved in the transactions keep the sales commissions they have earned along the way and the rat hole receives a generous gratuity.

As the narrator clarifies in the aborted mini-tutorial cited above, this sort of market manipulation is illegal. The film's Belfort, like the empirical broker that DiCaprio incarnates on the screen, spent twenty-two months in a federal penitentiary—presented in both Belfort's memoir and the movie as a resort community with a locked gate—for securities fraud and for laundering the proceeds of his scams in Swiss banks. But how different is Belfort's illegal pump-and-dump scheme from the deceptive but apparently legal ways that venerable Wall Street institutions make their money?

Is *The Wolf of Wall Street* about Wall Street?

Numerous film reviewers and finance specialists have argued that the movie's depiction of Belfort and his firm is not representative of finance more generally. The title of Andrew DeYoung's review, "*The Wolf of Wall Street* Isn't about Wall Street," distills a sentiment that recurs in many responses to the film.[10] "[Belfort and his buddies'] stock scam wasn't emblematic of greed in the Financial District," Ronald L. Rubin argues, for example, in the pages of the *Wall Street Journal*. "These guys were just shrewd crooks working out of Long Island."[11] In her summary of financial insiders' reactions to the film following an organized screening, Katie Allen cites an investment banker who declares that "it just isn't real." A fund manager cited in Allen's article, who "feels the story of greed and fraud at Stratton Oakmont brokerage is stretched well beyond the realm of possibility," concurs. Moreover, the unnamed fund manager argues, whether or not the film's depiction of Belfort's actions in the 1990s is accurate, his scams would be impossible now: "In reality people working in finance today are working in an immensely regulated environment," the money manager explains somewhat implausibly, given the massive bubble that had recently burst when unregulated "financial products" in the bond market suddenly became worthless.¹² Referencing that spectacular boom and bust of the bond market, Andrew Slocum, writing in *Forbes*, asserts that "any connection in the film between Stratton Oakmont's actual dealings in the 1990's and the ethics of big Wall Street firms' early trafficking of collateralized debt obligations (CDOs) [is] speculative, at best."¹³ Finally, in an article (to which I return below) appearing in the *New York Times*, Joe Nocera writes that "the rise and fall of Stratton Oakmont in the late 1980s and '90s has nothing to do with the events that brought the financial system to the brink" in 2008.¹⁴

In contrast to this loose faction of reviewers and industry insiders who argue, each in his or her own way, that "*The Wolf of Wall Street* isn't about Wall Street," the broker whose life is depicted in the movie states, in the sequel to his first book, that he is "no different from anybody else [on Wall Street]—no damn different!"¹⁵ Discussing the masters of the universe that populate Manhattan's financial district, he insists that "every last one of them is as crooked as me!"¹⁶ Although Belfort's assertions here are undoubtedly self-serving, as he is first to admit, there is a grain of truth to them.

It is noteworthy that among the cast of characters that Allen presents in her article, the bond market expert "is less quick to distance his industry from Scorsese's tale" than his peers: "We are only five years on from the crisis, so I wouldn't pretend it was ancient history," the anonymous bond specialist opines in response to the investment banker's expressed hope that "people see this in a historical context and not in the current context."¹⁷ The pride of place given to bond traders in general, and to the bond managers at Goldman Sachs in particular, in Akerlof and Schiller's book also indicates that the bond market has something peculiarly relevant to tell us about contemporary phishing schemes. Even Nocera, who unequivocally states that the story of Stratton Oakmont "has nothing to do with" the boom and bust of the bond market, concedes that "there is one important way in which they [Stratton Oakmont and, lo and behold, Goldman Sachs] are alike, and why using Stratton Oakmont as a proxy for Wall Street is not such a stretch": "The brokers (or traders in the case of Goldman) are, at bottom, salesmen."¹⁸ In Nocera's view, the film's Jordan Belfort "is an extreme example of the smooth-talking, I-can-sell-anything, [salesmen]" that populate the trading floors of investment centers around the world, without whom finance capitalism as we know it would cease to exist.¹⁹

Nocera's suggestion that Scorsese's Belfort epitomizes the smooth-talking salesman at the heart of the financial system contains the kernel of a far-reaching interpretation of the film's obsession with sales calls. As Rebecca Colesworthy writes in one of the surprisingly few scholarly articles on the film, "in returning again and again to scenes of sale, it is as if the film were returning to some primal scene of capitalism, to an originary *act* of exchange, and in this way it begins to allegorise a fundamental 'moment' of *real* abstraction."[20] In Colesworthy's view, although "the tools of commerce [by which she means technological innovations, but her statement applies equally to so-called 'financial instruments'] have changed, . . . the process of fictionalisation—that is, the *abstraction*—underwriting capital's flows is the same."[21] In contrast to theorists like Alberto Toscano and Jeff Kinkle, who interpret the film's fixation on Belfort's sales techniques as a deflection of the fundamental dynamics that structure capitalism, Colesworthy suggests here that, on the contrary, they reflect it.[22]

Colesworthy's reference to "the process of fictionalization" that supports capital's flows alludes to an important Marxian category, arguably more integral to understanding the current stage of capitalist development than any period since the Roaring Twenties, when the Dow Jones Industrial Average increased nearly sixfold (from around 70 points in 1921 to nearly 400 by mid-1929) before plummeting (shedding approximately 90 percent of its value) following the crash of 1929. The category of "fictitious capital," elaborated by Marx in volume 3 of *Capital*, sheds clear light on the obscure processes by which investment firms generate wealth, on ways that crafty financiers create vast fortunes seemingly out of thin air, on the widening disconnect between Wall Street and Main Street, and on the increasingly wild gyrations of global capital in recent decades. It also has a great deal to tell us about Stratton Oakmont's success in the 1990s and the boom of the bond market in the 2000s. In conclusion, let us examine this Marxian category and the ways it helps us understand both the film's world and ours.

Fictitious Capital in the Film's World and Ours

Marx introduces the notion of fictitious capital in order to distinguish claims on future wealth from the "real capital" invested in the means or the process of production. Examples of fictitious capital include stocks, bonds, commercial paper, treasury bills, public securities, and the like. Let us take the example of stock. Unlike the capital bound up in factories, machinery, raw materials, and so forth, capital invested in stock represents a claim to future surplus value that a company might produce. In theory, if the company performs well (if it creates surplus value), the investment will return dividends to the investor. From the company's perspective, the injection of capital from outside investors enables the enterprise to expand operations, modernize, research and develop new products, and so on. To a certain extent, the shares that an investor holds represent the capital invested in the company's operations. If a company uses the capital raised from selling shares to buy a new machine, for example, the shareholder becomes part owner of that machine. However, in the process, the capital seems to have miraculously doubled itself. It exists both in the purchased machinery and in a piece of paper that claims partial ownership of the new machine. The money has been spent, and yet it magically still exists. In the event that the company as a whole is owned by shareholders, as is the case with publicly traded corporations, the entire company takes on a dual existence, as both a real entity that makes and sells things and its spectral double, represented in its stock.

Marx takes the example of the major industries of his day to illustrate this duality:

> The shares in railway, mining, shipping companies, etc. represent real capital, i.e. capital invested and functioning in these enterprises, or the sum of money that was advanced by the shareholders to be spent in these enterprises as capital. . . . But the capital does not exist twice over, once as the capital value of the ownership titles, the shares, and then again as the capital actually invested or to be invested in the enterprises in question.[23]

In Marx's view, the capital exists only in the latter form. The capital invested in production is real, whereas the shares owned by stockholders are "paper duplicates of the real capital."[24] To illustrate his point, Marx compares these two forms of capital to a shipment of merchandise and the bill of lading that represents it, wryly commenting that it is "as if a bill of lading simultaneously acquired a value alongside the cargo it refers to."[25]

Moreover, these paper claims—these "nominal representatives of non-existent capitals," as Marx calls them—"can themselves be exchanged as commodities, and hence circulate as capital values."[26] Marx observes that the value of these illusory capitals "can rise and fall quite independently of the movement in value of the actual capital to which they are titles."[27] A company's stock can increase in value even as the value of its assets or its productive capacity decreases, or vice-versa. When this happens, the fictitious capital that seemed to duplicate the real capital it represented diverges from the capital it was meant to express and begins to obey its own logic. In sum, company stock, which is at one and the same time a genuine title to real capital and an illusory double of that capital, is also a commodity in its own right, which can be bought and sold in a market of its own—the *stock market*—where its value is determined by factors irreducible to those that govern a company's "real" value.

Let us take an example. In his lively and engaging graphic novel on how capitalism works (and does not work), Michael Goodwin recounts the story of how the corporate raider T. Boone Pickens bought a large number of Gulf Oil shares in the early 1980s. At that time, Gulf stock was selling at $40 a share, making the company "worth" $6.5 billion even though its oil fields were worth much more than that. This discrepancy between the company's nominal value and the value of its assets offers a fine example of the dissociation between real and fictitious forms of capital. In order to avoid being taken over by Pickens, whom they mistrusted, Gulf managers turned to Chevron, which engulfed the embattled company at $80 a share. "That meant that Pickens and his friends sold their stock for a $760 million profit, while Gulf disappeared."[28] Goodwin cites Pickens's assessment of what transpired: "At $40 the company's worth $6.5 billion, at $80 it's worth $13 billion. So everybody can see what was created here."[29] Indeed, everyone can see what was created: a heap of paper wealth and the disappearance of a Fortune 500 corporation. Goodwin's narrator sums up this outcome: "In real life, it's hard to see what was created except paper value. In fact, something had been *destroyed*."[30]

David Harvey approaches this type of situation from a different angle. "The problem," he writes, with an accumulation of fictitious capital is that it "can be transformed into actual money capital, thus making fictitious capital real."[31] This conversion of fictitious capital back into cash, which occurs during the "dump" stage in Belfort's pump-and-dump scheme, is what Harvey regrets here. In contrast to Goodwin, whose remarks above read like an ironic commentary on the notion of capitalist "creative destruction," Harvey laments here the financial speculator's ability to profit from his schemes by turning his fictitious profits into real wealth. For better or worse, it is the latter perspective that *The Wolf of Wall Street* adopts. In contrast to a film like Woody Allen's *Blue Jasmine* (examined in the next chapter), which shows the fallout of financial schemes and leaves the details of those schemes largely up to the viewer's imagination, *The Wolf of Wall Street* takes the opposite approach, depicting how Belfort and his cohorts make, spend, and launder their money while leaving us to imagine the consequences of their actions for the people they scammed.

Harvey takes the example of mortgage-backed securities to illustrate "the problem," as he calls it, with fictitious capital: "When mortgages were packaged into collateralized debt obligations they existed, as it were, in a doubly fictitious state; but when a hedge fund manager traded them to unsuspecting and gullible investors and made a cool billion, he acquired real money power that was not, unfortunately, in any way fictitious."[32] The collateralized debt obligations, or CDOs, existed in "a doubly fictitious state," in Harvey's estimation, because they duplicated the capital of mortgages, which themselves were paper duplicates of a real asset (a house). CDOs are "derivatives," so called because they derive their (fictitious) value from the (often fictitious) value of something else. However, Harvey observes, "what is fictitious capital at one moment can instantaneously be transformed into real money power (for capital or consumption) at another moment."[33] Therein lies the problem, as he sees it (although he enumerates others), with an accumulation of fictitious capital.

As indicated above, for Harvey, CDOs were doubly fictitious instruments. In fact, many were triply so. As Michael Lewis explains in *The Big Short*, the CDO was a financial instrument that bundled together a bunch of mortgages, which investment banks then sold as a bond to investors. The mortgages in the CDO were of varying quality. Some of them—the "prime" mortgages—were secure, with little chance of default, whereas others (the "subprime" ones) were at great risk of default. Rating agencies like Moody's and Standard & Poor's had the job of evaluating these newfangled investment products, which they did by placing the various mortgages comprising the CDO into different categories, called "tranches." Each tranche bore a rating reflecting its perceived risk. An AAA-rated tranche consisted of mortgages with virtually a zero-default-risk rate, while a BBB-rated tranche contained mortgages that were much more likely to go bad. However, Lewis explains, the clever bond managers at Goldman Sachs came up with a way to recycle the high-risk, BBB-quality mortgages—which he likens to the lower, more flood-prone floors of a building—into the low-risk, AAA-rated tranche (the penthouse) of a new CDO: "Having gathered 100 ground floors from 100 subprime mortgage buildings (100 different triple-B-rated bonds), they persuaded the rating agencies that these weren't, as they might appear, all exactly the same things: They were another diversified portfolio of assets!"[34] Out of ignorance or self-interest, the rating agencies "pronounced 80 percent of the new tower of debt [the new CDO built from the previously BBB-rated subprime mortgages] triple-A."[35] The remaining 20 percent could then, miraculously, be repackaged into yet another "diversified" CDO, which the agencies in turn pronounced 80 percent AAA. For Wall Street, Lewis concludes, the CDO was "a machine that turned lead into gold."[36]

The CDO accomplished, by virtue of its structure, the sort of duplicitous sale that Belfort trained his brokers at Stratton Oakmont to make during the preceding decade. Whereas he instructed his salespeople to lure in clients by pitching them high-quality blue-chip stocks and then, once they had suckered them in, to "unload the dog shit," the wise men at Goldman Sachs phished investment managers with secure-looking AAA-rated CDOs composed of what Steve Eisman, one of a handful of people to discern the quality of these bonds before they started to reek, characterized as "the equivalent of three levels of dog shit lower than the original bonds."[37] If Belfort ended up being indicted for securities fraud, the good people of Goldman Sachs, none of whom saw the inside of a prison cell, were engaged in a practice at least as deceptive as their predecessor. *"That's fraud,"* Charlie Ledley, one of the few people who foresaw the subprime mortgage crisis before it struck, said when he realized what a CDO was. "Maybe you can't prove it in a court of law. But it's fraud."[38]

Previous to the release of Adam McKay's cinematic adaptation of *The Big Short* in 2015, I would not have thought it possible to represent on film what a CDO is and how it works in an entertaining way that would appeal to a mass audience. McKay's film is as informative as it is witty and amusing. The viewer leaves the theater with a rich understanding of the precise mixture of shortsightedness and corruption that led to the biggest financial meltdown since 1929. However, while McKay's movie communicates with remarkable clarity *how* complex financial instruments work, it is less concerned with *why* they worked so well. By putting the spectator in the position of the gullible investor, *The Wolf of Wall Street*, by contrast, enables us to appreciate firsthand, as it were, how phools are phished. If, as Nocera reminds us, citing an old adage, "Stocks are sold, not bought," Scorsese's depiction of a flimflamming fleecer who doubles as a fast-talking narrator allows us to share the experience of the sucker that takes the bait.[39]

In addition to the similarity between Stratton Oakmont's deceptive sales techniques and the arcane schemes devised initially by Goldman Sachs and then replicated by all the major Wall Street firms to defraud investors in the 2000s, Nocera brings to light another important way in which the subprime mortgage scam resembles Belfort's stratagem:

> Fearing that a housing crash was nearing, Goldman bundled its worst mortgage bonds into a synthetic collateralized debt obligation—the kind of security the financial media would later label as "toxic mortgages." It also allowed John Paulson, the hedge-fund manager who was betting against mortgage bonds, to help choose the bonds that went into the deal. And then, just like Stratton Oakmont, Goldman sold these pigs in

a poke to the suckers.... When the housing bubble burst, the banks were stuck with big losses, while Goldman and Mr. Paulson racked up gains. Just like Stratton Oakmont.[40]

Lewis encapsulates this elaborate two-pronged strategy in a short sentence: "Goldman was in the position of selling bonds to its customers created by its own traders, so that they might bet against them."[41] Although neither Lewis nor Nocera use the term, the twofold scheme that they describe here bears similarities to the simple and effective yet inconveniently illegal pump-and-dump scheme that Belfort practiced in the 1990s. Although the pump and the dump are not as intimately tied in this case as they were at Stratton Oakmont, the idea of an investment firm packaging and selling bonds designed to go bad so that it can profit when the bonds self-destruct bears a family resemblance to the cruder technique that Belfort used in the previous decade to enrich himself at his clients' expense.

If Goldman Sachs has become the ugly poster child for the subprime mortgage debacle, it is in part because the firm not only survived the crisis but profited from it. Unlike Bear Stearns, for example, which was sold to J. P. Morgan Chase for $2 a share (later upgraded to $10), and Lehman Brothers, whose collapse in 2008 *The Wolf of Wall Street* echoes with the implosion of L. F. Rothschild in 1987, Goldman Sachs emerged from the crisis relatively unscathed. It did so thanks both to the winning bets it had placed against its customers and to the massive government handout that the firm received in 2008 when Henry Paulson, Goldman's former CEO, then serving as US Secretary of the Treasury, relieved the company of its remaining "troubled assets" at 100 cents on the dollar.

Goldman's role in the subprime mortgage fiasco and the global financial crisis that ensued earned it the unflattering nickname of the "great vampire squid."[42] The term calls to mind Marx's famous characterization, in volume 1, of capital as "dead labour which, vampire-like, lives only by sucking living labour."[43] Marx's description here pertains to industrial capitalism, which sucks the lifeblood out of its workforce. In a less celebrated passage from volume 3, he invokes a different type of predator to characterize finance capitalism: "Since ownership now exists in the form of shares, its movement and transfer become simply the result of stock-exchange dealings, where little fishes are gobbled up by the sharks, and sheep by the stock-exchange wolves."[44] Marx is describing here the process by which the stock market enables wealth to become concentrated into the hands of ever-fewer people. The characterization aptly applies to the current age of capitalism, when the wealthiest 1 percent of the world's population is using the stock market as a highly effective means to appropriate an ever-larger portion of the world's wealth at the expense of the rest of the population.

The Wolf of Wall Street allegorizes this process. If, as the resonant voice informs us at the beginning of the movie, "the world of investing can be a jungle," *The Wolf of Wall Street* warns us that the trained professionals that offer to guide us through this financial wilderness may be "stock-exchange wolves" in disguise. Such turned out to be the case, we now know, at all the major Wall Street firms in the early 2000s. Belfort plays a role in the film only too reminiscent of the investment bankers and fund managers that bamboozled their clients during the years leading up to the Great Recession. By addressing the spectator alternately (or simultaneously) as a confidant to whom he explains his system and the dupe in an elaborate charade, the film's Belfort also plays us for a phool even as he reveals how phishing schemes work. At the same time, by presenting the broker and his firm as emblematic of finance capitalism more broadly, the movie beckons us to generalize its image of the stock-market predator. Our lack of trust in Belfort should translate into a mistrust of the system he represents.

6

The Meltdown and the Bailout without the Recovery

Blue Jasmine

THE TITLE CHARACTER IN Woody Allen's 2013 *Blue Jasmine* (played by Cate Blanchett) is a New York socialite who has fallen on hard times. Her late ex-husband, Hal (Alec Baldwin), we learn in a series of flashbacks, was an extraordinarily successful businessman who amassed a fortune in fraudulent real estate ventures and shady investment schemes. Jasmine enjoyed a life of luxury on the proceeds of her husband's ventures. The flashback scenes of the couple entertaining guests at their sumptuous home on Central Park or relaxing at their beachfront mansion show her in her element, perfectly at ease with the lavish lifestyle she led on her husband's illicit earnings. It is only when she discovers that he has been having a string of affairs with other women, and that his latest fling, with a teenage au pair, has turned into a serious and potentially long-term relationship, that she looks at her husband's business dealings with a critical eye. In an impulsive act of revenge that brings about not only his downfall but hers, she phones the FBI to report what she knows about her husband's financial scams. Jasmine's ensuing demise takes two forms. On the one hand, following her husband's conviction and incarceration, she finds herself suddenly reduced to poverty. On the other hand, she suffers a nervous breakdown from which she only partially recovers. It is in this doubly precarious state that she moves to San Francisco to live with her sister Ginger (Sally Hawkins), a single mother raising two boys on a grocery clerk's salary, who offers Jasmine material and emotional support while the fallen socialite attempts to get back on her feet. We need only translate this scenario into the macroeconomic terms that had gained currency at the time of the film's release for the movie's allegorical dimensions to come into relief. Released several years after US taxpayers had bailed out the investment bankers whose arcane financial schemes had sunk their own institutions along with the rest of the economy, the film recasts the 2008 meltdown and bailout as a human drama played out on a micro-scale.

Two crucial plot developments enrich this allegorical tale. First, as we learn over the course of a series of flashback scenes, Ginger and her ex-husband, Augie (Andrew Dice Clay), a former building contractor who now moves furniture for a living, had an opportunity to improve their modest financial situation on a long-term basis. The couple had won $200,000 in the lottery and was planning to use the windfall to start a construction company, but Jasmine and Hal convinced them to invest their winnings in one of Hal's sham business ventures instead. Ginger and her ex-husband's dim financial prospects at the beginning of the movie are therefore a direct result of their mistaken belief that the investment manager was working in their interests, not against them. Second, undoubtedly the most engrossing aspect of the film is Jasmine's inability to accept the reality of her new situation. The numerous scenes showing her refusal to come to grips with the turn that her life has taken, and her sustained efforts to make her reality conform to her fantasy, culminate in the movie's brutal closing shot of Jasmine babbling incoherently on a park bench. If, as I suggest, the film can be interpreted as a recasting of the 2008 meltdown and bailout, one of the striking features of Allen's allegory is that the bailout does not lead to a recovery.

This chapter compares the narrative of *Blue Jasmine* to economic developments that unfolded on a national scale in the United States during the first decade of the twenty-first century. The interpretation begins with an overview of Jasmine's condition. Through comparative analyses of San Francisco–based scenes and flashbacks set in New York, I argue that the film depicts Jasmine as already deluding herself when she was living a carefree existence as a privileged member of the New York upper class. What Jasmine's descent into poverty brings about, I argue, is not the shattering of her idyllic fantasy world but the destruction of the material base on which it was founded. Analyzing the three stages through which the protagonist passes in her effort to overcome her empirical destitution, I examine Jasmine's successive attempts to recreate the material conditions for her imaginary life. When the last of those attempts fails and she suffers her final breakdown at the end of the movie, Jasmine goes into a freefall that, I argue, prefigures metaphorically the fate of the global economy. If, as David Graeber suggests in his magisterial anthropological study of debt, the world economy is "tumbling inexorably toward the next great catastrophe—the only real question being how long it will take," *Blue Jasmine* offers a poignant and poetic image of what that crash might look like on a personal scale.[1]

Jasmine's Delusions

The film's opening sequence gradually reveals Jasmine's condition. Following a computer-generated panoramic shot of an airplane flying through the sky, the movie begins with Jasmine reminiscing out loud to the woman seated beside her on the plane. The woman's reaction is hard to gauge. Although the conversation is mostly one-sided, with Jasmine doing almost all the talking, the fellow passenger maintains Jasmine's eye contact, says a word or two here and there to keep the conversation going, responds with a nod or a sympathetic shrug to almost everything Jasmine says, and returns her interlocutor's smiles. It looks like a pleasant and polite conversation, albeit a one-sided one, between two friendly strangers on a plane.

A series of shots then follows Jasmine and her fellow traveler through the San Francisco airport to the baggage claim area, where the two passengers wait for their luggage to arrive. Throughout these shots, Jasmine rambles on continuously about herself, giving intimate details about her sex life and her nervous breakdown, explaining that she will be staying in San Francisco with her sister Ginger, that she and Ginger are adopted sisters (not biologically related), that she couldn't stand Ginger's ex-husband, and so forth. We realize at this point that Jasmine has been blathering nonstop for hours. Her interlocutor's facial expression registers the exasperation, almost the desperation, that she feels from the barrage of endless unsolicited details that she has received about Jasmine's life over the past few hours. When the woman's husband arrives, she politely tells Jasmine that it was "really nice" talking to her and rushes off before Jasmine can get her phone number. "Who's that woman you were talking to?" the husband asks as the married couple walks away. "I was sitting next to her on the plane," the woman explains. "She was talking to herself. I thought she said something to me. I said, 'What?' But she couldn't stop babbling about her life."

By gradually introducing Jasmine's condition in this way, the film portrays the protagonist first as an outgoing conversationalist, not unlike the innumerable people that the spectator may have encountered in her own life. What initially comes across as sociability and self-confidence

Figure 6.1. The opening sequence of *Blue Jasmine* gradually reveals Jasmine's sociability and self-confidence to be antisocial self-absorption (Sony, 2013).

on Jasmine's part then reveals itself, over the course of the sequence, to be antisocial self-absorption. Not only does Jasmine go on and on about her life, not pausing to allow her interlocutor to get a word in edgewise (or, Heaven forbid, to do something other than talk to Jasmine); she is also oblivious to the suffocating effect that her prattle is having on her hapless interlocutor. Jasmine has, in effect, cast the poor woman, without the latter's consent, in the role of a minor character in the drama of her life. The woman's only function in the life story that Jasmine invents for herself—a story that she enacts in her every word and gesture—is to prop up the fantasy that Jasmine is an intriguing woman of the world with a fascinating life history.

The film further intertwines Jasmine's high self-esteem and her pathological narcissism via the striking similarity between the fallen socialite's interaction with the woman on the plane and earlier conversations, presented in subsequent flashbacks, that she had with her fellow socialites in New York. The scene of Jasmine and her friend Nora (Annie McNamara) walking down Madison Avenue as they discuss Ginger and Augie's dreaded visit to New York, for example, is roughly homologous to the scene of Jasmine and the woman on the plane. Jasmine's cadence, the characteristic Katharine Hepburn–like timbre of her voice, and the ways that her body language as well as her spoken language conveys a sense of self-importance are virtually identical in the two scenes. When Jasmine confides to Nora that Ginger "was never too bright. You know? And she was so wild and I, of course, was Miss Perfect," the dialogue could be lifted right out of (or transposed seamlessly into) the opening scene on the plane. The fact that Jasmine wears the same white Chanel cardigan with black trim, complemented by the same double string of pearls, in the two scenes visually reinforces the similitude between the fashionable socialite strolling down Madison Avenue and the babbling woman on the plane.

The paradigm here is the one that Jacques Lacan famously proposes in his 1946 presentation on psychical causality in order to exemplify delusion: "If a man who thinks he is a king is mad, a king who thinks he is a king is no less so."[2] If, as Lacan proposes here, a madman who takes himself for a king is no crazier than a king who thinks that he is a king, similarly, in *Blue Jasmine*, the babbling idiot who takes herself for a socialite is no madder than the rich and fashionable woman about town who takes herself for a socialite. Allen's genius here is to present first the blabbering woman on the plane, then to show the same woman engaged in the same type of conversation in a different context, where her demeanor distinguishes her as a member of the New York upper class. The suggestion is that the fashionable woman we see walking confidently down Madison Avenue with shopping bags in her hand as if she were a chic and sophisticated socialite is as deranged as the jabbering woman on the plane. The film implies that Jasmine's delusions of grandeur began before she found herself penniless on her sister's doorstep in San Francisco. They were already firmly in place when she was a carefree New York jetsetter. Jasmine was living in a fantasy world even when it was real.

When we see Jasmine animating the same sort of conversation with imaginary interlocutors, as she does, for example, while sitting alone in

Figure 6.2. The similarities between the flashback of Jasmine and her friend Nora strolling down Madison Avenue and the film's opening sequence reinforce the similitude between the fashionable New York socialite and the babbling woman on the plane (*Blue Jasmine*, Sony, 2013).

Ginger's empty apartment shortly after her arrival in San Francisco, we come to appreciate the severity of her condition. The scene of Jasmine sitting alone by the window in Ginger's empty flat, reminiscing aloud about how she changed her name from Jeanette to Jasmine because "'Jeanette' had no panache," directly follows a flashback of the glamorous socialite hosting a dinner party at her posh Fifth Avenue residence. In the flashback, Jasmine tells her guests that the song playing in the background, "Blue Moon," was playing when she and Hal first met. This remark, combined with Hal's follow-up comment—"I fell in love with the name Jasmine"—offers a partial explanation for the movie's title. "Blue Jasmine" refers initially to the heroine's self-made identity as one of the New York glitterati, a composite of her and Hal's song (in the sense of the expression "They're playing our song") and the name that the heroine chose to connote her elegance and charm. It is precisely this dinner-party scene that Jasmine is replaying while sitting by herself in Ginger's empty apartment. "This song was playing when we first met," she tells an imaginary interlocutor over Conal Fowkes's rendition of Rodgers and Hart's "Blue Moon," carried over on the sound track from the preceding scene. "You know it?" she asks the nonexistent guest beside her. "Yeah, we met at a party at Martha's Vineyard," she continues, as though responding to a guest's query. Throughout this simulated conversation, Jasmine's facial expressions and tone of voice mimic perfectly those of the glamorous hostess of an extravagant dinner party.

The juxtaposition of the dinner-party scene and its reenactment in Ginger's apartment suggests two contrasting yet complimentary ways

Figure 6.3. A flashback of Jasmine hosting a dinner party at her posh Fifth Avenue residence shows the glamorous socialite in her element (*Blue Jasmine*, Sony, 2013).

Figure 6.4. Jasmine's eerie reenactment of the dinner party scene as she sits alone, homeless and penniless, in her sister's apartment conveys the severity of the heroine's condition (*Blue Jasmine*, Sony, 2013).

to understand the movie's title. As indicated above, in the dinner-party scene, the title of *Blue Jasmine* represents a double inscription of the heroine's fictitious existence as a glamorous woman about town, combining the "blue" of "Blue Moon" with a name that has got some "panache." This is the meaning that the title would have "for her," as it were. The follow-up scene conjures Jasmine's condition in another way, by suggesting that she is "blue" in the idiomatic sense of being sad. By the end of the film, this is the primary sense that the title finally has "for us." By placing the dinner-party scene and its eerie reenactment side by side, Allen brings together these two senses of "Blue Jasmine" as though they described complementary facets of the same condition. In the first scene, we see the rich and fashionable socialite acting like a rich and fashionable socialite; in the next, the penniless and homeless woman playing the same role: first the fashion queen living a fantasy existence that she associates with the name of Jasmine and the song "Blue Moon," then "blue Jasmine" perpetuating the fantasy once its material support has crumbled.

Neoliberal Lifestyles

Much of the film depicts Jasmine's desperate attempts to make her empirical life conform to her fantasy existence after its material base has disintegrated. This sustained effort to recreate the material conditions for her fairy-tale life goes through three distinct stages. Each phase presents Jasmine with a new prospective love interest and a new profession in the form of a job prospect, an actual job, or a fictitious career. Let us take a moment to recap these stages, which reveal a great deal about the film's vision of contemporary neoliberalism, whether they mean to or not.

The first stage is short-lived. It lasts the duration of an afternoon during which Ginger and her new boyfriend, Chili (Bobby Cannavale), take out the newly arrived Jasmine for lunch and show her the sights. Knowing that Jasmine is new in town, Chili brings along his buddy Eddie (Max Casella), whom he jokingly introduces as a "sad excuse for a blind date" ("I'm the best he could do on short notice," Eddie self-mockingly adds with good humor). Jasmine has no interest in Eddie, Chili's "retarded boyfriend," as she later calls him. Nor does she have any interest in the job lead that he gives her. Hearing that Jasmine is unemployed, Eddie obligingly says that he knows a dentist who is looking for help. In a disdainful tone of voice, as though the idea of working in a dental office was beneath her dignity, she informs her suitor that she is planning on going back to school. "What would you be?" Eddie asks. "An anthropologist," Jasmine responds. Eddie seems perplexed: "Really? Like digging up old fossils?" "That's an archaeologist," Jasmine curtly replies, and the conversation drifts on to another topic.

The formulation of Eddie's first question here is telling. He does not ask Jasmine what she intends to study but what she would *be* if she went back to school. This formulation condenses a set of assumptions about what a university education is and why someone would bother getting one. One does not go to college to study something but to *be* something. Granted, Jasmine is broke and unemployed, with no marketable skills and no prospective source of income. To Eddie it seems obvious that what she needs is a job, not an education. Having undoubtedly never seen an ad in the paper for an anthropologist, he cannot fathom why she would consider studying an obscure-sounding subject of no obvious utility. The fact that he confuses anthropology with archaeology changes nothing. If Jasmine explained to him that anthropology is the study of human societies and cultures as opposed to the excavation and analysis of human artifacts, she would probably make him more skeptical rather than less so. As far as he is concerned, studies are useful to the extent that they provide applicable professional training. If there are no job listings for specialists in human cultures and societies, why bother studying these useless subjects?

For what it is worth, Jasmine agrees with Eddie's implicit views on the value of a college education. We know from the opening scene in the airplane that Jasmine was studying anthropology at Boston University when she met Hal: "One more year and I would have graduated," she tells her accidental traveling companion. "But I quit BU to marry him. I mean, what was I learning at school anyway? I mean, can you picture me as an anthropologist? Is that a joke?" Jasmine's self-assessment here rings true, of course, especially as the film progresses. The idea of Jasmine being an anthropologist is a joke. What is telling in her remarks is their unstated presupposition: people study anthropology to become anthropologists. Neither she nor Eddie shows an awareness that one might want to study human societies and cultures for any other reason.

The film shares by and large this perspective. The context of Jasmine's decision to return to school in order to complete her degree undercuts the inherent value that learning about other people and cultures (or gaining any not directly marketable skill) might have. Her decision to study anthropology functions, in the narrative, as a sign of her elitism and her detachment from reality. The film presents it as a perpetuation of her self-delusion, not a way for her to reengage with the world. What Jasmine needs, within the context of the narrative, is applied vocational training that she can transfer directly to a job. Jasmine's chosen field of study (a field chosen in the film by Jasmine, and for the film by Allen) connotes the precise opposite of that sort of training. "Anthropology" ultimately signifies, in the movie, what it does for Eddie: an arcane branch of the liberal arts of little or no value in the real world.

This assessment of the value of an academic discipline like anthropology is by no means restricted to *Blue Jasmine*. As philosopher Martha Nussbaum observes in her short and powerful book on the importance of the humanities and the social sciences for fostering a healthy democracy and for creating "a decent world culture capable of constructively addressing the world's most pressing problems," the liberal arts are under assault in nearly every country in the world: "Seen by policy-makers as useless frills, at a time when nations must cut away all useless things in order to stay competitive in the global market, they are rapidly losing their place in curricula, and also in the minds and hearts of parents and children."[3] For Wendy Brown, who dedicates the last chapter of her insightful, alarming, and depressingly convincing study of neoliberalism to post-secondary education, the phenomenon described by Nussbaum has reached a critical stage:

> We have lost a recognition of ourselves as held together by images, literatures, religions, histories, myths, ideas, forms of reason, grammars, figures, and languages. Instead, we are presumed to be held together by technologies and capital flows. That presumption, of course, is at risk of becoming true, at which point humanity will have entered its darkest chapter yet.[4]

Brown's chilling prognosis here—in effect, that the self-perpetuating demise of the liberal arts risks undermining the conditions for their future existence—should sound an alarm bell for anyone who cares about democracy, social equality, quality of life for the world's present and future inhabitants, or human societies and cultures more generally. It forecasts a vision of humanity in which an ever greater number of people will be reduced to the role of cogs in a machine as they lose their interest in and aptitude for thinking critically and methodically about the world they inhabit.

For Brown, the fate of the liberal arts is one of the hallmarks of neoliberalism. In contrast to the majority of political economists who write on neoliberalism, who analyze how the implementation of a broad range of economic policies over the past four decades constitutes a form of class warfare disguised as fiscal responsibility, Brown, basing her analysis on Michel Foucault's *Birth of Biopolitics* lectures, construes neoliberalism as a form of normative reason that generalizes the model of the free market to virtually all human endeavors, whether or not they entail the actual accumulation of wealth: "The point is that neoliberal rationality disseminates the *model of the market* to all domains and activities—even where money is not an issue—and configures human beings exhaustively as market actors, always, only, and everywhere *homo oeconomicus*."[5] In this vein, she proposes, a person might approach dating, personal health and fitness, unpaid charity work, relationships with friends and neighbors, and even interactions with family members as investments. *Blue Jasmine* adopts, more or less uncritically, this perspective in its depiction of the protagonist's career path.

When Jasmine eventually comes to terms with the idea that what she needs is a marketable skill in a practical trade and comes up with the idea of obtaining an interior decorator's license online, she therefore makes a career decision similar to those of an increasing number of her compatriots. Swallowing her pride, she follows up the lead that Eddie gave her and gets a job as a dental receptionist in order to save enough money to get her decorator's license. This second stage is in fact the most optimistic episode in the film. Although Jasmine hates working as a receptionist, is horrible at her job, is hopelessly incompetent on a computer, and suffers intermittent panic attacks when her work overwhelms her, she is nonetheless working toward financial independence. The film presents this stage in Jasmine's development as her "getting her feet back on the ground" and working toward a realistic goal. Unfortunately, her boss, Dr. Flicker (Michael Stuhlbarg), develops an unreciprocated crush on her and, after failing to seduce her at a bar, sexually harasses her at the office. Jasmine quits her job, leaving her unable to save up for her decorator's license, when he tries to force himself on her one afternoon after work.

The Meltdown and the Bailout without the Recovery 143

It is in this precarious position, on the verge of slipping back into the abject condition we saw her in at the beginning of the film, that Jasmine begins the third phase of her life in San Francisco. This episode begins, tellingly, with a shot of Jasmine dressed to the nines but standing alone and babbling to herself at an animated party in an upscale house overlooking San Francisco Bay. Jasmine went to the party with the express hope of meeting a socially appropriate man. It looks like the party is going to be a washout for Jasmine until she wanders into what she takes to be an empty room and stumbles onto Dwight Westlake (Peter Sarsgaard), a well-groomed and well-dressed ambitious young diplomat sitting by himself in the corner, thumbing through a book.

Jasmine and Dwight are immediately attracted to one another. In fact, Dwight's attraction to Jasmine preceded their encounter in the secluded room at the end of the hall. "I saw you in the other room before. I was hoping I'd get a chance to meet you," he tells her after introducing himself. He then divulges the basis for his attraction: "You have great style.... Chanel belt, Hermès bag, and Vivier shoes." Dwight's pick-up line here speaks volumes about both him and Jasmine. On the one hand, the fact that his initial overture to her takes the form of an enumeration of the labels of her designer clothes offers an indication of what he looks for in a woman. On the other hand, as Arlene Diane Landau observes in her film review in *Psychological Perspectives*: "Jasmine's clothes ... are, in their own way, an extremely collective representation of what a rich woman should wear—but in this case without a personal touch. All the clothes are label driven, labels we may recognize, handbags and sweaters that tell the knowing, 'I am rich.'"[6] Jasmine's feelings for Dwight are revealed in the extent to which she misleads him about herself. Whereas, in the other San Francisco–based scenes, Jasmine's detachment from reality takes the form of delusions about her present circumstances, here, for the first time, she lies outright about her past. In the fictional world that she invents for him, she is an interior decorator whose late husband, a surgeon, died of a heart attack (rather than being a financial crook who hung himself in his prison cell) before they could have children (unlike the actual Jasmine and Hal, who raised Hal's son from a previous marriage).

On this shaky foundation, Jasmine and Dwight begin a romantic relationship that leads to a marriage proposal. The flimsiness of the lovers' bond, subtly conveyed by Blanchett and Sarsgaard, who have the onscreen chemistry of wax and water, becomes blindingly apparent at the moment of their breakup. On their way into a jewelry store to pick out an engagement ring, the couple bumps into Ginger's ex-husband, Augie, who blows Jasmine's cover by bringing up inconvenient details from her past. Dwight immediately forces Jasmine back into the car, where he breaks off the engagement and launches a torrent of abuse at her. One understands his sense of betrayal, but the fact that he does such an instantaneous about-face without bothering to hear her side of the story bespeaks the tenuousness of his attachment to her. Jasmine's interpretation of Dwight's reaction—that he has come to the realization that she does not fit "in [his] future plans where [he needs] the appropriate wife"—rings true, even as his verdict on her conduct ("Your ethical behavior is equal to your ex-husband") also has a grain of truth to it.

The relationship between Jasmine and Dwight offers a fine illustration of Brown's suggestion that "one might approach one's dating life in the mode of an entrepreneur or investor, yet not be trying to generate, accumulate, or invest monetary wealth in this domain."[7] If, as Immanuel Kant proposes in his second formulation of the categorical imperative, ethical behavior demands that one treat other people "never merely as a means to an end, but always at the same time as an end," Jasmine and Dwight have a profoundly unethical relationship.[8] Each treats the other solely as a means to an end. The paradigm for the couple's interaction is, in essence, that of a free-market exchange. As Adam Smith, the father of economics, famously asserts in *The Wealth of Nations* (1776), on the free market, everything works for the best when each person looks out solely for his or her own personal interest (when each treats the other merely as a means to an end, in Kant's moral language).[9] In this light, the relationship between Jasmine and Dwight presents a mini-parable of dating in the entrepreneurial mode, a parable in which both parties involved in the transaction walk away from the encounter feeling like they have been ripped off.

Freefall

The breakup with Dwight precipitates Jasmine's final meltdown. With the disintegration of the fragile pedestal supporting her elaborate fantasy, Jasmine finds herself once again hovering above an abyss and, with no empirical base to support her elaborate fantasy, crashes to Earth. The film's devastating final sequence begins with a disheveled Jasmine arriving at Ginger's apartment, the prominent underarm sweat marks on her crêpe de chine designer dress betraying the fact that she has just walked across town in her ring-shopping outfit.[10] She arrives to a festive environment that only increases her sense of isolation and despair. Ginger and Chili are celebrating their reunion after having split up when Ginger, following Jasmine's advice, got involved with another man. Jasmine, who considers Chili to be a "loser" on par with Augie, finds the news of the couple's reunion nothing to celebrate. She chastises Ginger for settling for a menial existence as an unaspiring member of the urban proletariat, and, adopting the air of a high-class sister looking down on her working-class kin, gloatingly informs Ginger that she is going to be moving in with the upwardly mobile Dwight. She elaborates a detailed fairy-tale future for herself, explaining that she and Dwight are going to get married, live in Vienna for a few years, and then return to the area, where they will live in their house overlooking the bay. "Now, if you'll excuse me," she says in a tone of voice used for dismissing social inferiors, "I'm going to take a shower. I'll send for my luggage." The last line here reveals the absurdity of her actions. At this point in the film, we know that there is nowhere Jasmine could possibly have her luggage sent.

The film's last shot is gut-wrenching. It shows a washed-out Jasmine, fresh out of the shower but ungroomed and bleary-eyed, wearing her signature Chanel cardigan and the blouse she wore in the opening scene, wandering in a city park. The camera pans to follow her as she approaches and sits beside a woman reading a newspaper on a bench. It then tracks slowly into a close-up of Jasmine's face as she starts talking to herself. The woman on the bench glances at her out of the corner of her eye and then wordlessly folds her paper and silently slips off. The film's final image shows Jasmine in close-up rambling in a void about a series of tenuously connected topics, variously narrating them, reliving them in the first person, and commenting cryptically on them. "This was playing on the Vineyard," she remarks as we hear a reprise of Conal Fowkes's rendition of "Blue Moon." "I used to know the words," she says. "I knew the words. Now they're all a jumble." She then looks off into

Figure 6.5. *Blue Jasmine*'s gut-wrenching last shot shows Jasmine in freefall, with nothing to prevent her inevitable crash (Sony, 2013).

the distance and smiles as though she recognizes someone offscreen, her bloodshot eyes and disheveled hair providing a visual counterpoint to her Chanel sweater and her sociable smile. The screen then cuts to black as "Blue Moon" continues on the sound track. After a few seconds of pitch blackness, the closing credits start flashing on the screen.

This closing sequence represents both a catastrophe, in the theatrical sense (the final turning point in a drama, especially a tragedy), and the culmination of Jasmine's delusions. On the one hand, her final meltdown is the result of an unfortunate turn of events. Had Augie not blown her cover, the fantasyland existence that she describes to Ginger and Chili in the movie's penultimate scene might have congealed into a solid form. The lies that she spins for Ginger's benefit—and they do appear to be lies, as opposed to delusions—correspond quite closely to the future that she and Dwight were planning together. On the other hand, the projected fairy-tale ending in which she and Dwight live happily ever after, bathing in the glow of an eternal San Francisco sunset, is only the latest permutation of a fantasy life that Jasmine animates, in one way or another, in virtually every scene of the movie. Jasmine's final collapse at the end of the film represents both continuity and a rupture, simultaneously the logical culmination of her delusions and the traumatic shattering of her illusions.

The remarkable aspect of Jasmine's collapse at the film's end is that it entails not the dissolution of her fantasy but, on the contrary, her own dissolution into the fantasy. Rather than forcing a brutal confrontation with the fanciful aspects of her imaginary life, the breakup with Dwight pushes her deeper into her fantasy world. Forced to choose between her empirical existence as a fallen socialite and the perpetuation of a fantasy incompatible with her material existence, she chooses the fantasy. The last scene is tantamount to a suicide. We know from the scene in the airport at the beginning of the movie that Jasmine's parents are dead. In the course of the film, we learn (or see onscreen) that she has maintained no contact with her New York colleagues, that her ex-husband hanged himself in his cell, that her son has disowned her for what she did to his father, and that she has formed no lasting relationships with anyone in San Francisco. Ginger was the last person to whom she could turn. When Jasmine breaks her ties with her sister and haughtily walks off to live in her fantasy world, she wanders into an abyss from which there is no apparent return. The cut to black at the end of the movie functions, in this light, as an ominous ellipsis. In the best-case scenario, Jasmine will find herself in an insane asylum telling her fellow inmates, her caretakers, or the walls about how "Blue Moon" was playing when she and Hal met. The film has even eliminated the hope that she might recover from her illness under a doctor's care. With what, at the end of the film, suddenly seems like malicious foresight, Allen has made sure that we know that doctors' previous attempts to cure Jasmine, including shock treatment, lithium, Prozac, and a "cocktail" of other drugs, failed. The last shot shows Jasmine in freefall, with nothing to prevent her inevitable crash.

Blue Jasmine as National Allegory

What is striking is how much this scenario resembles in both its general outline and some of its finer details a grand narrative played out on a national scale in the first decade of the twenty-first century. The demise of a high-rolling financier at the center of an elaborate fictitious real estate scam, the bailout of the social class that had been benefitting from the scam before it went bust, the perpetuation of the fantasy that things can go on as before in the face of overwhelming evidence to the contrary, and the anticipated inevitable collapse of this unsustainable fantasy, all appear in refracted form in *Blue Jasmine*. In Allen's allegorical recasting of this national narrative, Hal stands in for the speculators that had figured out how to manipulate the system to their advantage while Jasmine plays the dual role of the bailed-out upper class and the complicit consumer who is only too happy to benefit from the arrangement as long as it works to her advantage (and, indeed, who cannot imagine living otherwise). Ginger, in turn, plays the twin parts of the unsuspecting victim of financial fraud and the hapless taxpayer called upon to save the fraudsters from ruin when their scheme went bust. The correspondences between the film text and its national context are not one-to-one, but they are close enough to enable the spectator to perceive the contours of the national narrative behind the film action, and to view the latter as an interpretation of the former.

One disadvantage of presenting Hal as a figure of the twenty-first century investment manager is the impression thereby created that the predatory financiers got their just deserts. We know that this is precisely what did not happen to the Wall Street bankers who caused the 2008 meltdown. As Michael Lewis reminds us, virtually all the major players involved in subprime mortgage fiasco—those on the losing end of the bet as well as those on the winning side, those who ran their institutions into bankruptcy as well as those who successfully shorted the banks—walked away from the mess with an enormous profit.[11] None of them went to jail. However, there is another iconic figure from the 2008–09 period who did get his comeuppance: a "bad apple" on Wall Street, as political elites and media pundits like to call such figures, who suffered the consequences that his peers in the subprime mortgage market did not.

Numerous critics have compared Hal to Bernie Madoff, the Wall Street fund manager who pleaded guilty in 2009 to eleven federal felonies and admitted that his wealth management business was, in his words, "a giant Ponzi scheme."[12] Verna Foster, for example, in her insightful interpretation of *Blue Jasmine* as a reworking of Tennessee Williams's 1947 *A Streetcar Named Desire* (a play to which virtually every reviewer compares Allen's film), dedicates a paragraph to enumerating the many similarities between Hal and Jasmine, on the one hand, and Bernie and Ruth Madoff, on the other. Acknowledging Allen's disavowal that he based the Hal character on Madoff, Foster notes:

> Like Madoff, Hal is a wealthy, respected businessman and a philanthropist. Jasmine, like Ruth Madoff, is the perfect "society wife" who raises money for charities and is a "world-class shopper." Through his fraudulent financial dealings Madoff ruined thousands of people, including his wife's sister and her husband. When Madoff's Ponzi scheme became unsustainable and his family members (sons rather than wife) reported him to the authorities, the Madoffs lost their money . . . ; Bernie went to jail and Ruth did indeed go to live for a while with her sister. . . . One of Madoff's sons committed suicide in 2010; the suicide by hanging gets transferred to Hal in jail.[13]

The paragraph continues in this vein, drawing a set of striking parallels and near parallels between the two couples and making a strong case for the extent to which Allen's film rewrites, even if inadvertently, the Madoff saga.

What I would add to Foster's compelling comparison of the Madoffs and the wealthy couple in *Blue Jasmine* is, first of all, the way that Madoff himself is emblematic of a larger social and economic trend. This is a point that Slavoj Žižek makes in *First as Tragedy, Then as Farce*, his fiery little book on the financial crisis of 2008–09: "The Madoff case presents us with an extreme but therefore pure example of what caused the financial breakdown itself."[14] As Žižek reminds us, Madoff was not a marginal figure running a fly-by-night boiler room in the financial boondocks. On the contrary, this prominent philanthropist and thrice-elected chairman of the NASDAQ stock market was "a figure from the very heart of the US financial establishment."[15]

According to a *Time* magazine article that Žižek cites in his book, Madoff ran an investment fund designed to "generate stable returns and also cap losses." Then, sometime around 2005, the *Time* article recounts, "Madoff's investment-advisory business morphed into a Ponzi scheme."[16]

To this analysis Žižek responds: "There is no exact point at which the Rubicon was crossed and the legitimate business morphed into an illegal scheme; the very dynamic of capitalism blurs the frontier between 'legitimate' investment and 'wild' speculation."[17] Arguing that "the temptation to 'morph' legitimate business into a pyramid scheme is part of the very nature of the capitalist circulation process," Žižek makes the case that Madoff's doomed venture, which *had* to collapse at some point, is not an aberration of the capitalist system but is "inscribed into the very system of capitalist relations."[18]

Žižek is not alone in making this argument. Authors as different as Nobel Prize–winning Keynesian economist Paul Krugman and a renowned Marxist like Harvey agree that, in Harvey's words, "the stock market has a Ponzi-like character even without the Bernie Madoffs of this world explicitly organising it so."[19] The most obvious example in recent years of this sort of blurring of lines between "'legitimate' investment and 'wild' speculation" is, of course, the booming subprime mortgage market of the 2000s. As Lewis asserts in his meticulously researched book on the subject, this burgeoning market "had the essential features of a Ponzi scheme": "To maintain the fiction that [the subprime lending companies] were profitable enterprises," Lewis writes, "they needed more and more capital to create more and more subprime loans."[20]

As Lewis's remark here suggests, the boom of the subprime mortgage market required—as all Ponzi schemes do—luring in an ever-greater number of investors. Pyramid schemes are successful to the degree that they expand. The moment they stop receiving injections of new capital, they collapse into rubble. Hal alludes in passing to this phenomenon when he tells Jasmine, at one point, how much money they would lose if they scaled back one of their investment schemes. "It's like a domino effect," he tells her. "One thing would follow the other." In order not only to thrive but to survive, the mortgage bond market, like Hal's cryptic real estate venture, therefore had to draw in more and more people. The mortgage-backed securities that, in Lewis's words, "were, increasingly, the beating heart of Wall Street" in the first decade of the twenty-first century did indeed attract a larger and larger number of investors, becoming a multi-trillion-dollar market by the mid-2000s.[21]

When the housing bubble burst, as all such bubbles must, it turned out that the investment banks that had been peddling their arcane mortgage bonds to unsuspecting investors were holding enough of the toxic securities to sink every last one of them. The collapse of the mortgage bond market would have annihilated every major Wall Street firm and decimated the global financial system had the US government not stepped in and bailed out the banks. As Harvey insists, the term "national bailout" to describe this sort of financial relief is misleading: "Taxpayers are simply bailing out the banks, the capitalist class, forgiving them their debts."[22] The actions of Treasury Secretary Henry Paulson, who, in September 2008, persuaded Congress that he needed $700 billion of taxpayers' money to buy subprime mortgage assets from banks, are well known. Equally well known is the use to which he put the funds: "Once handed the money," Lewis reminds us, "Paulson abandoned his promised strategy and essentially began giving away billions of dollars to Citigroup, Morgan Stanley, Goldman Sachs, and a few others."[23] But this $700 billion bailout, known as TARP (for Troubled Asset Relief Program), which represents an average contribution of $3,447 from every US citizen between the ages of eighteen and sixty-five, is only the tip of the iceberg.[24] In addition to the cash handouts that Paulson distributed to favored banks—banks which, in turn, doled out much of the money to their high-ranking executives, as though these scoundrels deserved multi-million-dollar bonuses for their actions—he also guaranteed the remaining subprime assets that the banks were holding. The $306 billion guarantee extended to just one of those institutions (Citigroup), which the treasury secretary "presented as an undisguised gift" to the firm, represented "roughly the combined budgets of the departments of Agriculture, Education, Energy, Homeland Security, Housing and Urban Development, and Transportation."[25] This is an extraordinary reward for having run the global economy into the ground. The government that, for decades, had been arguing that it could not afford to subsidize healthcare, daycare, afterschool programs for kids, free high-quality K-12 education for everyone, adequate benefits to war veterans, or a public university system that would enable people to get a college education without accumulating mountains of debt, suddenly produced, in the blink of an eye, the equivalent of nearly 5 percent of US gross domestic product, with the promise of much more to come, in order to bail out the institutions that had swindled countless investors of their savings.[26]

The compensation that the Wall Street bankers received for their pains is especially curious given the bankers' notorious scorn for government interference in the workings of the supposedly "free" market. As Lewis writes, the investment firms, "which disdained the need for government regulation in good times, insisted on being rescued by government in bad times."[27] The relationship here takes a recognizable form in Allen's depiction of Jasmine's rapport with her sister. The flashback scenes of Ginger and Augie visiting Jasmine and Hal in New York leave little doubt that the upper-class couple wanted to have as little involvement as possible with their working-class relatives. Augie reminds his ex-wife of this dynamic in an early scene in the movie: "When she had all that money,

The Meltdown and the Bailout without the Recovery   151

she wanted nothing to do with you," he reminds her. "Now that she's broke, all of a sudden she's moving in." Midway through the film, Chili makes a similar point: "Where was she when she was loaded and you were tending bar, waiting tables?" he rhetorically asks Ginger. "Now family's family?" Even when Jasmine arrives in San Francisco, she continues to treat her sister with thinly veiled contempt. The relationship between the two sisters inflects interactions played out on a national scale between the upper classes, who regard taxes as fetters and the lower classes as tax burdens, and the working people that bailed out their high-rolling compatriots when it turned out that the gamblers had misplaced their bets.

In his award-winning book on debt, anthropologist David Graeber gives two readings of this debacle, both of which appear in refracted form in Allen's film. On a certain level, Graeber recognizes, echoing many of his peers on the left, the global financial crisis was what it appeared to be: "a scam, an incredibly sophisticated Ponzi scheme designed to collapse in the full knowledge that the perpetrators would be able to force the victims to bail them out."[28] Yet, on another level, he argues, it can also be seen as "the outcome of years of political tussles between creditors and debtors, rich and poor."[29] The latter tussles, which form the guiding thread in Graeber's fascinating book, achieved a moment of clarity in 2008, when the US government, forced to choose between bailing out creditors (the rich) and rescuing debtors (the poor), made the predictable choice and bailed out the financiers with taxpayer money.

Graeber's two interpretations of the financial crisis each correspond to a character or set of characters in *Blue Jasmine*. His first reading pinpoints the architects of the great Ponzi scheme as the culprits responsible for the financial breakdown. In the film, Hal plays this role, with Jasmine acting as an accomplice. Graeber's second interpretation shifts emphasis from the fraudulent actions of a bunch of unscrupulous financiers to a conception of the meltdown and the bailout as pivotal episodes in a class struggle of long duration. This second explanation corresponds, in the film, to tensions between the two sisters, with Hal playing a supporting role on Jasmine's side, and Augie and Chili figuring on Ginger's side. Both Graeber's analysis and Allen's film show a keener interest in the second of these two dynamics than the first, leading us to perceive the crash of 2008 (in Graeber's case) or its allegorical refraction (in Allen's) as a climactic moment in an ongoing class struggle.

When Jasmine arrives uninvited in San Francisco at the beginning of the movie to stay with the sister she swindled, she, in effect, continues this class warfare by other means. The irony is that, in bailing out her sister, Ginger unintentionally becomes an "enabler," in the pejorative sense of the term. By obligingly saving Jasmine from immediate ruin, she enables her deluded sister to continue living in her fantasy world, inadvertently setting her up for her ultimate downfall at the end of the film. Here again, the implicit parallel with the national bailout is hard to miss. When the US government diverted hundreds of billions of tax dollars to rescue the big banks and guaranteed trillions more worth of toxic assets, without demanding that any substantial changes be made to the financial system that had proven to be so self-destructive, it too became an "enabler," allowing the dream of endless capitalist accumulation to continue.

This idea, that in bailing out the banks, the US government perpetuated the fantasy that global capitalism can continue indefinitely on its current trajectory, is essentially the point that Žižek makes in his intervention at an Occupy Wall Street rally in 2011, by way of reference to the proverbial cartoon cat that has run over the edge of a cliff but remains suspended in mid-air: "We all know the classic scene from cartoons. The cat reaches a precipice but it goes on walking, ignoring the fact that there is nothing beneath this ground. Only when it looks down and notices it, it falls down. This is what we are doing here. We are telling the guys there on Wall Street, 'Hey, look down!'"[30] Countering the accusation that the Occupy protestors are "dreamers," Žižek argues that, on the contrary, "the true dreamers are those who think things can go on indefinitely the way they are."[31] Implicitly recalling his earlier remarks, from his 2009 book on the financial crisis, in which he warned that "the predominant narrative of the meltdown will be the one which, instead of awakening us from a dream, will enable us to *continue dreaming*," here, addressing his fellow protestors at Liberty Square in 2011, Žižek affirms: "We are awakening from a dream that is turning into a nightmare."[32] *Blue Jasmine* offers a poetic image of what that nightmare might look like if we do not wake up—if, aided and abetted by a sympathetic sister, for example, we *continue dreaming*. The film's blue Jasmine functions as a metaphor for what lies in store for us if we do not look down.

Conclusion

Allegories for the Present

THE EPILOGUE TO THE HISTORICAL narrative sketched in this book is well known. In 2011, restive populations in places as remote from one another as Cairo, Madrid, and New York took to the streets to protest the global status quo. Although the 2011 uprisings in the Middle East, collectively known as "the Arab Spring," did not present themselves as explicitly anti-capitalist in orientation, the other two international protest movements of 2011 did. Both the anti-austerity encampment protests in Europe, launched by the "indignados" (angry ones) in Madrid on May 15, 2011, and the Occupy Wall Street movement, begun in Lower Manhattan in September of the same year, pinpointed neoliberal capitalism as the source of gross social inequalities. The message of these demonstrators resonated around the world. By mid-October of 2011, encampment protests had occurred or were currently underway in nearly a thousand cities on six continents. These protestors were demonstrating against precisely the sorts of socioeconomic developments examined in this book.

Numerous films gave allegorical form to the spirit of revolt visible on city streets around the world in 2011. Lars von Trier's *Melancholia* (2011), David Cronenberg's *Cosmopolis* (2012), Quentin Tarantino's *Django Unchained* (2012), Neill Blomkamp's *Elysium* (2013), Bong Joon-ho's *Snowpiercer* (2013), and Sarah Gavron's *Suffragette* (2015) come to mind. These movies would constitute an allegorical "sequel" to the overarching narrative sketched in the pages of this book. Examining them would form a different study, covering the short historical sequence running, roughly, from the tumultuous events of 2011 to the Brexit vote in June 2016 and the election of Donald Trump as the forty-fifth president of the United States in November of that year.

The difference between the events marking the beginning and the end of the five-year sequence running from 2011 to 2016 is remarkable. This difference is perhaps nowhere more striking than in the United States, where the popular discontent of 2011, coming from the anti-capitalist left, was followed five years later by the election of the one of the most brazen right-wing capitalists (as well as one of the most openly racist and overtly misogynist presidents) ever to sit in the Oval Office. Close ties between industry and the US government are, of course, nothing new. They date back to the founding of the country in 1776, as Naomi Klein acknowledges in *No Is Not Enough*, her 2017 book on Trumpism. "The difference with Trump," Klein asserts, "is one of volume, and shamelessness."[1] "Up to now in US politics there's been a mask on the corporate state's White House proxies," she observes. "Now the mask is gone."[2] Although it is too early, at the time of writing, for feature films responding directly to the Trump election to have appeared in theaters, a number of recent movies, such as J. C. Chandor's *A Most Violent Year* (2014), Dan Gilroy's *Nightcrawler* (2014), and Jean-Marc Vallée's *Demolition* (2015), shed retrospective light on the Trump phenomenon. Although it would be anachronistic to qualify the latter set of films as allegories of the post-2016 present, they do function as timely allegories *for* the present.

The films examined in the present study can also be interpreted as allegories for the present. Based on Trump's first few months in office, Cuarón's dystopian vision of a society on the verge of collapse is looking eerily premonitory. Many of the crises presented in the film—including the erosion of democracy, the breakdown of social solidarity across racial and ethnic lines, the degradation of the environment, and the ongoing process of corporate downsizing—promise to enter into a more critical phase under the current administration than they did during the Bush-Cheney years of 2001–2009. Cuarón's hyperbolic vision of England in 2027 as a rigorously segregated police state in which immigrants have been declared illegal and are therefore rounded up and quarantined like animals in cages in anticipation of their expulsion from the homeland seems less implausible in the present context than it did during even the darkest moments of the "war on terror." Regarding the fate of the planet as such, the presence in the White House of a president who has claimed that global warming is "a Chinese hoax" and who, since entering office, has "[taken] aim at any and all climate protections," imbues Cuarón's vision of environmental catastrophe with a renewed sense of urgency.[3] As far as Trump's campaign promises to revive manufacturing and create jobs in the United States are concerned, Klein's analysis of the president's track record of offshoring and subcontracting, combined with his appointment of a slate of corporate executives and supply-side economists to prominent cabinet positions, offers little hope that either employment rates or labor conditions will improve under the current administration.[4]

The issues raised in *Syriana* also gain new currency following the Trump election. When, shortly after coming into office, the president signed executive orders approving construction of the controversial Keystone XL and Dakota Access oil pipelines, he signaled his willingness to use his executive power to further the interests of multinational oil and gas companies. His own investments in energy companies like Shell, Chevron, and ExxonMobil cast these actions in a self-serving light, reminiscent of those of the members of the fictional Committee for the Liberation of Iran in Gaghan's film.[5] His appointment of Rex Tillerson, CEO of ExxonMobil from 2006 to 2016, to the post of secretary of state only reinforces the suspicion that the president may be using his public office for private financial gain. By contrast, Trump's notorious speech on August 21, 2017, to a crowd gathered at the Fort Myer military base in Arlington, Virginia, in which the president stated that the US objective in Afghanistan is "killing terrorists," not "nation building," reveals the naked brutality of the current administration's foreign policy.[6] Unlike the members of both the fictional Committee for the Liberation of Iran and the empirical Committee for the Liberation of Iraq—members who strove, in both cases, to maintain at least the appearance of respect for norms of international engagement—Trump's August 21 announcement unabashedly cast US foreign policy as mass murder. If Gaghan's "cognitive map" of geopolitics is accurate, we should expect to see an escalation of international terrorist activity in the coming years in response to Trump's actions. If the scenario presented in Cuarón's film offers an indication of the events to follow, we should not be surprised to see President Trump declare a state of emergency curtailing the civil liberties of US citizens and suspending the human rights of suspected terrorists: in sum, permutations of the film narratives of *Children of Men* and *Syriana* played out in the real world of a hypothetical near-future United States.

Trump's investments in multinational pharmaceutical companies provide a thread linking the shenanigans presented in *Syriana* to those depicted in *The Constant Gardener*.[7] The reptilian Sir Bernard Pellegrin in Meirelles's film, the investor-*cum*-politician who orders the "corporate murder" of whistleblowers that threaten to publicize the diplomat's unsavory backroom dealings, comes across as a comparatively warm-blooded version of Trump. Indeed, bearing in mind the argument presented in chapter 3 of this book, if one were to imagine what a flesh-and-blood incarnation of "corporate personhood" might look like, one could do worse than the current US president. As Klein astutely remarks, Trump is "the personification of the merger of humans and corporations—a one-man megabrand."[8] Recalling that, according to Joel Bakan, the corporate "person" is a psychopath, it would be worth considering which of the attributes and behaviors that Bakan associates with pathological personalities Trump exhibits. Bakan's list includes a propensity for manipulative behavior, a lack of empathy, asocial tendencies, self-aggrandizing tendencies, a refusal to accept responsibility for one's actions, and an inability to feel remorse.

Continuing in this vein, the title character of *Inside Man*, the political and economic insider that "used his position with the Nazis to enrich himself while all around him people were being stripped of everything they owned," calls to mind both Trump's unethical business practices and his notorious connection to white supremacists and neo-Nazis.[9] In this light, the interracial coalition of bank robbers and detectives that collaborate to bring down the shady tycoon in the film combine two groups targeted by Trump supporters in the so-called "alt-right" movement: African Americans and Jews. The film is very much of its time, rooted as it is in the Bush family legacy, but it may well prove, depending on how history plays out in the next few years, to be a timely allegory for our time as well.

In sum, numerous characters encountered in this book retrospectively come across as Trump-like figures. *Syriana*'s Dean Whiting, *The Constant Gardener*'s Bernard Pellegrin, and *Inside Man*'s Arthur Case all bear a certain family resemblance to the sitting president. Included on this list would be Jordan Belfort, the eponymous "Wolf of Wall Street" who devised a cagy scheme to rip off investors and pocket their money. In particular, "Jordan Belfort's Straight Line" seminar—a hands-on workshop where attendees learn Belfort's method of wealth creation—has shades of the scandal-plagued and now defunct Trump University (also known as the Trump Wealth Institute and Trump Entrepreneur Initiative). Belfort's monologue in the mock infomercial for the "Straight Line" seminar in Scorsese's film, in which the dapper Belfort declares that "no matter who you are, no matter where you came from, you too can become financially independent in just a matter of months," reads like a reworked version of an ad for Trump University, in which Trump claims that he "can turn anyone into a successful real estate investor, including you."[10] The two men here are "phishing for phools" by promising to teach a bunch of prospective phools how to phish. The parallels continue. The liberties that Belfort takes, in the film, with women within his reach (such as groping flight attendants) visualizes for the viewer the sort of scenario that Trump described in his infamous remark, made in 2005 to

Billy Bush on the set of *Days of Our Lives*, that if you are as rich and famous as he is, "you can do anything" to women.[11] The extravagant parties that the film's Belfort organizes on the floor of Stratton Oakmont and in a Las Vegas casino recall Trump's elaborate parties for investors and financiers in his own casinos. Whereas, at Stratton Oakmont, the festivities include dwarf-tossing contests and a marching band of high school students stripped to their underwear, at Trump's casinos they include the spectacle of Donald Trump, sporting satin gym shorts and boxing gloves, punching through a paper wall to the musical accompaniment of the *Rocky* theme song.[12] At both venues, spectators are treated to the sight of the host CEO publicly shaving the head of a designated "loser" to the cheers of an enthusiastic crowd.[13] In sum, these two self-proclaimed "winners," who shamelessly gloat over their success while deriding the "losers" that they prey upon, have so much in common that if the film were released today, after the entrance of Trump into the most prominent public office in the world, spectators would undoubtedly view it as a thinly veiled allusion to the contemporary Wolf of Washington.

However, the figure that most readily calls to mind Donald Trump is *Blue Jasmine*'s Hal, an investor who made his fortune in shady real estate ventures. Hal is Jasmine's super-rich husband whose corruption leads to her ruin. By a juicy coincidence, he is played by Alec Baldwin, whose uncanny impersonation of Trump on *Saturday Night Live* retrospectively enables us to perceive the caricatured Trump in the figure of Hal. According to his detractors, Hal is "a con man and a hypocrite" "up to his ass in phony real estate and bank fraud." In his own estimation, he is a clever businessman who "[knows] how not to give half of [his] money to the government." These differing opinions of Hal anticipate the contrasting assessments of Trump. When, during the first presidential debate, for example, Hillary Clinton accused her rival, who presented himself as a savvy entrepreneur able to run the country like a successful megacorporation, of paying no federal income tax in some years, Trump's retort could easily have come out of Hal's mouth: "That makes me smart."[14] In his critics' view, Trump's business acumen lies largely in this ability to cheat the system and manipulate it to his advantage. "What Trump is definitely not is a successful, productive and innovative capitalist," Slavoj Žižek writes, for instance, in his chronicle of the events of 2016; "he excels in getting into bankruptcy and then making the taxpayers cover his debts."[15] He excels, in other words, in performing precisely the sort of operations that Hal's activities allegorize in *Blue Jasmine*.

The irony of this argument will not be lost on the reader. If films that allegorize the vicissitudes of capitalism during the short first decade of the twenty-first century also function as allegories for the post-2016 period, then some essential element of the first period must persist or repeat itself in the second. That fundamental element is, of course, global capital itself, which resurged with a vengeance following a short period of contraction and a brief heyday of anti-capitalist protest in the aftermath of the meltdown. Capitalism not only survived the financial crisis that began in 2008, it emerged from the turmoil stronger and more robust than before. The system that looked to be teetering on the verge of collapse a decade ago is now firmly back on its feet. If, as Angus Fletcher proposes, allegory is the representational mode endemic to multinational capitalism in its advanced stage, we should expect to see cinematic allegories of the type examined in this book continue to come out of Hollywood in the years to come.

Notes

Introduction

1. Alberto Toscano and Jeff Kinkle, *Cartographies of the Absolute* (Winchester, UK: Zero Books, 2015), 183.
2. Christopher Sharrett, "False Criticism: Cinema, Bourgeois Society, and the Conservative Complaint," in *Cinema and Modernity*, ed. Murray Pomerance (New Brunswick, NJ: Rutgers University Press, 2006), 140, 141.
3. Angus Fletcher, *Allegory: The Theory of a Symbolic Mode*, with a foreword by Harold Bloom and a new afterword by the author (Princeton, NJ: Princeton University Press, 2012), 2.
4. Cited in Rita Copeland and Peter T. Struck, "Introduction," in *The Cambridge Companion to Allegory*, ed. Rita Copeland and Peter T. Struck (Cambridge: Cambridge University Press, 2010), 2.
5. Ibid., 2–3.
6. David Harvey, *The Enigma of Capital and the Crises of Capitalism*, with a new afterword (Oxford: Oxford University Press, 2011).
7. Fletcher, *Allegory*, 370.
8. Ibid., 394.
9. Ibid., 396.
10. Ibid., 395.
11. Ibid., 371.
12. Ibid.
13. See Fredric Jameson, "Cognitive Mapping," in *Marxism and the Interpretation of Culture*, ed. Cary Nelson and Lawrence Grossberg (Urbana: University of Illinois Press, 1988), 347–60.
14. Fredric Jameson, *Postmodernism, or, The Cultural Logic of Late Capitalism* (Durham, NC: Duke University Press, 1991), 416.
15. Ibid., 51.
16. Toscano and Kinkle, *Cartographies*, 7.
17. Fredric Jameson, *The Political Unconscious: Narrative as a Socially Symbolic Act* (Ithaca, NY: Cornell University Press, 1981), 10.

18. Copeland and Struck, "Introduction," in *Cambridge Companion*, 2.
19. Ibid., 10.
20. The fictional world I have in mind here is the one presented in "Pierre Menard, Author of the *Quixote*." This witty and delightful piece of fiction presents itself as a commentary on a literary scholar who attempts to go beyond a mere "translation" of Miguel de Cervantes' *Don Quixote* by "re-creating" the text, word for word, in Cervantes' original Spanish. See Jorge Luis Borges, *Ficciones*, ed. and with an introduction by Anthony Kerrigan (New York: Grove Press, 1962), 45–56.
21. Jameson, *Political Unconscious*, 17, 20.
22. Robert Sklar, *Movie-Made America: A Cultural History of American Movies*, rev. and updated ed. (New York: Vintage/Random House, 1994).
23. Max Horkheimer and Theodor W. Adorno, *Dialectic of Enlightenment: Philosophical Fragments*, ed. Gunzelin Schmid Noerr, trans. Edmund Jephcott (Stanford, CA: Stanford University Press, 2002), 108–9.
24. Ibid., 97.
25. Ibid., 98.
26. Mark Crispin Miller, "Introduction," in *Seeing through Movies*, ed. Mark Crispin Miller (New York: Pantheon, 1990), 13.
27. Adam Davidson, "How Does the Film Industry Actually Make Money?" *New York Times Magazine*, June 26, 2012, http://www.nytimes.com/2012/07/01/magazine/how-does-the-film-industry-actually-make-money.html.
28. Miller, *Seeing through Movies*, 4.
29. Horkheimer and Adorno, *Dialectic*, 105.
30. Siegfried Kracauer, *From Caligari to Hitler: A Psychological History of the German Cinema*, rev. and expanded ed. (Princeton, NJ: Princeton University Press, 2004), 5–6.
31. Ibid., 8.
32. Leonardo Quaresima, "Introduction," in Kracauer, *Caligari*, xxv.
33. Francesco Casetti, *Theories of Cinema: 1945–1995*, trans. Francesca Chiostri and Elizabeth Gard Bartolini-Salimbeni with Thomas Kelso (Austin: University of Texas Press, 1999), 125. Cited in Quaresima, "Introduction," in Kracauer, *Caligari*, xxviii.
34. Fredric Jameson, *Signatures of the Visible* (New York: Routledge, 1992), 38.
35. Phillip E. Wegner, *Life between Two Deaths, 1989–2001: U.S. Culture in the Long Nineties* (Durham, NC: Duke University Press, 2009).
36. Mark Fisher, *Capitalist Realism: Is There No Alternative?* (Winchester, UK: Zero Books, 2009).
37. The characterization of Žižek as a "one-person culture mulcher" appears on the back cover of Žižek's *Looking Awry: An Introduction to Jacques Lacan through Popular Culture* (Cambridge, MA: MIT Press, 1992), which attributes the phrase to Edward Ball of the *Voice Literary Supplement*.
38. Kirk Boyle and Daniel Mrozowski, eds., *The Great Recession in Fiction, Film, and Television: Twenty-First Century Bust Culture* (Lanham, MD: Rowman & Littlefield, 2013).

39. Clint Burnham, *Fredric Jameson and "The Wolf of Wall Street"* (London: Bloomsbury, 2016); Todd McGowan, *Spike Lee* (Urbana: University of Illinois Press, 2014); David Sterritt, *Spike Lee's America* (Cambridge: Polity, 2013).

40. Todd McGowan, "The Temporality of the Real: The Path to Politics in *The Constant Gardener*," *Film-Philosophy* 11, no. 3 (2007): 59–86; McGowan, *Out of Time: Desire in Atemporal Cinema* (Minneapolis: University of Minnesota Press, 2011), 111–34.

41. Fredric Jameson, "Future City," *New Left Review* 21 (May–June 2003), 76.

42. Chris Harman, *Zombie Capitalism: Global Crisis and the Relevance of Marx* (Chicago: Haymarket Books, 2010), 11.

43. Karl Marx, *Capital*, vol. 1, trans. Ben Fowkes (London: Penguin, 1976), 342.

44. Walter Benjamin, *The Origin of German Tragic Drama*, trans. John Osborne (London: Verso, 1998), 175.

Chapter 1

1. Cited in Susan Buck-Morss, *The Dialectics of Seeing: Walter Benjamin and the Arcades Project* (Cambridge, MA: MIT Press, 1991), 161. John Osborne's translation of this passage reads: "[The importance of] the allegorical way of seeing . . . resides solely in the stations of its decline." Benjamin, *Origin*, 166.

2. Benjamin, *Origin*, 223–24.
3. Buck-Morss, *Dialectics*, 168.
4. Benjamin, *Origin*, 178.
5. Ibid., 166.
6. Ibid., 175.
7. "The Siege of Seattle," *Newsweek*, December 12, 1999, http://www.newsweek.com/siege-seattle-162706.
8. Shawn Reese, "Defining Homeland Security: Analysis and Congressional Considerations" (report prepared for the Congressional Research Service, January 8, 2013). Cited in "Homeland Security," *Wikipedia*, https://en.wikipedia.org/wiki/Homeland_security.
9. Ibid.
10. Giorgio Agamben, *State of Exception*, trans. Kevin Attell (Chicago: University of Chicago Press, 2005), 3.
11. Ibid.
12. Ibid.
13. Ibid., 4.
14. Giorgio Agamben, *Homo Sacer: Sovereign Power and Bare Life*, trans. Daniel Heller-Roazen (Stanford, CA: Stanford University Press, 1998), 52–54.
15. Ibid., 47–48.
16. Slavoj Žižek, *Iraq: The Borrowed Kettle* (London: Verso, 2005), 55.
17. Judith Butler, *Precarious Life: The Powers of Mourning and Violence* (London: Verso, 2004), 77.

18. I thank Marjana Bilandzic for her translation of the woman's Serbo-Croatian lines.

19. Slavoj Žižek, *Welcome to the Desert of the Real: Five Essays on September 11 and Related Dates* (London: Verso, 2002), 100.

20. Sara Ahmed, *The Promise of Happiness* (Durham, NC: Duke University Press, 2010), 185.

21. Ibid., 170.

22. Ibid.

23. David Harvey, *Seventeen Contradictions and the End of Capitalism* (Oxford: Oxford University Press, 2014), 108.

24. Ibid.

25. Ibid., 110.

26. "The Possibility of Hope," directed by Alfonso Cuarón, DVD extra in *Children of Men*, directed by Alfonso Cuarón (Universal, 2007). Transcription modified to correct minor grammatical mistakes.

27. Terry Gilliam, "Audio commentary," *Brazil*, directed by Terry Gilliam, disc 1 (New York: Criterion, 1999), DVD, 3 discs.

28. "Possibility of Hope."

29. Zahid R. Chaudhary, "Humanity Adrift: Race, Materiality, and Allegory in Alfonso Cuarón's *Children of Men*," *Camera Obscura* 24, no. 3 (2009): 82.

30. According to Cuarón, "Caine wanted to play his role as an older John Lennon." Alfonso Cuarón, interview by Richard von Busack, *Metroactive*, April 22, 2007, http://www.metroactive.com/metro/01.10.07/alfonso-cuaron-0702.html.

31. The fact that the only pop icon directly linked to Julian, Theo, and Dylan is the Jamaican-born Bob Marley, whose image appears in the family shrine, lends credence to the idea that Dylan's parents appreciate music originating from regions outside of the British Isles.

32. Fredric Jameson, *The Cultural Turn: Selected Writings on the Postmodern, 1983–1998* (London: Verso, 2009), 74.

33. Ibid., 75.

34. Slavoj Žižek, "Comments on *Children of Men*," DVD extra in *Children of Men*, directed by Alfonso Cuarón (Universal, 2007).

35. See, for example, Chaudhary's fine analysis of the way the background becomes the foreground in this scene in "Humanity Adrift," 82–83.

36. Slavoj Žižek, *Did Somebody Say Totalitarianism?* (London: Verso, 2001), 78.

37. Giorgio Agamben, *Remnants of Auschwitz*, trans. Daniel Heller-Roazen (Brooklyn: Zone Books, 1999), 68.

38. Agamben, *State of Exception*, 16–22.

39. Agamben, *Homo Sacer*, 168; Agamben, *Remnants*, 49.

40. Agamben, *State of Exception*, 2.

41. Carl Schmitt, *Political Theology: Four Chapters on the Concept of Sovereignty*, trans. George Schwab (Chicago: University of Chicago Press, 2005), 5.

42. Benjamin, *Origin*, 65.

43. Walter Benjamin, *Selected Writings*, vol. 4, ed. Howard Eiland and Michael W. Jennings (Cambridge, MA: Harvard University Press, 2006), 392.

44. Agamben, *State of Exception*, 58.
45. Ibid.
46. Ibid.
47. Chaudhary, "Humanity Adrift," 88–89.
48. Ibid., 89.
49. Ahmed, *Promise*, 187.
50. Ibid.
51. Chaudhary, "Humanity Adrift," 91.
52. Ibid., 87.
53. Buck-Morss, *Dialectics*, 174.
54. Benjamin, *Origin*, 232. Italics in original. See Buck-Morss, *Dialectics*, 174–75.
55. Buck-Morss, *Dialectics*, 175.
56. Ibid.
57. For a particularly rich (and decidedly critical) interpretation of *Children* as a Christian allegory, see Chaudhary, "Humanity Adrift," 92 and elsewhere.
58. Žižek, "Comments on *Children of Men*."
59. Ahmed, *Promise*, 197.
60. Ibid.
61. Kirk Boyle, "*Children of Men* and *I Am Legend*: The Disaster-Capitalism Complex Hits Hollywood," *Jump Cut* 51 (Spring 2009), http://www.ejumpcut.org/archive/jc51.2009/ChildrenMenLegend/index.html.

Chapter 2

1. Douglas Kellner, *Cinema Wars: Hollywood Film and Politics in the Bush-Cheney Era* (Malden, MA: Wiley-Blackwell, 2010), 169.
2. Jameson, *Postmodernism*, 409.
3. Toscano and Kinkle, *Cartographies*, 10.
4. "*Syriana* Production Notes," *Cincinnati World Cinema*, http://www.cincyworldcinema.org/z_syriana2.php, accessed September 9, 2015. These production notes state that "a crew of approximately 200 and a cast of more than 100 covered three continents over a period of five months to complete filming of *Syriana*," but elsewhere they name filming locations on four continents. Casablanca, Morocco (Africa), stands in for Tehran, Beirut, and an unnamed country in the Persian Gulf; Dubai, United Arab Emirates (Asia), serves as a metropolis in the anonymous Persian Gulf state; scenes set in Geneva, Switzerland (Europe), are filmed on location, as are the scenes set in a variety of locations in the United States (North America). The six languages we hear in the film are English, Arabic, Urdu, Farsi, Mandarin, and French.
5. Daniel Fisher, "ExxonMobil's Kazakhstan Quagmire," *Forbes*, April 23, 2003, http://www.forbes.com/2003/04/23/cz_df_0423xom.html.
6. Robert Baer, *See No Evil: The True Story of a Ground Soldier in the CIA's War on Terrorism* (New York: Three Rivers Press, 2002), 241.
7. Stephen Gaghan, interview by Kamla Bhatt, *The Kamla Show*, July 31, 2014, https://www.youtube.com/watch?v=2xoDC3LF72s.

8. "Committee for the Liberation of Iraq," *Right Web: Tracking Militarists' Efforts to Influence U.S. Foreign Policy. Institute for Policy Studies,* http://rightweb.irc-online.org/profile/Committee_for_the_Liberation_of_Iraq, accessed September 9, 2015.

9. Ibid.

10. Harvey, *New Imperialism,* 18–19.

11. Ibid., 19.

12. Ibid.

13. Ibid.

14. Ibid.

15. Klein, *Shock Doctrine,* 394.

16. Ibid.

17. See ibid., 437–39.

18. Ibid., 394–95.

19. Ibid., 395.

20. Robert Baer, interview by Robert Siegel, "All Things Considered," *National Public Radio,* December 6, 2005, http://www.npr.org/templates/story/story.php?storyId=5041385.

21. Ibid.

22. Stephen Gaghan, interview by Emanuel Levy, *Cinema 24/7,* November 11, 2005, http://emanuellevy.com/interviews/syriana-with-writer-director-gaghan-2/.

23. Tom Conley, *Cartographic Cinema* (Minneapolis: University of Minnesota Press, 2007), 5.

24. Ibid., 2.

25. Ibid., 6.

26. Ibid., 20.

27. Andrew Sarris, review of *Syriana,* directed by Stephen Gaghan, *New York Observer,* December 4, 2005, http://observer.com/2005/12/soderbergh-clooney-and-co-make-mideast-mess-too-simple-2/.

28. Aristotle, *Poetics,* trans. H. S. Butcher (London: Macmillan, 1902), 35/1451 a.

29. Ibid., 35/1451 b.

30. Charles Krauthammer, review of *Syriana,* directed by Stephen Gaghan, *Washington Post,* March 3, 2006, http://www.washingtonpost.com/wp-dyn/content/article/2006/03/02/AR2006030201209.html.

Chapter 3

1. John le Carré, *The Constant Gardener* (Toronto: Penguin Canada, 2001), 129.

2. "John le Carré: From the Page to the Screen." *The Constant Gardener,* directed by Fernando Meirelles (Montreal: Alliance, 2010), DVD.

3. As this narrative strategy suggests, the film interpolates a Western viewer. Numerous scholars have criticized the movie on these or related grounds, arguing that it marginalizes the African characters—and by implication, African viewers—in relation to the white ones. While these criticisms raise important

issues about cultural hegemony in a global context, they tell us little about this particular film. For, as the most original and thought-provoking of the articles that criticize the film's Anglo-European perspective concludes following a lengthy analysis of the way the film encodes African and European archetypes, "what this film is really about (and has been about all along) is the white love story and not Africa at all." Diana Adesola Mafe, "(Mis)Imagining Africa in the New Millennium: *The Constant Gardener* and *Blood Diamond*," *Camera Obscura* 25, no. 3 (2011): 82. I would push the argument even further and contend that Africa functions as a metaphor in much the same way that the pharmaceutical industry does. The film is not "about" Kenya any more than it is "about" the pharmaceutical industry per se. What the film is about, in my view—or, in any case, what makes it timely and compelling—is the ways that multinationals, working in collusion with Western governments, exploit the developing world with impunity. In the terms of one of the film's key metaphors, it is about how global corporations and the governments that do their bidding "get away with murder."

4. Joel Bakan, *The Corporation: The Pathological Pursuit of Profit and Power* (London: Constable, 2005), 2.

5. McGowan, *Out of Time*, 114–15.

6. Ibid., 114–17.

7. Ibid., 117.

8. Ibid., 117–18.

9. "Save Our Bees," *National Resources Defense Council*, http://www.nrdc.org/wildlife/animals/bees.asp, accessed October 4, 2015.

10. Bryan Walsh, "The Plight of the Honeybee," *Time*, August 19, 2013, http://time.com/559/the-plight-of-the-honeybee/.

11. McGowan, *Out of Time*, 125.

12. "The 14 Worst Corporate Evildoers," *International Labor Rights Forum*, http://www.laborrights.org/in-the-news/14-worst-corporate-evildoers, accessed October 4, 2015; Grace Kiser, "The 12 Least Ethical Companies in the World," *Huffington Post*, March 30, 2010, http://www.huffingtonpost.com/2010/01/28/the-least-ethical-compani_n_440073.html; Michelle Schoffro Cook, "Monsanto Wins Worst Company of 2011 Award," *Care2*, February 1, 2012, http://www.care2.com/greenliving/monsanto-wins-worst-company-of-2011-award.html; Connor Adam Sheets, "Monsanto Named 2013's 'Most Evil Corporation' in New Poll," *International Business Times*, June 10, 2013, http://www.ibtimes.com/monsanto-named-2013s-most-evil-corporation-new-poll-1300217.

13. "Infant Formula: Hawking Disaster in the Third World," *Multinational Monitor* 8, no. 4 (April 1987), http://multinationalmonitor.org/hyper/issues/1987/04/formula.html.

14. Le Carré, *Constant Gardener*, 104.

15. Ibid., 155.

16. Marcia Angell, "The Body Hunters," *New York Review of Books*, October 6, 2005, http://www.nybooks.com/articles/archives/2005/oct/06/the-body-hunters/.

17. Ibid.

18. Ibid.

19. Ibid.

20. Bakan, *Corporation*, 1–2.
21. Ibid., 35.
22. Ibid., 37.
23. Ibid., 57.
24. Angell, "Body Hunters."
25. The novel describes a substantially similar process in relation to the theft of Tessa's computer, but it does not name the procedure. See le Carré, *Constant Gardener*, 312.
26. Angell, "Body Hunters."
27. McGowan, *Out of Time*, 131.
28. Le Carré, *Constant Gardener*, 474.
29. Angell, "Body Hunters."
30. Le Carré, *Constant Gardener*, 474.
31. McGowan, "Temporality of the Real," 59–68. In the revised version of the essay, McGowan renders Lacan's *pas-toute* as "incompletion" (*Out of Time*, 119–33). I cite here the original version of McGowan's piece, which uses the more technical terms "not-all" and "not-whole." For the theory of sexual difference that McGowan brings into play here, see Jacques Lacan, *On Feminine Sexuality, the Limits of Love and Knowledge: The Seminar of Jacques Lacan, Book XX, Encore*, ed. Jacques-Alain Miller, trans. and notes by Bruce Fink (New York: Norton, 1998), 49–89.
32. McGowan, "Temporality of the Real," 60.
33. Ibid., 68.

Chapter 4

1. David Edelstein, "Explosive Action," *New York*, March 27, 2006, 74.
2. Peter Rainer, review of *Inside Man*, directed by Spike Lee, *Christian Science Monitor*, March 24, 2006, http://www.csmonitor.com/2006/0324/p11s03-almo.html.
3. Kevin Maher, review of *Inside Man*, directed by Spike Lee, *Sight & Sound* 16, no. 5 (May 2006): 57.
4. David Walsh, review of *Inside Man*, directed by Spike Lee, *World Socialist Web Site*, https://www.wsws.org/en/articles/2006/04/insi-a12.html, accessed November 11, 2015.
5. Ali Jaafar, review of *Inside Man*, directed by Spike Lee, *Sight & Sound* 16, no. 5 (May 2006): 5.
6. Hamilton Carroll, "September 11 as Heist," *Journal of American Studies* 45, no. 4 (2011): 835–51; Lori Harrison-Kahan, "*Inside Man*: Spike Lee and Post-9/11 Entertainment," *Cinema Journal* 50, no. 1 (Fall 2010): 39–58.
7. Macheath aka Mack the Knife's original line is: "What is a picklock to a bank share? What is the burgling of a bank to the founding of a bank?" Bertolt Brecht, *The Threepenny Opera*, trans. Desmond Vesey (New York: Grove Press, 1949), 92, act 3, scene 3.
8. Both David Gerstner and David Sterritt make minor errors regarding the diamonds, which lead them to simplify or misconstrue Russell's motives. Sterritt states: "The items in the safe-deposit box are indeed priceless, but only

to Case." *Spike Lee's America* (Cambridge: Polity, 2013), 181. Although Case says almost these exact words to White, Russell makes clear toward the end of the movie that the diamonds in the safe deposit box have value to him. We realize that White has intuited Russell's interest in the stones when she tells Case, near the end of the film, "There had to have been something in that box that was worth more to him than your envelope. You don't have to tell me. There's only one thing it could be anyway: diamonds." For his part, Gerstner writes: "Before they depart, Dalton tells his crew that he has only the Nazi-Case documents but not the diamonds. After all the spectacle had nothing to do with profit and everything to do with principle." "De Profondis: A Love Letter from the Inside Man," in *The Spike Lee Reader*, ed. Paula J. Massood (Philadelphia: Temple University Press, 2008), 249. Just to clarify, it is the ring that Russell leaves behind, not the diamonds. In addition to White's remarks to Case, cited above, three moments in the film suggest that Russell takes the diamonds: (1) Frazier does not find them in the safety deposit box; (2) the fact that Russell drops one of the diamonds into Frazier's pocket on the way out of the bank suggests that he has them on his person; and (3) Russell's closing monologue clarifies that he made a profit from his venture even though he did not take any cash from the bank: "I'm no martyr. I did it for the money. But it's not worth much if you can't face yourself in the mirror." Although the narrative would be a neater and cleaner moral tale if, as Gerstner proposes, "the spectacle had nothing to do with profit and everything to do with principle," Russell's actual motivations make the film messier and more complex. For a sample of the theories that fans have put forward to explain the movie's plot twists, see the exchanges on the Metafilter chat room (accessed November 11, 2015) at: http://ask.metafilter.com/35101/Held-me-understand-the-twist-of-Inside-Man.

 9. Sterritt, *Spike Lee's America*, 180–81.
 10. Carroll, "September 11 as Heist," 846.
 11. Ibid.
 12. One of the rare critics to trace Lee's "double dolly" shot to Demy is Murray Pomerance, in the context of an analysis of Michael Lehmann's use of the technique in *40 Days and 40 Nights* (2002). Murray Pomerance, *The Eyes Have It: Cinema and the Reality Effect* (New Brunswick, NJ: Rutgers University Press, 2013), 228n4.
 13. Sterritt, *Spike Lee's America*, 180.
 14. Gerstner, "De Profondis," 249.
 15. "Inside," *Reverso*, http://dictionary.reverso.net/english-definition/inside.
 16. I focus here mostly on the mise-en-scène in the dolly shot of Case at his desk. For a compelling interpretation of how Lee's signature dolly shots work in general, intellectually as well as technically and aesthetically, see McGowan, *Spike Lee*, 41–46.
 17. Ibid., 44.
 18. Žižek, *Violence*, 21–22.
 19. David Harvey, *A Brief History of Neoliberalism* (Oxford: Oxford University Press, 2005), 97–98.
 20. Žižek, *Violence*, 20.
 21. Ibid., 22.

22. It could also be that, like Donald Sterling, the former owner of the NBA's Los Angeles Clippers, he donates to causes such as the NAACP in order to inoculate himself from possible charges of racism in the future and thereby acquire defenders in advance. I thank Eric Schramm for sharing this observation.

23. Bakan, *Corporation*, 87.

24. Edwin Black interview in *The Corporation*, directed by Mark Archabar and Jennifer Abbot, written by Joel Bakan et al., disc 1 (Montreal: Mongrel Media, 2004), DVD, 2 discs.

25. Bakan, *Corporation*, 88.

26. Ben Aris and Duncan Campbell, "How Bush's Grandfather Helped Hitler's Rise to Power," *The Guardian*, September 25, 2004, http://www.theguardian.com/world/2004/sep/25/usa.secondworldwar.

27. Ibid.

28. Ibid.

29. Ibid.

30. Ibid.

31. "Prescott Bush," *Wikipedia*, https://en.wikipedia.org/wiki/Prescott_Bush.

32. Marx, *Capital*, vol. 1, 873.

33. David Harvey, *A Companion to Marx's "Capital"* (London: Verso, 2010), 291.

34. Marx, *Capital*, vol. 1, 873–74.

35. Ibid., 874.

36. Ibid., 875.

37. Hannah Arendt, *Imperialism* (New York: Harcourt Brace Jovanovich, 1968), 22; Harvey, *Companion to Marx's "Capital,"* 304–13; Harvey, *New Imperialism*, 137–82; Rosa Luxemburg, *The Accumulation of Capital*, trans. Agnes Schwarzchild (London: Routledge, 2003), 432.

38. Harvey, *New Imperialism*, 145.

39. Ibid., 144.

40. Harvey, *Brief History*, 160–64; Harvey, *Companion to Marx's "Capital,"* 307–11; Harvey, *Enigma*, 244–47; Harvey, *New Imperialism*, 145–52.

41. Harvey, *Companion to Marx's "Capital,"* 309.

42. Harvey, *Brief History*, 161.

43. Ibid., 33.

44. Jameson, *Cultural Turn*, 142.

45. Ibid., 153.

46. Ibid., 142, 154.

47. Wendy Brown, *Undoing the Demos: Neoliberalism's Stealth Revolution* (Cambridge, MA: MIT Press, 2015), 17. See Harvey, *Brief History*, for a concise synthesis of his thoughts on neoliberalism.

48. Gérard Duménil and Dominique Lévy, *Capital Resurgent: Roots of the Neoliberal Revolution*, trans. Derek Jeffers (Cambridge, MA: Harvard University Press, 2004), 1–2.

49. See, for example, figure 1.1 in Thomas Piketty, *Capital in the Twenty-First Century*, trans. Arthur Goldhammer (Cambridge, MA: Harvard University Press, 2014), 24. This figure graphs income inequality in the United States

between 1910 and 2010. Other data produced in Piketty's book, some reaching as far back as the eighteenth century, show similar trends in other countries.

50. Harvey, *Brief History*, 11.
51. See figure 9.5 in Piketty, *Capital in the Twenty-First Century*, 319.
52. Harvey, *Brief History*, 48.
53. Ibid., 23.
54. Ibid., 25–26.
55. Arrighi studies regimes of *accumulation* rather than regimes of *production*, which explains his inclusion of hegemonic regimes, such as Florence, Venice, and Genoa, that predate the capitalist mode of production.
56. Giovanni Arrighi, *The Long Twentieth Century: Money, Power and the Origins of Our Times*, new and updated ed. (London: Verso, 2010), 220.
57. See graph in Harvey, *Enigma*, 22.
58. Arrighi, *Long Twentieth Century*, 221.
59. Ibid., 384.
60. Susan Buck-Morss, "A Commonist Ethics," in *The Idea of Communism 2*, ed. Slavoj Žižek (London: Verso, 2013), 72.
61. For fascinating insight into cinematographer Matthew Libatique's work on the film as well as Lee's directing style, see John Calhoun, "Cop vs. Robber," *American Cinematographer*, April 2006, http://www.theasc.com/ac_magazine/April 2006/InsideMan/page1.php. See also the illuminating director's commentary included as a bonus feature on *Inside Man*, directed by Spike Lee (Universal City, CA: Universal, 2006), DVD.
62. Craig Garcia, "Should You Buy When There Is Blood in the Streets?" Streetdirectory.com, http://www.streetdirectory.com/travel_guide/196604/property_tips/should_you_buy_when_there_is_blood_in_the_streets.html, accessed October 9, 2015.
63. Among the innumerable articles available on the internet urging investors to follow the Baron de Rothschild's advice, see, for example, Daniel Myers, "When There's Blood in the Streets," *Forbes*, February 23, 2009, http://www.forbes.com/2009/02/23/contrarian-markets-boeing-personal-finance_investopedia.html; Barry Popik, "Rothschild Moment (Buy When There's Blood in the Streets)," New York City Banking/Finance/Insurance, June 28, 2013.

Chapter 5

1. Joseph E. Stiglitz, *Freefall: America, Free Markets, and the Sinking of the World Economy* (New York: Norton, 2010), 1.
2. Mark Hayward, "Settling Accounts: On the Subject of Economic Confessions," *Topia* 30–31 (Fall 2013–Spring 2014): 168.
3. The film does not give us a shot of the speedometer, so we do not actually know Jordan's speed as he whizzes down the highway. I get the 200 mph rate from the prologue to *Catching the Wolf of Wall Street*, the sequel to Belfort's first memoire, where the narrator writes: "We were careening down the fast lane, at 200 miles per hour, with one fingertip on the steering wheel, never signaling, and never looking back." Jordan Belfort, *Catching the Wolf of Wall*

Street: More Incredible True Stories of Fortunes, Schemes, Parties, and Prison (New York: Bantam, 2011), 2.

4. David Harvey, *The Limits to Capital*, new and fully updated ed. (London: Verso, 2007), 95.

5. Burnham, *Fredric Jameson and "The Wolf,"* 188–89.

6. The 1992 Dreyfus ad, featuring an encounter between a bull and a lion at the foot of a statue across from the New York Stock Exchange, ends with the roaring lion morphing into a logo. The Dreyfus commercial lasts virtually the exact same length of time as the fake Stratton ad, and concludes with a tagline very similar to the one in the film: "In the jungle, among money funds, there is only one king." The Dreyfus ad is available at https://www.youtube.com/watch?v=2xO5W7b0aoU, accessed February 3, 2016.

7. For an intriguing alternate reading of this infomercial, which situates it in relation to archival TV commercials that Scorsese incorporates into the movie, see Burnham, *Fredric Jameson and "The Wolf,"* 187–88.

8. George A. Akerlof and Robert J. Schiller, *Phishing for Phools: The Economics of Manipulation and Deception* (Princeton, NJ: Princeton University Press, 2015).

9. Most of the mechanics of Belfort's pump-and-dump scheme can be gleaned from the film. I fill in the gaps here with details provided in Belfort's two memoirs, *The Wolf of Wall Street* (New York: Bantam, 2007) and *Catching the Wolf of Wall Street*.

10. Andrew DeYoung, "*The Wolf of Wall Street* Isn't about Wall Street," *The Stake*, January 7, 2014, http://thestake.org/2014/01/07/the-wolf-of-wall-street-isnt-about-wall-street/.

11. Ronald L. Rubin, "How the 'Wolf of Wall Street' Really Did It," *Wall Street Journal*, January 3, 2014, http://www.wsj.com/articles/SB10001424052702 3034530045792904507079 20302.

12. Katie Allen, "*The Wolf of Wall Street*: 'Not Sure If View of Bankers Can Sink Any Lower,' " *The Guardian*, January 15, 2014, http://www.theguardian.com/business/2014/jan/15/wolf-of-wall-street-bankers.

13. David Slocum, "Here's What *The Wolf of Wall Street* Teaches Us about Corporate Storytelling," *Forbes*, April 9, 2014, http://www.forbes.com/sites/berlinschoolofcreativeleadership/2014/04/09/heres-what-the-wolf-of-wall-street-teaches-us-about-corporate-story-telling/#2715e4857a0b55a74cbf74d7.

14. Joe Nocera, "Sex and Drugs and I.P.O.'s," *New York Times*, December 22, 2013, http://www.nytimes.com/2013/12/22/movies/martin-scorseses-approach-in-the-wolf-of-wall-street.html?_r=0.

15. Belfort, *Catching the Wolf*, 22.

16. Ibid.

17. Allen, "View of Bankers."

18. Nocera, "Sex and Drugs and I.P.O.'s."

19. Ibid.

20. Rebecca Colesworthy, "Capital's Abstractions," *Textual Practice* 28, no. 7 (2014): 1171.

21. Ibid.

22. Toscano and Kinkle, *Cartographies*, 44.

23. Karl Marx, *Capital*, vol. 3, trans. David Fernbach (London: Penguin, 1981), 597.

24. Ibid., 608.

25. Ibid.

26. Ibid.

27. Ibid.

28. Michael Goodwin, *Economix: How Our Economy Works (and Doesn't Work) in Words and Pictures*, illustrated by Dan E. Burr (New York: Abrams, 2012), 211.

29. Ibid.

30. Ibid.

31. David Harvey, *A Companion to Marx's "Capital," Volume 2* (London: Verso, 2013), 254.

32. Ibid., 254–55.

33. Ibid., 254.

34. Michael Lewis, *The Big Short: Inside the Doomsday Machine*, with a new afterword (New York: Norton, 2011), 73. Adam McKay's 2015 cinematic adaptation of Lewis's book presents this recycling of low-grade debt into highly rated tranches of a new CDO by way of a comical analogy with fish stew. The Wall Street firms, stuck with unsold bonds, were like a chef stuck with unsold fish. "So what am I going to do?" celebrity chef Anthony Bourdain asks rhetorically. "Throw all this unsold fish in the garbage and take the loss? No way. Whatever crappy levels of the bond I don't sell, I throw into the seafood stew. See, it's not old fish; it's a whole new thing!"

35. Lewis, *Big Short*, 73.

36. Ibid.

37. Cited in ibid., 140.

38. Cited in ibid., 129.

39. Nocera, "Sex and Drugs and I.P.O.'s."

40. Ibid.

41. Lewis, *Big Short*, 77.

42. The phrase, coined by Matt Taibbi in 2010, was later taken up by protestors in the Occupy Wall Street movement in 2011. See Matt Taibbi, "The Great American Bubble Machine," *Rolling Stone*, April 5, 2010, http://www.rollingstone.com/politics/news/the-great-american-bubble-machine-20100405; Kevin Roose, "The Long Life of the Vampire Squid," *New York Times*, December 13, 2011, http://dealbook.nytimes.com/2011/12/13/the-long-life-of-the-vampire-squid-metaphor/?_r=0.

43. Marx, *Capital*, vol. 1, 342.

44. Ibid., vol. 3, 571. I owe this set of associations to Toscano and Kinkle, who, in their fascinating reading of Michael Wadleigh's *Wolfen* (1981), link the "great vampire squid" of Goldman Sachs to both Marx's famous vampire reference in volume 1 of *Capital* and his kindred remarks on werewolves, also in volume 1. See Toscano and Kinkle, *Cartographies*, 130–31. For my purposes here,

Marx's evocation of the "stock-exchange wolves" in volume 3 is more pertinent than the image of the industrialist as werewolf in volume 1.

Chapter 6

1. David Graeber, *Debt: The First 5,000 Years*, updated and expanded ed. (Brooklyn: Melville House, 2014), 17.

2. Jacques Lacan, *Écrits: The First Complete Edition in English*, trans. Bruce Fink (New York: Norton, 2006), 139. Žižek, who frequently references this passage, translates Lacan's dictum in the form: "A madman is not only a beggar who thinks he is a king, but also a king who thinks he is a king." See for example Žižek, *The Plague of Fantasies* (London: Verso, 1997), 142.

3. Martha C. Nussbaum, *Not for Profit: Why Democracy Needs the Humanities* (Princeton, NJ: Princeton University Press, 2010), 2, 7.

4. Brown, *Undoing the Demos*, 188.

5. Ibid., 31.

6. Arlene Diane Landau, review of *Blue Jasmine*, directed by Woody Allen, *Psychological Perspectives* 57, no. 3 (2014): 346.

7. Brown, *Undoing the Demos*, 31.

8. Immanuel Kant, *Grounding for the Metaphysics of Morals*, trans. James W. Ellington (Indianapolis: Hackett, 1993), 30.

9. Adam Smith, *An Inquiry into the Nature and Causes of the Wealth of Nations* (Indianapolis: Liberty Classics, 1976), 25–30, Book 2, chapter 2.

10. For a detailed description of Jasmine's wardrobe, complete with illustrations, see Deborah L. Jacobs, "An Insider's Guide to Cate Blanchett's Designer Outfits in *Blue Jasmine*," *Forbes*, August 29, 2013, http://www.forbes.com/sites/deborahljacobs/2013/08/29/an-insiders-guide-to-cate-blanchetts-designer-outfits-in-blue-jasmine/#311a422d139e.

11. Lewis, *Big Short*, 256–57.

12. Stephen Gandel, "Wall Street's Latest Downfall: Madoff Charged with Fraud," *Time*, December 12, 2008. Cited in Slavoj Žižek, *First as Tragedy, Then as Farce* (London: Verso, 2009), 35.

13. Verna A. Foster, "White Woods and *Blue Jasmine*: Woody Allen Rewrites *A Streetcar Named Desire*," *Literature Film Quarterly* 43, no. 3 (2015): 195–96.

14. Žižek, *First as Tragedy*, 36.

15. Ibid.

16. Gandel, "Wall Street's Latest Downfall." Cited in ibid., 35.

17. Žižek, *First as Tragedy*, 36.

18. Ibid.

19. Harvey, *Enigma*, 22. See also: Paul Krugman, *The Return of Depression Economics and the Crisis of 2008*, with a new epilogue (New York: Norton, 2009), 147.

20. Lewis, *Big Short*, 14–15.

21. Harvey, *Enigma*, 21; Lewis, *Big Short*, 123, 225.

22. Harvey, *Enigma*, 30.

23. Lewis, *Big Short*, 260.

24. The $3,447 figure is based on a population of 203,085,087 US citizens between the ages of eighteen and sixty-five, which is the United States Census Bureau's estimate for 2008. See United States Census Bureau, Population Estimates, Vintage 2008: National Tables, http://www.census.gov/popest/data/historical/2000s/vintage_2008/.

25. Lewis, *Big Short*, 261.

26. Based on World Bank estimates, US gross domestic product in 2008 was $14.89 trillion, making the $700 billion TARP payment the equivalent of 4.76% of GDP. Statistics available on the World Bank web site at http://data.worldbank.org/indicator/NY.GDP.MKTP.CD/countries/US?display=graph.

27. Lewis, *Big Short*, 210.

28. Graeber, *Debt*, 373.

29. Ibid.

30. Slavoj Žižek, "We Are the Awakening," Occupy Wall Street talk at Liberty Square, October 10, 2011, https://vimeo.com/30367180. Transcript available at http://www.imposemagazine.com/bytes/slavoj-zizek-at-occupy-wall-street-transcript.

31. Ibid.

32. Ibid., Žižek, *First as Tragedy*, 19–20.

Conclusion

1. Naomi Klein, *No Is Not Enough: Resisting the New Shock Politics and Winning the World We Need* (Toronto: Knopf Canada, 2017), 149.

2. Ibid., 4.

3. Ibid., 77.

4. See ibid., 103–7.

5. See Jennifer Wang, "Trump's Stock Portfolio: Big Oil, Big Banks and More Foreign Connections," *Forbes*, November 29, 2016, https://www.forbes.com/sites/jenniferwang/2016/11/29/trumps-stock-portfolio-big-oil-big-banks-and-more-foreign-connections/#6cb4adc0464e.

6. See: "Trump Calls Terrorists Losers," *CNN Video*, August 22, 2017, http://www.cnn.com/videos/politics/2017/08/22/president-trump-afghanistan-war-plan-terrorists-predators-losers-sot-ac.cnn/video/playlists/the-war-in-afghanistan/.

7. See Wang, "Trump's Stock Portfolio."

8. Klein, *No Is Not Enough*, 10.

9. For Trump's ethically dubious business practices, see Adam Davidson, "Trump's Business of Corruption," *New Yorker*, August 21, 2017, https://www.newyorker.com/magazine/2017/08/21/trumps-business-of-corruption.

10. Cited in Klein, *No Is Not Enough*, 50.

11. See Ashley Feinberg, "Donald Trump on Getting Women: 'Grab Them by the Pussy,'" *The Concourse*, October 7, 2016, http://theconcourse.deadspin.com/donald-trump-on-getting-women-grab-them-by-the-pussy-1787545407.

12. See Klein, *No Is Not Enough*, 55.

13. See ibid., 52.
14. See Daniella Diaz, "Trump: 'I'm Smart' for Not Paying Taxes," *CNN*, September 27, 2016, http://www.cnn.com/2016/09/26/politics/donald-trump-federal-income-taxes-smart-debate/index.html.
15. Slavoj Žižek, *The Courage of Hopelessness: Chronicles of a Year of Acting Dangerously* (London: Allen Lane, 2017), 260.

Bibliography

Agamben, Giorgio. *Homo Sacer: Sovereign Power and Bare Life*. Trans. Daniel Heller-Roazen. Stanford, CA: Stanford University Press, 1998.
———. *Remnants of Auschwitz*. Trans. Daniel Heller-Roazen. Brooklyn: Zone Books, 1999.
———. *State of Exception*. Trans. Kevin Attell. Chicago: University of Chicago Press, 2005.
Ahmed, Sara. *The Promise of Happiness*. Durham, NC: Duke University Press, 2010.
Akerlof, George A., and Robert J. Schiller. *Phishing for Phools: The Economics of Manipulation and Deception*. Princeton, NJ: Princeton University Press, 2015.
Allen, Katie. "*The Wolf of Wall Street*: 'Not Sure If View of Bankers Can Sink Any Lower.'" *The Guardian*, January 15, 2014. http://www.theguardian.com/business/2014/jan/15/wolf-of-wall-street-bankers.
Angell, Marcia. "The Body Hunters." *New York Review of Books*, October 6, 2005. http://www.nybooks.com/articles/archives/2005/oct/06/the-body-hunters/.
———. *The Truth about the Drug Companies: How They Deceive Us and What To Do about It*. New York: Random House, 2005.
Arendt, Hannah. *Imperialism*. New York: Harcourt Brace Jovanovich, 1968.
Aris, Ben, and Duncan Campbell. "How Bush's Grandfather Helped Hitler's Rise to Power." *The Guardian*, September 25, 2004. http://www.theguardian.com/world/2004/sep/25/usa.secondworldwar.
Aristotle. *Poetics*. Trans. H. S. Butcher. London: Macmillan, 1902.
Arrighi, Giovanni. *The Long Twentieth Century: Money, Power and the Origins of Our Times*. New and updated ed. London: Verso, 2010.
Baer, Robert. Interview by Robert Siegel. "All Things Considered." *National Public Radio*, December 6, 2005. http://www.npr.org/templates/story/story.php?storyId=5041385.
———. *See No Evil: The True Story of a Ground Soldier in the CIA's War on Terrorism*. New York: Three Rivers Press, 2002.
Bakan, Joel. *The Corporation: The Pathological Pursuit of Profit and Power*. London: Constable, 2005.

Belfort, Jordan. *Catching the Wolf of Wall Street: More Incredible True Stories of Fortunes, Schemes, Parties, and Prison.* New York: Bantam, 2011.

———. *The Wolf of Wall Street.* New York: Bantam, 2007.

Benjamin, Walter. *The Origin of German Tragic Drama.* Trans. John Osborne. London: Verso, 1998.

———. *Selected Writings.* Volume 4. Ed. Howard Eiland and Michael W. Jennings. Cambridge, MA: Harvard University Press, 2006.

Blue Jasmine. Directed by Woody Allen. 2013. Culver City, CA: Sony, 2014. DVD.

Borges, Jorge Luis. *Ficciones.* Ed. and with an introduction by Anthony Kerrigan. New York: Grove Press, 1962.

Boyle, Kirk. "*Children of Men* and *I Am Legend*: The Disaster-Capitalism Complex Hits Hollywood." *Jump Cut* 51 (Spring 2009). http://www.ejumpcut.org/archive/jc51.2009/ChildrenMenLegend/index.html.

Boyle, Kirk, and Daniel Mrozowski, eds. *The Great Recession in Fiction, Film, and Television: Twenty-First Century Bust Culture.* Lanham, MD: Rowman & Littlefield, 2013.

Brecht, Bertolt. *The Threepenny Opera.* Trans. Desmond Vesey. New York: Grove Press, 1949.

Brown, Wendy. *Undoing the Demos: Neoliberalism's Stealth Revolution.* Cambridge, MA: MIT Press, 2015.

Buck-Morss, Susan. "A Commonist Ethics." In *The Idea of Communism 2*, ed. Slavoj Žižek, 57–75. London: Verso, 2013.

———. *The Dialectics of Seeing: Walter Benjamin and the Arcades Project.* Cambridge, MA: MIT Press, 1991.

Burnham, Clint. *Fredric Jameson and "The Wolf of Wall Street."* London: Bloomsbury, 2016.

Butler, Judith. *Precarious Life: The Powers of Mourning and Violence.* London: Verso, 2004.

Carroll, Hamilton. "September 11 as Heist." *Journal of American Studies* 45, no. 4 (2011): 835–51.

Casetti, Francesco. *Theories of Cinema: 1945–1995.* Trans. Francesca Chiostri and Elizabeth Gard Bartolini-Salimbeni with Thomas Kelso. Austin: University of Texas Press, 1999.

Chaudhary, Zahid R. "Humanity Adrift: Race, Materiality, and Allegory in Alfonso Cuarón's *Children of Men*." *Camera Obscura* 24, no. 3 (2009): 73–109.

Children of Men. Directed by Alfonso Cuarón. 2006. Universal City, CA: Universal, 2007. DVD.

Colesworthy, Rebecca. "Capital's Abstractions." *Textual Practice* 28, no. 7 (2014): 1169–79.

Conley, Tom. *Cartographic Cinema.* Minneapolis: University of Minnesota Press, 2007.

The Constant Gardener. Directed by Fernando Meirelles. 2005. Montreal: Alliance, 2010. DVD.

Copeland, Rita, and Peter T. Struck, eds. *The Cambridge Companion to Allegory.* Cambridge: Cambridge University Press, 2010.

The Corporation. Directed by Mark Archabar and Jennifer Abbot. Written by Joel Bakan et al. 2004. Toronto: Mongrel Media, 2004. DVD. 2 discs.
Cuarón, Alfonso. Interview by Richard von Busack. *Metroactive*, April 22, 2007. http://www.metroactive.com/metro/01.10.07/alfonso-cuaron-0702.html.
DeYoung, Andrew. "*The Wolf of Wall Street* Isn't about Wall Street." *The Stake*, January 7, 2014. http://thestake.org/2014/01/07/the-wolf-of-wall-street-isnt-about-wall-street/.
Duménil, Gérard, and Dominique Lévy. *Capital Resurgent: Roots of the Neoliberal Revolution*. Trans. Derek Jeffers. Cambridge, MA: Harvard University Press, 2004.
Edelstein, David. "Explosive Action." *New York*, March 27, 2006. http://nymag.com/movies/reviews/16450/.
Fisher, Mark. *Capitalist Realism: Is There No Alternative?* Winchester, UK: Zero Books, 2009.
Fletcher, Angus. *Allegory: The Theory of a Symbolic Mode*. With a foreword by Harold Bloom and a new afterword by the author. Princeton, NJ: Princeton University Press, 2012.
Foster, Verna A. "White Woods and *Blue Jasmine*: Woody Allen Rewrites *A Streetcar Named Desire*." *Literature Film Quarterly* 43, no. 3 (2015): 188–201.
Gaghan, Stephen. Interview by Emanuel Levy. *Cinema 24/7*, November 11, 2005. http://emanuellevy.com/interviews/syriana-with-writer-director-gaghan-2/.
———. Interview by Kamla Bhatt. *The Kamla Show*, July 31, 2014. https://www.youtube.com/watch?v=2xoDC3LF72s.
Gerstner, David A. "De Profondis: A Love Letter from the Inside Man." In *The Spike Lee Reader*, ed. Paula J. Massood, 243–54. Philadelphia: Temple University Press, 2008.
Gilliam, Terry. "Audio commentary." Disc 1. *Brazil*, directed by Terry Gilliam. New York: Criterion, 1999. DVD. 3 discs.
Goodwin, Michael. *Economix: How Our Economy Works (and Doesn't Work) in Words and Pictures*. Illustrated by Dan E. Burr. New York: Abrams, 2012.
Graeber, David. *Debt: The First 5,000 Years*. Updated and expanded ed. Brooklyn: Melville House, 2014.
Hansen, Miriam Bratu. *Cinema and Experience: Siegfried Kracauer, Walter Benjamin, and Theodor W. Adorno*. Berkeley: University of California Press, 2012.
Harman, Chris. *Zombie Capitalism: Global Crisis and the Relevance of Marx*. Chicago: Haymarket, 2010.
Harrison-Kahan, Lori. "*Inside Man*: Spike Lee and Post-9/11 Entertainment." *Cinema Journal* 50, no. 1 (Fall 2010): 39–58.
Harvey, David. *A Brief History of Neoliberalism*. Oxford: Oxford University Press, 2005.
———. *A Companion to Marx's "Capital."* London: Verso, 2010.
———. *A Companion to Marx's "Capital," Volume 2*. London: Verso, 2013.
———. *The Enigma of Capital and the Crises of Capitalism*. With a new afterword. Oxford: Oxford University Press, 2011.
———. *The Limits to Capital*. New and fully updated ed. London: Verso, 2007.

———. *The New Imperialism*. Oxford: Oxford University Press, 2005.

———. *Seventeen Contradictions and the End of Capitalism*. Oxford: Oxford University Press, 2014.

Hayward, Mark. "Settling Accounts: On the Subject of Economic Confessions." *Topia* 30–31 (Fall 2013–Spring 2014): 165–82.

Horkheimer, Max, and Theodor W. Adorno. *Dialectic of Enlightenment: Philosophical Fragments*. Ed. Gunzelin Schmid Noerr. Trans. Edmund Jephcott. Stanford: Stanford University Press, 2002.

Inside Man. Directed by Spike Lee. 2006. Universal City, CA: Universal, 2006. DVD.

Jaafar, Ali. Review of *Inside Man*, directed by Spike Lee. *Sight & Sound* 16, no. 5 (May 2006): 5.

Jacobs, Deborah L. "An Insider's Guide to Cate Blanchett's Designer Outfits in *Blue Jasmine*." *Forbes*, August 29, 2013. http://www.forbes.com/sites/deborahljacobs/2013/08/29/an-insiders-guide-to-cate-blanchetts-designer-outfits-in-blue-jasmine/#311a422d139e.

Jameson, Fredric. "Cognitive Mapping." In *Marxism and the Interpretation of Culture*, ed. Cary Nelson and Lawrence Grossberg, 347–60. Champaign: University of Illinois Press, 1988.

———. *The Cultural Turn: Selected Writings on the Postmodern, 1983–1998*. London: Verso, 2009.

———. "Future City." *New Left Review* 21 (May–June 2003): 65–79.

———. *The Geopolitical Aesthetic: Cinema and Space in the World System*. Bloomington: Indiana University Press, 1992.

———. *The Political Unconscious: Narrative as a Socially Symbolic Act*. Ithaca, NY: Cornell University Press, 1982.

———. *Postmodernism, or, The Cultural Logic of Late Capitalism*. Durham, NC: Duke University Press, 1991.

———. *Signatures of the Visible*. New York: Routledge, 1992.

Kant, Immanuel. *Grounding for the Metaphysics of Morals*. Trans. James W. Ellington. Indianapolis: Hackett, 1993.

Kellner, Douglas. *Cinema Wars: Hollywood Film and Politics in the Bush-Cheney Era*. Malden, MA: Wiley-Blackwell, 2010.

Klein, Naomi. *No Is Not Enough: Resisting the New Shock Politics and Winning the World We Need*. Toronto: Knopf Canada, 2017.

———. *The Shock Doctrine: The Rise of Disaster Capitalism*. Toronto: Vintage Canada, 2008.

Kracauer, Siegfried. *From Caligari to Hitler: A Psychological History of the German Cinema*. Revised and expanded ed. Ed. Leonardo Quaresima. Princeton, NJ: Princeton University Press, 2004.

Krauthammer, Charles. Review of *Syriana*, directed by Stephen Gaghan. *Washington Post*, March 3, 2006. http://www.washingtonpost.com/wp-dyn/content/article/2006/03/02/AR2006030201209.html.

Krugman, Paul. *The Return of Depression Economics and the Crisis of 2008*. With a new epilogue. New York: Norton, 2009.

Lacan, Jacques. *Écrits: The First Complete Edition in English*. Trans. Bruce Fink. New York: Norton, 2006.

———. *On Feminine Sexuality, the Limits of Love and Knowledge: The Seminar of Jacques Lacan, Book XX, Encore*. Ed. Jacques-Alain Miller. Translated and with notes by Bruce Fink. New York: Norton, 1998.

Landau, Arlene Diane. Review of *Blue Jasmine*, directed by Woody Allen. *Psychological Perspectives* 57, no. 3 (2014): 344–48.

Le Carré, John. *The Constant Gardener*. Toronto: Penguin Canada, 2001.

Lewis, Michael. *The Big Short: Inside the Doomsday Machine*. With a new afterword. New York: Norton, 2011.

Luxemburg, Rosa. *The Accumulation of Capital*. Trans. Agnes Schwarzchild. London: Routledge, 2003.

Maher, Kevin. Review of *Inside Man*, directed by Spike Lee. *Sight & Sound* 16, no. 5 (May 2006): 57.

Mafe, Diana Adesola. "(Mis)Imagining Africa in the New Millennium: *The Constant Gardener* and *Blood Diamond*." *Camera Obscura* 25, no. 3 (2011): 68–99.

Marx, Karl. *Capital*. Volume 1. Trans. Ben Fowkes. London: Penguin, 1976.

———. *Capital*. Volume 3. Trans. David Fernbach. London: Penguin, 1981.

McGowan, Todd. *Out of Time: Desire in Atemporal Cinema*. Minneapolis: University of Minnesota Press, 2011.

———. *Spike Lee*. Urbana: University of Illinois Press, 2014.

———. "The Temporality of the Real: The Path to Politics in *The Constant Gardener*." *Film-Philosophy* 11, no. 3 (2007): 59–86.

Miller, Mark Crispin, ed. *Seeing through Movies*. New York: Pantheon, 1990.

Nocera, Joe. "Sex and Drugs and I.P.O.'s." *New York Times*, December 22, 2013. http://www.nytimes.com/2013/12/22/movies/martin-scorseses-approach-in-the-wolf-of-wall-street.html?_r=0.

Nussbaum, Martha C. *Not for Profit: Why Democracy Needs the Humanities*. Princeton, NJ: Princeton University Press, 2010.

Piketty, Thomas. *Capital in the Twenty-First Century*. Trans. Arthur Goldhammer. Cambridge, MA: Harvard University Press, 2014.

Pomerance, Murray. *The Eyes Have It: Cinema and the Reality Effect*. New Brunswick, NJ: Rutgers University Press, 2013.

Rainer, Peter. Review of *Inside Man*, directed by Spike Lee. *Christian Science Monitor*, March 24, 2006. http://www.csmonitor.com/2006/0324/p11s03-almo.html.

Rubin, Ronald L. "How the 'Wolf of Wall Street' Really Did It." *Wall Street Journal*, January 3, 2014. http://www.wsj.com/articles/SB10001424052702 303453004579290450707920302.

Sarris, Andrew. Review of *Syriana*, directed by Stephen Gaghan. *New York Observer*, December 4, 2005. http://observer.com/2005/12/soderbergh-clooney-and-co-make-mideast-mess-too-simple-2/.

Schmitt, Carl. *Political Theology: Four Chapters on the Concept of Sovereignty*. Trans. George Schwab. Chicago: University of Chicago Press, 2005.

Sharrett, Christopher. "False Criticism: Cinema, Bourgeois Society, and the Conservative Complaint." In *Cinema and Modernity*, ed. Murray Pomerance, 130–51. New Brunswick, NJ: Rutgers University Press, 2006.

Sklar, Robert. *Movie-Made America: A Cultural History of American Movies*. Revised and updated ed. New York: Vintage/Random House, 1994.

Slocum, David. "Here's What *The Wolf of Wall Street* Teaches Us about Corporate Storytelling." *Forbes*, April 9, 2014. http://www.forbes.com/sites/berlinschoolofcreativeleadership/2014/04/09/heres-what-the-wolf-of-wall-street-teaches-us-about-corporate-story telling/#2715e4857a0b55a74cbf74d7.
Smith, Adam. *An Inquiry into the Nature and Causes of the Wealth of Nations*. Indianapolis: Liberty Classics, 1976.
Sterritt, David. *Spike Lee's America*. Cambridge: Polity, 2013.
Stiglitz, Joseph E. *Freefall: America, Free Markets, and the Sinking of the World Economy*. New York: Norton, 2010.
Syriana. Directed by Stephen Gaghan. 2005. Hollywood, CA: Warner Bros., 2005. DVD.
Toscano, Alberto, and Jeff Kinkle. *Cartographies of the Absolute*. Winchester, UK: Zero Books, 2015.
Walsh, David. Review of *Inside Man*, directed by Spike Lee. *World Socialist Web Site*. Accessed November 11, 2015. https://www.wsws.org/en/articles/2006/04/insi-a12.html.
Wegner, Philip E. *Life between Two Deaths, 1989–2001: U.S. Culture in the Long Nineties*. Durham, NC: Duke University Press, 2009.
The Wolf of Wall Street. Directed by Martin Scorsese. 2013. Hollywood, CA: Paramount, 2014. DVD.
Žižek, Slavoj. *The Courage of Hopelessness: Chronicles of a Year of Acting Dangerously*. London: Allen Lane, 2017.
———. *Did Somebody Say Totalitarianism?* London: Verso, 2001.
———. *First as Tragedy, Then as Farce*. London: Verso, 2009.
———. *Iraq: The Borrowed Kettle*. London: Verso, 2005.
———. *Looking Awry: An Introduction to Jacques Lacan through Popular Culture*. Cambridge, MA: MIT Press, 1992.
———. *The Plague of Fantasies*. London: Verso, 1997.
———. *Violence: Six Sideways Reflections*. New York: Picador, 2008.
———. "We Are the Awakening." Occupy Wall Street talk at Liberty Square, October 10, 2011. https://vimeo.com/30367180.
———. *Welcome to the Desert of the Real: Five Essays on September 11 and Related Dates*. London: Verso, 2002.
———. *The Year of Dreaming Dangerously*. London: Verso, 2012.

Index

Abu Ghraib, 5, 14, 19–20
accumulation by dispossession, xxxi, 82, 95–100
Adorno, Theodor, xxi–xxii, xxiii
Agamben, Giorgio, xxviii, 5, 20–22
Ahmed, Sara, 6, 8, 24, 26
Akerlof, George, 122, 125
allegory, xvi–xx, xxxi, 46, 79–80, 102, 134, 147, 156; as allegoresis, xx; Benjamin's conception of, xxviii, xxix, 1–2, 25; definitions of, xvii; de Man's conception of, xx; and enigma, xvii; films as, xvi, 154–58; Fletcher's conception of, xvii–xix, xx, 158; Jameson's conception of, xx, xxv; Kracauer as practitioner of, xxiv–xxv; Quintilian's conception of, xvii; resurgence of, xvii–xix
Allen, Katie, 124–25
Allen, Woody, xv, xxvii, 128, 133; as allegorist, xvi, xxxii, 134, 147, 150–51; and Madoff case, 148; narrative strategies of, 137, 139, 147; and neoliberalism, 141; and Tennessee Williams, 148. See also *Blue Jasmine*
Althusser, Louis, xix, 45
American Psycho (film), xxix
Angell, Marcia, xxviii, 57, 66–67, 69–70, 71, 73
apocalypse, films about, xxviii, 12
Arab Spring (2011), 153

Arendt, Hannah, 96
Aris, Ben, 95
Aristotle, 46
Arrighi, Giovanni, xxviii, xxxi, 82, 101–102, 169n55

Baer, Robert, 36, 38, 41, 42
Bakan, Joel, xxviii, 57, 68, 71, 81, 94, 156
bank bailout (2008), xvi, 150, 151; *Blue Jasmine* as allegory of, xxxii, 134, 147, 151, 152
bare life, 5, 23
Benjamin, Walter, xxviii; on allegory, xxix, 1, 2, 24–26; on state of emergency, 3, 21–22
Big Short, The (film), xvi, 130
Black, Edwin, 94
Blanchard, Terrence, 102
Blomkamp, Neill, 153
Blue Jasmine, xv, xvi, xxxii; as allegory of bank bailout, 134, 147, 151, 152; as allegory of financial crisis, 134, 147, 151; class warfare in, 151–52; delusion in, 135–39, 141, 143, 146; freefall in, 144–47; Madoff and, 148; neoliberalism in, 139–44; plot summary of, 133–34; title of, 139. *See also* Allen, Woody
Boiler Room (film), 114
Borges, Jorge Luis, xx
Boyle, Kirk, xxvii, 26–27

Brazil (film), 11–12
Brecht, Bertolt, 81
Bremer, L. Paul III, 41
Brown, Wendy, xxviii, 98, 141–42, 144
Buchanan, John, 95
Buck-Morss, Susan, 1, 25, 102
Burnham, Clint, xxvii, 133, 170n7
Bush, Barbara, 82, 91
Bush, George H. W., 81, 100; in *Inside Man*, xxxi, 82, 91, 98, 99–100; and signal crisis, 101
Bush, George W., 32, 46, 81, 82, 98, 100, 154; and invasion of Iraq, xxx, 39, 40; and terminal crisis, 102; and war on terror, 4–5, 6, 21
Bush, Prescott, xxxi, 81, 82, 94–95, 98, 100
Butler, Judith, 5

Campbell, Duncan, 95
Cape Fear (Scorsese film), xxvi
Carroll, Hamilton, 80, 87–88
Chandor, J. C., xvi, 154
Chaudhary, Zahid, 13, 22–23, 24–26
Children of Men (film), xvi, xxviii, xxix–xxx; as documentary, 12–13; ending of, 24–28; *entwürdigen* in, 20; environmental degradation in, 13–14; infertility metaphor in, xxix, 2, 9, 14, 29; labor in, 8–12; nostalgia for 1960s in, 14–18; social satire in, 10–12; state of exception in, 3–8, 18–24; suffering in, 6; tracking shots in, 6; as *Trauerspiel*, xxix, 1–2, 21, 25–26; uprising in, 22–24. *See also* Cuarón, Alfonso
Children of Men, The (novel), 16
Coen brothers, 103
cognitive mapping, xxvi, xix, 32–33, 45, 47
Colesworthy, Rebecca, 125–26
Committee for the Liberation of Iraq (CLI), 34, 39, 41, 43
concentration camps, 5, 86, 94
Conley, Tom, 44–45

Constant Gardener, The (film), xvi, xxvii, xxviii, xxx–xxxi; audience in, 54, 56, 75–77; corporate murder in, 69–74; corporation in, 60–69; cyclical structure of, 72, 74–78; pharmaceutical metaphor in, 55–56; strategies of deception in, 57–60; subcontracting in, 70, 71, 74, 77; subplots of, 56–57. *See also* Meirelles, Fernando
Constant Gardener, The (novel), 55–56, 57, 65–66, 67, 73, 76
Copeland, Rita, xvii, xx
Coppola, Francis Ford, 48
Corporation, The (film), 68
Cosmopolis (film), 153
crisis, global financial (2008), xv, xvi, xxix, 102, 107, 125; *Blue Jasmine* as allegory of, xxxii, 134, 147, 151; effects of, 9; emergence from, 158; films representing, xxvi–xxvii; Goldman Sachs's role in, 131; and Madoff case, 148; severity of, 108; *Wolf of Wall Street* as allegory of, xxxi, 107
crisis, signal, 101
crisis, terminal, 101–102
Cronenberg, David, 153
Cuarón, Alfonso, xv, xxix, 1–2, 13, 21; as allegorist, xvi, 25–26; as co-producer of *This Changes Everything*, 14; dystopian vision of, xxx, 27, 28, 154–55; and P. D. James, 16; as social commentator, 10; use of tracking shots, 5–6. *See also Children of Men* (film)
culture industry, xxi–xxiii

Davis, Angela, 14
Decree for the Protection of People and State (1933), 5, 21
Deleuze, Gilles, 97
de Man, Paul, xx
democracy, xviii, xxix, 40, 142, 154
Demolition (film), 154

Demy, Jacques, 89, 167n12
Desplat, Alexandre, 35
DeYoung, Andrew, 124
Django Unchained (film), 153
Dog Day Afternoon (film), xxv, 80, 84
Do the Right Thing (film), 80
Duménil, Gérard, 98
Dylan, Bob, 16–17, 24, 162n31

Edelstein, David, 80
Elysium (film), 153
environmental degradation, 62, 154; depictions of, 13, 14, 28
Evans, Bruce, xxix
ExxonMobil, 38

Fassbinder, Rainer Werner, 114
fictitious capital, xxviii, 109, 126–29
Fight Club (film), xxvi
film studios, xxi–xxiv
finance, xvi, 125, 131, 132; films about, xvii; *Inside Man* as critique of, 79; vs. productive capital, 101; rise of, 97–98; Wall Street as emblematic of, 81, 114; *Wolf of Wall Street* as critique of, 124–25
Fincher, David, xxix
Fisher, Mark, xxvi
Fletcher, Angus, xvii–xx, xxix, 158
Foster, Verna, 148
Foucault, Michel, 98, 142
Friedman, Thomas, 41

Gaghan, Stephen, xv, xvi, 29, 45–46; as allegorist, xvi, 47; and cognitive mapping, 32–33, 47; on *Syriana*, 38; on title of *Syriana*, 41–42. See also *Syriana*
Gates, Bill, 39
Gavron, Sarah, 153
Gerstner, David, 89–90, 166–67n8
Gewirtz, Russell, 79, 88
Ghost Dog (film), xxvi
Giffen, James, 38
Gilliam, Terry, 11, 12

Gilroy, Dan, 154
Girl with the Dragon Tattoo, The (Fincher film), xxix
Girl with the Dragon Tattoo, The (Oplev film), xxix
Giuliani, Rudy, 91, 99
Goldman Sachs, 114, 125, 129, 130–31, 150
Goodwin, Michael, 128
Graeber, David, xxviii, 135, 151
Great Depression, 9, 107
Great Recession, xxvii, 9, 107, 132
Guantánamo Bay, 5

Harman, Chris, xxviii
Harrison-Kahan, Lori, 80
Harron, Mary, xxix
Harvey, David, xxvii–xxviii, 82; on accumulation by dispossession, xxxi, 82, 96–97; on bank bailout, 149; and enigma of capital, xvii; on fictitious capital, 109, 128–29; on neoliberalism, 98, 100; on petro-politics, xxx, 33, 39–40, 41, 47; on Ponzi-like character of stock market, 149; on redundancy of human labor, 9–10
Hayward, Mark, 108
Hegel, G. W. F., 12
Hepburn, Katharine, 136
Holocaust, 86, 91, 93, 94, 96, 105
Homeland Security Act, US (2002), 4, 19
homo sacer (figure), 5–6
Horkheimer, Max, xxi–xxiii

I Am Legend (film), 26
In a Year with Thirteen Moons (film), 114
Independence Day (film), xxvii
indignados, 153
Inside Man (film), xv, xviii, xxxi; accumulation by dispossession in, xxxi, 99–100; acting styles in, 102–103; George H. W. Bush and,

Inside Man (film) *(continued)* 82, 91, 98, 99–100; George W. Bush and, 81, 82, 98, 100, 102; Prescott Bush and, 81, 82, 94–95, 98, 100; camerawork in, 102; as class allegory, 102–106; Holocaust in, 91, 93, 96; music in, 102; neoliberalism in, xxviii, 99; plot summary of, 82–87; plot twists in, 84–87, 166–67n8; primitive accumulation in, 96; race in, 80, 103; reviews of, 79–80; Rothschild moment in, 104–105; short American century and, 99–102; signature shot in, 89, 91; strategies of deception in, 87–88; terminal crisis in, 101–102; title character of, 88–91; Wall Street banker in, 91–95; Wall Street location in, 81. *See also* Lee, Spike

Iraq, invasion of (2003), xvi, xvii, xxx, 5, 33, 39–41, 155; in *Children of Men*, 14, 16; in *Constant Gardener*, 53, 55; in *Syriana*, 46, 50

Islamic State of Iraq and Syria (ISIS), xxx, 33, 50

Jaafar, Ali, 80
James, P. D., 16
Jameson, Fredric, xxvi, xxvii, xxviii, 45, 113; allegorical approach of, xxi; on allegory, xx; on cognitive mapping, xix, 32–33; on film industry, xxv; on finance capital, 97; on political unconscious, xx–xxi; on politics of the 1960s, 17
Jonze, Spike, 118
Joon-ho, Bong, 153
Judge, Mike, 11

Kant, Immanuel, xviii, 144
Kellner, Douglas, 32
Keynesian economics, 100
Kinkle, Jeff, xvii, xix, xxvi, 32, 126
Klein, Naomi, xxviii, xxx; in *Children of Men*, 14; on environmental degradation, 14; on "model" theory, 33, 40–41; on Trump, 154, 156
Kracauer, Siegfried, xxiii–xxiv, xxv
Krauthammer, Charles, 47, 51
Krugman, Paul, 149

labor, xxiv, xxix, 10, 14, 17, 97, 155
Lacan, Jacques, 74, 137, 166n31
Landau, Arlene Diane, 143
Larsson, Stieg, xxix
Lawrence, Francis, 26
le Carré, John, 55–56, 57, 65–66, 67, 69
Lee, Spike, xv, xxviii, xxxi; as allegorist, xvi, 79; cinematography of, 102, 169n61; and class, 80; and coalition politics, xxxi; as inside man, 90; and race, 80; reputation of, 80; signature shot, xxxi, 89, 91, 167n12, 167n16; use of wide shots, 106. *See also Do the Right Thing*; *Inside Man*
Lehman Brothers, 114, 131
Lennon, John, 14, 16, 17, 162n30
Lévi, Dominique, 98
Lewis, Avi, 14
Lewis, Michael, xxviii, 129, 131, 147, 149–50
Loftus, John, 95
Lumet, Sidney, xxv, 80, 84
Luxemburg, Rosa, 96
Lynch, Kevin, xix

Madoff, Bernie, 148–49
Madoff, Ruth, 148
Maher, Kevin, 80
Margin Call (film), xvi
Marx, Karl, xxviii, 82, 98, 131, 171–72n44; on fictitious capital, 109, 126–27; on primitive accumulation, 95–96, 105
Massood, Paula, 89
McGowan, Todd, xxvii; on *Constant Gardener*, 57, 58–60, 62–64, 73, 74–75; on *Inside Man*, 93; on Spike Lee signature shot, 167n16

McKay, Adam, xvi, 130, 171n34
Meirelles, Fernando, xv, xxvii, xxx, 53, 79, 155; as allegorist, xvi; and le Carré, 56, 66–67; narrative strategies of, 58, 60, 63–66, 76. See also *Constant Gardener* (film)
Melancholia (film), 153
Melville, Jean–Pierre, 103
Mensch, Gerhard, 101
Miller, Mark Crispin, xxi, xxii–xxiii
Miller's Crossing (film), 103
"model" theory, xxviii, 33, 40–41
Monsanto, 64
Moore, Michael, 94
mortgage bond market, crash of (2008), xxviii, 102, 107, 108, 125–26, 129–30, 131, 147, 149, 150
Most Violent Year, A (film), 154
mourning play. See *Trauerspiel*
Mr. Brooks (film), xxix
Mrozowski, Daniel, xxvi

neoliberalism, xxviii; in *Blue Jasmine*, 140; and class warfare, 102; definitions of, 98; history of, 98–99, and post-secondary education, 141–42; and war profiteering, 100
Nestlé boycott (1977), 64–65
Nightcrawler (film), 154
Nocera, Joe, 125, 130–31
Nussbaum, Martha, 141

Occupy Wall Street (2011), 152, 153
Office Space (film), 11–12
Oplev, Niels Arden, xxix
Outsiders, The (film), 48

Parapluies de Cherbourg, Les (film), 89
Parks, Rosa, 14
Patriot Act, USA (2001), 4–5
Paulson, Henry, 131, 150
Pfizer scandal, 67
Piketty, Thomas, 98
political action committees (PACs), xvii, xxx, 38
Pomerance, Murray, 167n12
primitive accumulation, 95–96, 99, 105
protest movements, 3–4, 14–17, 24, 152, 153

Quintilian, xvii

Rainer, Peter, 80
Reagan, Ronald, xxi, 82, 91, 99, 100–101
Rothschild, Baron de, 104–105
Rothschild, L. F., 118, 131
Rubin, Ronald R., 124
Rumsfeld, Donald, 46

Salgado, Sebastião, 35
Samouraï, Le (film), 103
Sarris, Andrew, 46
Schiller, Robert, 122, 125
Schmitt, Carl, 21–22
Schweitzer, Eva, 95
Scorsese, Martin, xv, xxvi, 107, 125, 156; as allegorist, xvi, xxxi; narrative strategies of, 109, 114–16, 119, 130. See also *Cape Fear*; *Wolf of Wall Street*
serial killers, films about, xviii
Sharrett, Christopher, xvii
Sklar, Robert, xxi
Slocum, Andrew, 125
Smith, Adam, 95, 144
Snowpiercer (film), 153
Soros, George, 93
state of exception, xxviii, 3, 5, 20, 21–23
Sterritt, David, xxvii, 85, 89–90, 166–67n8
Stiglitz, Joseph, 108
stock market, 112, 128, 131–32, 151; crash of (1929), 108, 126, 130; crash of (1987), 108, 118, 131; cyclical nature of, 108; Ponzi-like character of, 149
Struck, Peter, xvii, xx
subcontracting, 70, 71, 74, 77, 154
sublime, xviii, xix

Suffragette (film), 153
Syriana, xvi, xxviii, xxx; camerawork in, 31; as cognitive map, 32, 47; Committee for the Liberation of Iraq (CLI) in, 34, 39, 41, 43; ExxonMobil and, 38; filming locations, 34; and history, 46–51; and Iraq invasion, xxviii, xxx, 33, 39–41, 46, 50; and Islamic State of Iraq and Syria (ISIS), 50; maps in, 30–31, 42–46; "model" theory in, xxviii, 33, 40–41, 42, 50, 51; plot summary of, 33–37; suicide bombers in, 33, 36, 47, 49–51; timeliness of, 51; title of, 39–42; topicality of, 37–39; and *USS Cole* attack, 47. *See also* Gaghan, Stephen

Tarantino, Quentin, 153
Thatcher, Margaret, 91, 98, 99
This Changes Everything (film), 15
Thyssen, Fritz, 95
Toscano, Alberto, xvii, xix, xxvi, 32, 126
tragic drama, German baroque. See *Trauerspiel*
Trauerspiel, xxix, 1–2, 21, 25–26
Trump, Donald, 153–57

Vallée, Jean-Marc, 154
vampires, xxviii, 131, 171–72n44
Volcker, Paul, 100–101
von Trier, Lars, 153

Walsh, David, 80
war on terror, xv, 6, 21, 154

Wegner, Philip, xxv–xxvi
Weyerhaeuser timber company, 62
Williams, J. Bryan, 83
Williams, Tennessee, xvi, 148
Winter, Terence, 107, 109, 115
Wolfen (film), xxvi
Wolf of Wall Street, The (film), xvi, xxviii, xxxi–xxxii; as allegory of financial crisis, xv, xvi, 125; as economic confession, 108; fictitious capital in, 126–32; and Goldman Sachs, 125, 130–31; investor in, 123, 129, 130; liar's paradox in, 109; as mock infomercial, 110–18; and mortgage bond market, 129–31; narrative strategy of, 110; phishing for phools in, 122; pump-and-dump scheme in, 123–24, 128; reviews of, 124–25; sales techniques in, 118–19; spectator in, 102–103, 130; Stratton Oakmont in, 110–16, 119–20, 123–24; and Stratton Oakmont investment firm, 110, 114, 124–25, 130–31
World Trade Organization (WTO), 3
Wire, The (TV series), xxvi

Younger, Ben, 114

Žižek, Slavoj, xxvi, xxviii; on *Children of Men*, 12–13, 17, 26; on dehumanization of Jews, 19, 20; on financial crisis, 152; on *homo sacer*, 5, 6; on Madoff case, 148–49; on Trump, 157; on violence, 82, 93
zombies, xxviii

THE SUNY SERIES

HORIZONS OF CINEMA

MURRAY POMERANCE | EDITOR

Also in the series

William Rothman, editor, *Cavell on Film*

J. David Slocum, editor, *Rebel Without a Cause*

Joe McElhaney, *The Death of Classical Cinema*

Kirsten Moana Thompson, *Apocalyptic Dread*

Frances Gateward, editor, *Seoul Searching*

Michael Atkinson, editor, *Exile Cinema*

Paul S. Moore, *Now Playing*

Robin L. Murray and Joseph K. Heumann, *Ecology and Popular Film*

William Rothman, editor, *Three Documentary Filmmakers*

Sean Griffin, editor, *Hetero*

Jean-Michel Frodon, editor, *Cinema and the Shoah*

Carolyn Jess-Cooke and Constantine Verevis, editors, *Second Takes*

Matthew Solomon, editor, *Fantastic Voyages of the Cinematic Imagination*

R. Barton Palmer and David Boyd, editors, *Hitchcock at the Source*

William Rothman, *Hitchcock: The Murderous Gaze, Second Edition*

Joanna Hearne, *Native Recognition*

Marc Raymond, *Hollywood's New Yorker*

Steven Rybin and Will Scheibel, editors, *Lonely Places, Dangerous Ground*

Claire Perkins and Constantine Verevis, editors, *B Is for Bad Cinema*

Dominic Lennard, *Bad Seeds and Holy Terrors*

Rosie Thomas, *Bombay before Bollywood*

Scott M. MacDonald, *Binghamton Babylon*

Sudhir Mahadevan, *A Very Old Machine*

David Greven, *Ghost Faces*

James S. Williams, *Encounters with Godard*

William H. Epstein and R. Barton Palmer, editors, *Invented Lives, Imagined Communities*

Lee Carruthers, *Doing Time*

Rebecca Meyers, William Rothman, and Charles Warren, editors, *Looking with Robert Gardner*

Belinda Smaill, *Regarding Life*

Douglas McFarland and Wesley King, editors, *John Huston as Adaptor*
R. Barton Palmer, Homer B. Pettey, and Steven M. Sanders, editors, *Hitchcock's Moral Gaze*
Nenad Jovanovic, *Brechtian Cinemas*
Will Scheibel, *American Stranger*
Amy Rust, *Passionate Detachments*
Steven Rybin, *Gestures of Love*
Seth Friedman, *Are You Watching Closely?*
Roger Rawlings, *Ripping England!*
Michael DeAngelis, *Rx Hollywood*
Ricardo E. Zulueta, *Queer Art Camp Superstar*
John Caruana and Mark Cauchi, editors, *Immanent Frames*
Nathan Holmes, *Welcome to Fear City*
Homer B. Pettey and R. Barton Palmer, editors, *Rule, Britannia!*

www.ingramcontent.com/pod-product-compliance
Lightning Source LLC
Chambersburg PA
CBHW030651230426
43665CB00011B/1045